Sommaire

Introduction

Françoise Le Jeune et Michel Prum

En 2007, les Britanniques commémorèrent le deux centième anniversaire de la loi qui mettait fin au commerce des esclaves dans l'Empire britannique. Un service religieux fut tenu à l'abbaye de Westminster le 25 mars, en présence de la Reine, des dignitaires de l'Église anglicane et du Premier ministre. Selon Tony Blair, cette commémoration devait permettre aux Britanniques de se souvenir de la longue campagne qu'avaient menée des leaders religieux comme William Wilberforce auquel le service était dédié. Blair rappelait aussi le nom de quelques esclaves libres comme Olaudah Equiano et le rôle des hommes et des femmes de bonne volonté dans cette campagne pour l'abolition de la traite. C'est donc le peuple britannique et son engagement dans la campagne en faveur de l'abolition que le Premier ministre souhaitait féliciter en appelant leurs descendants à se souvenir de cet engagement humaniste, inscrit dans l'histoire des nations : « *Slavery's impact upon Africa, the Caribbean, the Americas and Europe was profound. Thankfully, Britain was the first country to abolish the trade.* »

Dans un deuxième temps, Blair rappelait qu'il fallait aussi prendre en compte le fait que la Grande-Bretagne avait construit sa richesse économique grâce à l'esclavage d'hommes et de femmes pendant plus de deux siècles. Puis, Blair s'exprima personnellement en tant que Chrétien en condamnant l'apport de l'esclavage dans la construction de l'Empire britannique, appelant les Britanniques à se souvenir de ce passé peu glorieux et du poids de cette culpabilité. Mais le discours politique prenait le pas sur l'emphase religieuse lorsque Blair, n'oubliant pas son projet de *New Britain*, invita les Britanniques à se réjouir de l'apport multiculturel de ce passé colonial.

> *Personally I believe the bicentenary offers us a chance not just to say how profoundly shameful the slave trade was—how we condemn its existence utterly and praise those who fought for its abolition, but also to express our deep sorrow that it ever happened, that it ever could have happened and to rejoice at the different and better times we live in today.*

La presse dans les anciennes colonies des Caraïbes, en Jamaïque, à Trinidad et Tobago, et certains journaux africains, lui reprochèrent son refus de s'excuser plus clairement au nom de la nation britannique. Les excuses étaient faites à titre personnel, là où les descendants d'esclaves attendaient des compensations[1]. On reprocha à Tony Blair de choisir de commémorer une date qui n'avait pas marqué l'abolition de l'esclavage, qui n'était intervenu qu'en 1833. Cette même presse reprocha à la Reine son mutisme sur le passé peu glorieux de son peuple. On sait aussi que le service religieux fut interrompu par l'intervention d'un homme noir, aussitôt arrêté pour trouble de l'ordre public[2]. Comme on peut le constater le moment était toujours pénible, et la réconciliation et l'oubli proposés par Tony Blair restaient une aspiration des Britanniques.

Dans cet ouvrage, il nous a paru important de revenir sur cette partie de l'histoire britannique contemporaine. Les chercheurs du présent volume se sont penchés sur les différents moments clés de l'histoire de l'esclavage et de son abolition en Grande-Bretagne entre 1787 et 1840. Les articles soulignent une réelle mobilisation de la population britannique autour de deux campagnes importantes tout en s'intéressant au contexte idéologique dans lequel ce débat s'était tenu.

Laurent Curelly étudie la mise en place et le développement de la Traite anglaise, depuis les premières expéditions du XVIe siècle jusqu'à son essor final dans la seconde moitié du XVIIIe. Les proportions exceptionnelles que prend ce commerce dans cette dernière phase est une des raisons qui expliquent l'intérêt que suscite la question de la Traite et les polémiques qui font rage à cette époque. Mais ces polémiques sont précédées, un siècle plus tôt, par un autre débat tout aussi vif, portant non sur la légitimité morale d'une telle pratique, alors incontestée et appréciée pour sa forte rentabilité, mais sur son mode opératoire. À la logique protectionniste de l'État anglais, qui défend ses intérêts nationaux contre les Néerlandais, s'oppose la logique libérale, défendue entre autres par Adam Smith, qui critique les monopoles octroyés par la Couronne et défend la dérégulation du marché. S'il est difficile d'évaluer les bénéfices soutirés par le commerce négrier, on peut néanmoins affirmer qu'il a beaucoup contribué au développement des ports, comme Liverpool ou Bristol, et à la prospérité de nombreux secteurs économiques (banques, assurances, chantiers navals…). Cette prospérité va servir d'argument aux adversaires de l'abolition, qui prédiront non seulement la faillite des compagnies négrières, mais l'effondrement de l'ensemble de l'économie anglaise en cas de victoire de leurs adversaires.

1. Voir « Carribean Leaders do not Wish to Commemorate », *Jamaica Observer*, 1er avril 2007. « *The bicentennial events, mostly concentrated in Britain, stirred the first official support for reparations, says Aaron Larrier, a Christian minister and Black heritage activist. After the March 25 anniversary of the end of the British slave trade, the Barbadian Parliament passed a resolution acknowledging for the first time that slavery was a crime against humanity. Prime Minister Owen Arthur has expressed support for reparations, though he has urged those drafting the appeal to focus on educational exchanges and technology transfers rather than cash payments. Talk of reparations has been heard in the Caribbean since the islands began gaining their independence in the 1960s.* »
2. http://news.bbc.co.uk/2/hi/uk_news/6497935.stm.

Les thèses de ces antiabolitionnistes sont étudiées en détail par Eric Molina, qui distingue deux groupes d'auteurs : les chroniqueurs esclavagistes qui résident dans les colonies et les propriétaires d'esclaves demeurant en Grande-Bretagne. Les premiers (comme Beckford et Edwards), qui côtoient et connaissent les esclaves, sont souvent des pragmatiques qui considèrent l'esclavage comme allant de soi et ne cherchent pas à lui trouver une légitimation théorique. Ils sont certes convaincus de l'infériorité des Noirs et s'emploient à défendre la « suprématie blanche », mais ils rêvent de rapports apaisés entre maîtres et travailleurs asservis. Ils développent un discours « presque humaniste » et imaginent un système dont chacun, Noirs et Blancs, tirerait satisfaction.

Au contraire les « *absentee landlords* », comme Holroyd, profitent financièrement de l'esclavage sans pour autant connaître de près cette institution, puisqu'ils résident en Angleterre. L'argument économique est bien sûr primordial à leurs yeux, mais c'est dans la Bible qu'ils cherchent, comme le Révérend Harris, leur légitimité morale. Même le publiciste William Cobbett, qui rejoindra plus tard le mouvement « radical », estime que l'esclavage est établi par la « loi divine ». À l'instar des autres antiabolitionnistes anglais, il croit en l'infériorité naturelle des Africains. On retrouve chez lui comme chez d'autres la comparaison entre l'esclavage colonial et l'« esclavage » des ouvriers anglais, celui-ci étant posé comme plus rude encore que celui-là. Reprenant cette comparaison, Flora Tristan écrira en 1840, à l'issue de sa visite à Londres : « L'esclavage n'est plus à mes yeux la plus grande des infortunes humaines depuis que je connais le prolétariat anglais[1]. »

Le postulat de l'infériorité des Noirs, qui semble être le point commun de tous les antiabolitionnistes anglais, trouve curieusement une caution intellectuelle prestigieuse en la personne du philosophe David Hume, défenseur de la tolérance, pourfendeur des préjugés et illustre représentant des Lumières écossaises. Michel Prum revient sur la polémique qu'a suscitée une simple note de bas de page, ajoutée à l'essai *Of National Character*, dans laquelle Hume affirme qu'aucun Noir n'a jamais apporté de contribution intellectuelle, scientifique ou artistique, à l'histoire de l'humanité. Tous les contre-exemples proposés par James Beattie et d'autres n'y feront rien : il semble que l'empirisme de Hume se heurte ici à un *a priori* rédhibitoire : une aversion viscérale des Noirs, qui pousse le philosophe à contredire son propre credo universaliste. Paradoxalement, l'auteur du *Treatise of Human Nature* contribue ainsi à renforcer, par sa négrophobie, les intérêts des partisans de la traite négrière.

1. Flora Tristan, *Promenades dans Londres* (1840), Paris, Maspéro, 1978.

La première campagne britannique contre la traite et l'esclavage de 1787, n'aurait pas pu prendre forme idéologiquement sans le dynamisme du mouvement antiesclavagiste dans les colonies américaines. C'est ce que démontre Marie-Jeanne Rossignol en reprenant la chronologie du discours antiesclavagiste nord-américain depuis 1688. C'est l'influence des écrits Quakers publiés en Amérique du Nord, puis diffusés en Grande-Bretagne au sein de leur congrégation, qui convainc les Quakers britanniques de la nécessité de prendre position contre l'immoralité de la détention et de la vente d'esclaves. C'est aussi de l'Amérique du Nord que viennent les idées du Grand réveil religieux qui influencèrent le discours évangélique, au-delà des dénominations non-conformistes. Puis dans un troisième temps, Marie-Jeanne Rossignol revient sur le moment marquant de la guerre d'indépendance américaine (1775-1783) durant laquelle le débat d'idées porte sur les droits « naturels » des hommes, sur la nécessité de libérer les esclaves dans les colonies du nord pour des opérations militaires et la nécessité d'inscrire la fin de la traite dans le projet de la nouvelle République. Selon l'auteur, ces avancées américaines constituèrent un élément déterminant dans l'ouverture du débat britannique après 1783. Il fallait à la Grande-Bretagne désormais relever le défi de la « liberté », en cherchant à s'affranchir de la nation américaine et en prouvant au monde qu'elle restait une nation et un empire vertueux où les droits naturels étaient respectés.

L'implication des congrégations religieuses dans la campagne contre la traite et l'esclavage est essentielle au cours du XVIIIe siècle. Olivette Otele montre que l'engagement des Quakers américains marque la première étape de cette campagne. Leurs textes polémiques publiés en Grande-Bretagne dans la seconde moitié du XVIIIe siècle trouvent un écho parmi les Quakers britanniques et les Méthodistes. Ainsi, John Wesley fut influencé par sa visite dans les plantations esclavagistes dans les colonies américaines. Puis, sensibilisé à la cause des esclaves noirs sur le sol britannique, à la suite de la campagne juridique menée par Granville Sharp, le prédicateur méthodiste prit position dans un sermon, *Thoughts Upon Slavery,* publié en 1774. Quant aux Quakers de Londres, ils fondèrent une société en 1783 pour mobiliser les membres de leur communauté et ainsi diffuser à travers leurs réseaux, les premiers textes polémiques contre l'esclavage. En dernier lieu, l'Église anglicane, peu sensible au discours antiesclavagiste au départ, se rallia aux mouvements des autres congrégations en 1787, influencée par le discours évangélique.

Parmi les principaux acteurs et entrepreneurs de cette première campagne contre l'abolition en Grande-Bretagne, Thomas Clarkson est considéré comme un inlassable ambassadeur de la cause auprès des cercles Quakers et Anglicans, auprès des parlementaires et du grand public, ainsi qu'auprès des Français en 1789. Françoise Le Jeune analyse ses écrits les plus importants. Ses textes polémiques font appel aux arguments utilisés par le discours évangélique mais aussi par les économistes, juristes et philosophes du XVIIIe siècle. Maniant savamment discours humaniste, discours religieux et discours politique, Clarkson traverse le pays inlassablement pour convaincre les classes moyennes de signer les pétitions qui représenteront leurs idées antiesclavagistes auprès d'un Parlement très oligarchique en cette fin de XVIIIe siècle.

Si les femmes n'étaient pas très remarquées dans le mouvement lors de la première campagne de 1787 à 1792, car leur présence et leur participation étaient souvent occultées par l'implication très visible des acteurs principaux Clarkson, Sharp et Wilberforce, Véronique Molinari montre que leur engagement dans la seconde partie de la campagne pour l'abolition de l'esclavage fut essentiel. Grâce à l'activisme de quelques figures importantes comme Elizabeth Heyrick, le mouvement en faveur de l'abolition de l'esclavage reprit à partir des années 1820. Alors qu'une grande partie de la population ainsi que les activistes de la première campagne étaient en faveur d'une abolition progressive de l'esclavage dans les colonies britanniques, Elizabeth Heyrick s'engagea en publiant des textes polémiques rappelant au public l'urgence de l'émancipation des esclaves en raison des conditions inhumaines dans lesquelles ils étaient exploités dans les Antilles. À sa suite, plusieurs associations de femmes s'organisèrent à travers la Grande-Bretagne pour rallier les femmes de la classe moyenne à la cause. Elizabeth Heyrick préconisait la levée de fonds pour une campagne nationale, la circulation d'informations sur les conditions inhumaines de l'esclavage auprès du public pour obtenir des signatures aux pétitions et pour finir le boycott des produits en provenance des plantations esclavagistes. Bien que s'engageant pour une cause publique, les femmes devaient néanmoins prendre en compte leur domaine d'action qui restait limité à la « sphère » féminine. Après l'abolition de l'esclavage dans les colonies britanniques, obtenue en 1833, Véronique Molinari rappelle que les femmes s'engagèrent à nouveau dans le combat pour l'émancipation des esclaves du système des apprentis auquel les planteurs eurent recours après la fin de l'esclavage. C'est l'envoi au parlement d'une pétition massivement signée par les femmes qui fut décisif dans l'émancipation des esclaves dans les colonies.

Françoise Orazi poursuit l'analyse de l'implication des femmes de la classe moyenne dans la campagne contre l'esclavage, en examinant les écrits d'Harriet Martineau, intellectuelle et écrivain britannique. Dans un premier texte de 1832, « Demerara » publié dans ses *Illustrations on Political Economy*, Martineau démontre par la « fiction » que l'esclavage est une pratique économiquement peu viable et, contrairement au discours des lobbies de planteurs, coûteuse à la métropole. Par ailleurs, lors de son voyage en Amérique en 1837-38, dont elle consigne les impressions dans *Society in America*, Martineau put observer les pratiques esclavagistes dans les colonies du Sud. Le système fut donc dénoncé par l'écrivain, ainsi que le lobby esclavagiste dont elle eut à subir les foudres après s'être exprimée dans la presse américaine avant son retour en Grande-Bretagne. Comme le montre Françoise Orazi, Martineau ne s'engage pas directement au sein d'une association de femmes militant pour l'émancipation des esclaves, sa santé le lui interdit à cette époque, mais elle se sert de sa plume pour dénoncer l'inhumanité de l'esclavage et pour soutenir les diverses rébellions contre les planteurs à Demerara ou à Saint-Domingue. Ce soutien est au cœur de *The Hour and the Man*, un texte fictionnel de 1841 prenant Toussaint Louverture pour héros. Martineau n'oublie pas pour autant sa « cause », la condition des femmes de son époque, en suggérant une comparaison radicale entre la cause des esclaves dans les colonies et la cause des épouses dans les sociétés civilisées, et en prenant l'image du « *bondage* » pour illustrer son propos.

Les Irlandais font partie, à double titre, de l'histoire de l'esclavage des Îles Britanniques : en tant qu'esclaves et en tant que propriétaires d'esclaves. Joyce Fereres rappelle cette dimension peu connue de l'histoire qu'est l'esclavage blanc, en particulier durant la seconde partie du XVIIe siècle. Il ne s'agit pas ici de l'« esclavage » au sens métaphorique dont parleront, au début du XIXe siècle, tous les radicaux et socialistes à propos du prolétaire anglais. Les esclaves irlandais sont embarqués de force, vendus et même parfois marqués au fer rouge. Et ils se révoltent aux côtés de leurs frères africains et sont comme eux réprimés dans le sang. Encore moins connue est la participation irlandaise au commerce négrier. Cette histoire-là dérange sans doute encore plus. Pourtant parmi les nombreux immigrés irlandais qui rejoignent l'Angleterre, les États-Unis, voire la France, quelques-uns parviennent à s'enrichir grâce à la traite. Outre l'attrait du gain, la brutalité envers les Noirs est pour ces immigrés de fraîche date un moyen de rejoindre la communauté *mainstream*, d'affirmer leur propre identité blanche. C'est en particulier le cas aux États-Unis, où le chemin de l'intégration irlandaise passe par l'oppression des Africains.

L'Écosse est, plus encore que l'Irlande, impliquée dans la question de l'esclavage, comme le montre William Findlay dans le dernier chapitre de ce volume. Elle l'est d'abord par la vigueur de son combat pour l'abolition. Cette forte mobilisation est d'autant plus inattendue que les travailleurs serviles en Écosse sont loin de représenter des populations très nombreuses, mais ce qu'ils représentent, symboliquement, est d'un poids sans commune mesure avec la réalité sociologique. Si la hiérarchie de l'Église d'Écosse ne s'empresse pas de soutenir la cause abolitionniste, le clergé de base, lui, fait feu de tout bois pour défendre les esclaves fugitifs. La société civile, qu'il s'agisse du secteur éducatif ou du mouvement ouvrier, se mobilise aussi lors des batailles juridiques, et la branche écossaise de la *Society for the Abolition of the Slave Trade* n'a rien à envier à son homologue anglaise. Mais il ne faut pas voir pour autant l'Écosse comme unanimement abolitionniste. Certaines villes écossaises, comme Glasgow, doivent à l'époque une grande part de leur prospérité au commerce négrier. L'Écosse est donc présente, pour le meilleur comme pour le pire, dans les combats qui font rage autour de l'esclavage. Les débats qui opposent abolitionnistes et antiabolitionnistes ne peuvent certainement pas s'étudier dans un contexte simplement anglo-anglais.

The Origins of the British Transatlantic Slave Trade (1560s-1760s): a Survey and an Assessment

Laurent Curelly

The British came to dominate the transatlantic slave trade in the course of the eighteenth century; yet, they had been rather late comers compared with other European nations. While the Portuguese had embraced the trade as early as the 1470s, transporting shiploads of enslaved Africans first to Portugal and later to Brazil, and forging an enduring link between slave labour and sugar cultivation, the British did not enter the European competition for African slaves until the 1640s at a time when sugar and other commodities produced in the Americas were beginning to change consumer tastes in Europe, including Britain.[1] English merchants only began to take an active part in the transatlantic slave trade in the mid-seventeenth century; similarly, only in the 1650s did the English government pass a series of laws to gain control of what was to become a lucrative trade involving England, the West African coast and the newly-conquered territories in North America and the Caribbean Sea.[2]

1. Spain followed the Portuguese lead as early as the 1490s, and its territories in the Americas were soon turned into slave-owning colonies. In the early sixteenth century, the Spanish Crown granted Portugal the *asiento*, a licence authorising it to enjoy a monopoly in the supply of enslaved Africans to Spanish colonies in America. The *asiento* changed hands in the next centuries until it was given to Britain following the Treaty of Utrecht in 1713. Other European powers, like the Netherlands and France, broke into the market for African slaves in the seventeenth century, thus turning the transatlantic slave trade into a source of commercial and diplomatic rivalry. For more information on the very beginnings of European involvement in the slave trade with Africa, see James Walvin, *A Short History of Slavery* (London: Penguin, 2007), pp.37-49, and Hugh Thomas, *The Slave Trade. The History of the Transatlantic Slave Trade 1440-1870* (New York: Simon & Schuster; London: Picador, 1997), pp.68-86.
2. The transatlantic trade, which involved three continents—Europe, Africa and America—, is often referred to as the triangular trade, the first leg of the trade consisting in European manufactured goods being shipped to Africa and bartered for enslaved Africans while the second leg consisted in the slaves captured or bought in Africa being forcibly transported across the Atlantic to the Americas. There they were supplied to planters to grow crops which were in high demand in Europe, such as tobacco, cacao, coffee, and especially sugar, an increasingly popular product initially used as a sweetener for hot drinks. Hence the third leg of the triangular trade was the homeward-bound voyage to Europe, with English ships delivering their cargoes of tropical products to English ports typically one year or so after their departure. This paper covers both the periods prior to and after the 1707 Act of Union, which marked the official birth of Great Britain, although the realms of England and Scotland were associated through the so-called Union of the Crowns as early as 1603 when James VI of Scotland ascended the English throne. As a result, the words "England" and "English" will generally be used to refer to the period of time before the 1707 Act of Union while "Britain" and "British" will be used to refer to history after 1707. In addition, the slave trade itself essentially concerned England rather than Scotland even if, in the eighteenth century, Glasgow thrived on the tobacco trade from the Chesapeake region in North America.

The eighteenth century was unquestionably the heyday of the British slave trade. It was the time when Britain came to outstrip Portugal as the leading exporter of African slaves, with over three million of them shipped to the Americas compared with approximately two million transported in Portuguese ships. British exports of enslaved Africans throughout the eighteenth century accounted for slightly less than half of the total number of slaves removed from Africa.[1] Over the whole of its slave-trading history from the 1640s to 1807, when the slave trade was officially abolished, Britain exported some three and a half million enslaved Africans to the Americas, which shows how big a role Georgian Britain actually played in the transatlantic trade with no less than 40,000 slaves shipped annually in the 1740s.[2] Thus, the sheer size of the British slave trade in the eighteenth century may be one of the reasons why the abolitionist movement came into its own in the 1770s-1780s with written accounts of former slaves popularised in Britain and religious dissenters voicing their opposition to the slave traffic operated by British merchants.[3] Although the impact of the transatlantic trade on the British economy is still a contentious issue among historians Britain's involvement was by no means marginal and may have caused the debate on the abolition of the trade to take a hold in Parliament and in the country at large.

The beginnings of the British slave trade

The British slave trade expanded steadily from the 1640s onwards; yet, there had been attempts before that time to secure African slaves, the first of which can be traced back to the 1560s. The first slaving voyage ever recorded in England was pioneered by John Hawkins in 1562. With the support of a syndicate including people who had traded with Africa

1. See David Richardson, "Slave exports from West and West-Central Africa, 1700-1810: new estimates of volume and distribution" (1988) in Jeremy Black ed., *The Atlantic Slave Trade. Volume III: Eighteenth Century* (Aldershot: Ashgate Publishing Ltd), pp.1-22. It should be noted that such estimates are merely educated guesses as there are no comprehensive records of the slave trade but only sketchy information, which is why slave trade figures are still a matter of debate among historians.
2. See Robin Law ed., *The British Transatlantic Trade. Vol.1: The Operation of the Slave Trade in Africa* (London: Pickering and Chatto, 2003), pp.xxxii. According to Law, the British slave trade seems to have reached a peak in the 1740s while Richardson (*op.cit.*) argues that it peaked in the 1790s and Kenneth Morgan in *Slavery, Atlantic Trade and the British Economy, 1660-1800* (Cambridge: Cambridge University Press, 2000) has the late 1760s as record high years for British slave exports. Numbers, therefore, provide a general view of trends and developments but should preferably be taken with a pinch of salt.
3. One such account was the autobiography of a former slave, Olaudah Equiano, published in 1789 under the title *The Interesting Narrative of the Life of Olaudah Equiano, or Gustavus Vassa, the African*. As regards the role played by religious groups in the struggle against the slave trade, American Quakers were instrumental in influencing those in Britain—initially fellow-Quakers and then Evangelicals—who spearheaded the abolitionist campaign.

before—albeit not in slaves—Hawkins captured Africans on the Guinea Coast and delivered them to Hispaniola, present-day Haiti, six months later, to be sold to Spanish settlers. As a private merchant, he had clearly infringed Portuguese and Spanish slave-trading monopolies but, back in England, he had been able to persuade the government that there was good money to be made from the triangular trade and had even received Queen Elizabeth's backing for a second and a third voyage which he completed between 1564 and 1569. From then on, however, English slaving voyages became occasional private ventures, hardly an organised and state-sponsored form of trade, and remained so until the 1640s.

Hawkins's slaving enterprises are worth mentioning, though, because they gave rise to contrasting readings when the slave trade issue was hotly debated in the Westminster Parliament in the late eighteenth century. Thus, Hawkins went down in history, clearly enjoying a fair amount of posterity with a staunch slave trade supporter like the Duke of Clarence, the future William IV, who duly named him in a speech to the House of Lords in 1799:

> That able navigator, Hawkins, in 1562, first sailed to Sierra Leone; and at that time the African Trade was considered of such importance in this country, that Queen Elizabeth, the ensuing year, sent Hawkins to trade there. He gives an account of their barbarity, and states, that the people were at that time mere slaves. He also mentions, that he found the French trading in that quarter of the world; so that your Lordships may perceive, that even so early as the latter part of the sixteenth century, the different nations of Europe that had possessions in the West Indies, considered the Slave Trade as absolutely necessary for the existence of those colonies. It is said, that Queen Elizabeth gave the first charter, and I believe the fact, as it comes from a very respectable channel.[1]

Clarence's view of Hawkins was challenged by abolitionist Thomas Clarkson who, in his *History of the Rise, Progress and Accomplishment of the Abolition of the African Slave Trade*, belittles the Elizabethan seafarer portraying him as the unscrupulous father of the English slave trade, while denying Queen Elizabeth I any responsibility in it:

> The first importation from Africa by our countrymen was in the reign of Elizabeth, in the year 1562. This great princess seems on the very

1. The Duke of Clarence's speech was incorporated under the auspices of the West India lobby and Liverpool merchants into a pamphlet entitled *Substance of the Speech of His Royal Highness The Duke of Clarence in The House of Lords on the Motion for the Recommitment of the Slave Trade Limitation Bill on the Fifth Day of July, 1799*. See John Pinfold, ed. *The Slave Trade Debate. Contemporary Writings For and Against* (Oxford: Bodleian Library, 2007) pp.331-366. Interestingly, the Duke of Clarence draws upon English history to put forward two major arguments consistently used by anti-abolitionists, the first being that enslaved Africans were no worse off working on plantations than they would be in Africa and the second being that abolishing the slave trade would mean undermining Britain's economy beyond repair.

> commencement of the trade to have questioned its lawfulness. She seems to have entertained a religious scruple concerning it, and indeed, to have revolted at the very thought of it. [...] When Captain Hawkins (afterwards Sir John) Hawkins returned from his first voyage to Africa and Hispaniola, whither he had carried slaves, she sent for him, and, as we learn from Hill's *Natural History*, expressed her concern lest any of the Africans should be carried off without their free consent. [...] Captain Hawkins promised to comply with the injunctions of Elizabeth in this respect. But he did not keep his word; for when he went to Africa again, he seized many of the inhabitants and carried them off as slaves.[1]

These two contrasting visions of England's past clearly serve two different purposes but the very reconstruction of history is intended by both men as a way to reach out to their respective audiences more effectively. It is doubtful whether Hawkins's slaving voyages played a major role in the actual development of the English transatlantic trade but they certainly contributed to building up a shared slaving past which would be either revered or rejected.

It is a fact, though, that until the mid-seventeenth century English merchants traded in Africa for other commodities than slaves, mainly gold. Official voyages to Africa under the early Stuarts were the sole responsibility of the Guinea Company, a joint-stock organisation which was set up in 1618 and was granted by King James I a monopoly over trade in that part of the world. Private merchants also joined in, in breach of the Guinea Company's monopoly, acting as interlopers. Meanwhile, England was keen to expand its empire in North America, with the foundation of Jamestown, Virginia, in 1607, and St Mary's, Maryland, in 1634 as well as in the Caribbean, with the establishment of colonies in St Kitts in 1623, Barbados in 1625, Nevis in 1628 and Montserrat and Antigua in 1632. These territories became the backbone of the British Empire in the west when it was discovered that the Chesapeake region in North America and the Caribbean islands could accommodate cash crops, respectively tobacco and sugar. In the 1640s, there was a high demand for labourers who would be physically able to grow the crops, which is why thousands of indentured servants[2] ended up working on plantations in the Americas. But the need

1. Thomas Clarkson, *History of the Rise, Progress and Accomplishment of the Abolition of the African Slave Trade, by the British Parliament* (London, 1808), volume I, chapter II.
2. Indentured servants were white immigrants who bought themselves to a planter for a certain period of time after which they were released from their servitude. During the Interregnum (1649-1660) they were typically paupers, convicts and political opponents who were thus kept away from Britain. They accounted for roughly 40 per cent of all whites in Britain's transatlantic colonies. Their numbers gradually declined as more and more African slaves were shipped across the Atlantic. See Hillary McD. Beckles, "The 'Hub of Empire': The Caribbean and Britain in the Seventeenth Century" in Nicholas Canny, ed. *The Origins of Empire. Oxford History of the British Empire* (Oxford: Oxford university Press, 1998) pp.222-4.

for labourers in the American colonies, especially in the sugar islands, was so great that England soon turned to African slaves to keep production going.

Barbados shifted its production to sugar in the mid-1640s, thus becoming the richest of all British colonies, but it soon lost the lead it held because of sugar production to Jamaica. 1655 marked a watershed in the expansion of England's commercial empire. A few months after Cromwell had launched his "Western Design", Jamaica was captured from the Spanish and was subsequently peopled by English settlers who turned the island into a major sugar production centre. Ultimately, but for the conquest of Jamaica, Cromwell's plan to secure the much-coveted island of Hispaniola and thus to undermine the Spanish economic dominance in the Caribbean failed. Yet, building on Cromwell's political vision and economic ambitions for England the English state was committed to asserting its transatlantic presence on an unprecedented scale, which was all the more crucial as the Dutch were also showing a keen interest in the region.[1]

From the 1660 Restoration until the late eighteenth century, when opponents began to call for its abolition, the British transatlantic trade continued unabated. Between the 1660s and the 1760s the number of slaves shipped from Africa to the Americas per decade increased almost tenfold. Over their slave trading period the British undertook 12,000 slaving voyages out of a total of 34,000 with 5,000 of them originating in Liverpool. Due to mass-imports, the slave population in Barbados soared from a little over 5,500 in 1645 to 20,000 in 1651 and 50,000 in 1700. In the early 1700s Jamaica took over from Barbados as the major destination for African slaves in the British Americas and, by 1750, it was home to nearly 120,000 enslaved Africans. Compared with the Caribbean islands, British settlements in North America imported fewer African slaves as the fertility rate among slaves became higher there and fewer supplies were needed as a result. The staggeringly large number of slave imports to the British Caribbean resulted in shifting population patterns among blacks and whites on those

1. Cromwell's political vision consisted in keeping Spain in check which, after a fair amount of dithering, was branded as England's arch-enemy. Cromwell's "Western Design" was presented by the propagandists of the regime as a spiritual crusade led by a Protestant nation against a Catholic power—a "popish state" as Spain was called in those days—although the rationale behind this plan was certainly much more mundane. Its essential aim was clearly to challenge the power of Spain overseas. England's commercial expansion was aided by the passing of protectionist laws, the so-called Navigation Acts (see further down). For a discussion of why, quite ironically, the slave trade was boosted during the Interregnum, an age when the English had broken free from the tyranny of the Stuart monarchs, see Carla Gardina Pestana, *The English Atlantic in an Age of Revolution, 1640-1661* (Cambridge, Mass. & London: Harvard University Press, 2004) pp.177-180.

islands: by the 1670s, indeed, black slaves had outnumbered white people with over 75 per cent of blacks in 1700 and 90 per cent in 1780.[1]

All these figures are an obvious sign that, shortly after joining in the slave trade, England acquired a leading position, which it retained until the 1807 Abolition Act. By the mid-seventeenth century it had emerged as the main rival of the Netherlands, which eventually led to the second Anglo-Dutch War of 1665-67, and the English soon outran the Dutch in the fierce competition for African slaves. British hegemony over the transatlantic trade was further consolidated by the fact that in 1713 Britain was able to secure the *asiento* as a result of the Treaty of Utrecht which ended the Spanish War of Succession. The *asiento* meant that, from then on, the British South Sea Company was granted a monopoly right to ship enslaved Africans to Spanish colonies in America[2], so that by the early eighteenth century Britain clearly dwarfed its European competitors in terms of slave exports to the Americas.

The organisation of the British transatlantic slave trade

In 1713, the South Sea Company was by no means the only slaving operator in Britain. It actually partnered up with the Royal African Company (R.A.C.) which, until the 1690s, had been a key-player in the transatlantic trade although by the early eighteenth century it was overshadowed by private merchants who competed ferociously for the provision of slaves to British colonies in the Americas. A successor to the Company of Royal Adventurers into Africa which received a royal charter in 1660, the Royal African Company was established in 1672 and granted by King Charles II a monopoly right over English trade with Africa. This meant that private merchants, who had been in favour during the Interregnum while the trade was still in its infancy but was beginning to grow, were officially denied any participation in the supplying of slaves to English colonies in the Americas.

Setting up monopoly companies to conduct trade overseas was far from uncommon in early modern times. No later than 1618 was the Company of Adventurers of London Trading to the Parts of Africa founded, whose remit was to trade with Africa, albeit not in slaves. This company, better known as the "Guinea Company", was granted a royal charter by James I.

1. For these figures and more, see James Walvin, *A Short History of Slavery*, *op.cit.*; Kenneth Morgan, *Slavery and the British Empire from Africa to America* (Oxford: Oxford University Press, 2007); David Richardson, "The British Empire and the Transatlantic Slave Trade 1660-1807" in P.J. Marshall, *The Oxford History of the British Empire. Vol.II: The Eighteenth Century* (Oxford, New York: Oxford University Press, 1998).
2. The *asiento* was in fact discontinued when Britain and Spain were in conflict, in 1718-21, 1727-29 and 1739-48, and it ended in 1748.

It was reorganised in 1631 and continued to enjoy royal patronage as a fresh charter was issued by Charles I but lost its monopoly in the wake of the Civil War and the abolition of monarchy in 1649, when private companies were encouraged to enter the African trade. It was a period of time when England was beginning to deal in African slaves on a much larger scale than the occasional ventures of the previous decades. Private merchants rushed in to enter the trade and began to tap the slave market. Soon after the Restoration, however, Charles II made private trading to Africa illegal by granting a charter to the Company of Royal Adventurers Trading to Africa, the first joint-stock company of its kind to pursue the slave trade, among other activities. The Company of Royal Adventurers sustained financial losses and went bust in the late 1660s before being replaced by the Royal African Company in 1672. British monarchs at that time were keen to endorse monopoly companies which they assumed would boost trade and thus bolster the economy. The R.A.C. could rely on the king's protection and was instrumental in the development of England's transatlantic trade in the late seventeenth century.[1] This, however, did not stop interlopers from trading illegally and increasingly challenging the R.A.C.'s leadership.

With the demise of royal absolutism in 1688 and the rise of parliamentary monarchy, the Royal African Company's monopolistic position came under constant criticism from private traders who pushed for a more open trade to Africa in order to further their interests. Private merchants especially combated the R.A.C. in Parliament by continuously petitioning MPs and conducting intense lobbying. This power struggle was successful, for they were able to have a law passed in 1698 which rescinded the R.A.C.'s monopoly and henceforth opened the transatlantic trade to competitors. However, the latter had to pay a 10 per cent duty on their outward cargoes to Africa towards maintenance costs for the forts operated by the R.A.C on the African coast.[2]

Such a guarantee was only short-lived as the 10 per cent tax provision included in the 1698 act was due to be scrapped in 1712. Private merchants, thus, had dealt the R.A.C. a severe blow from which it never recovered and, from 1712 onwards, the British slave trade became deregulated with private traders vying for market shares. In the early eighteenth century the R.A.C. was almost extinct; in 1730 its market share accounted for a mere

1. The R.A.C. often minted gold coins featuring an elephant's head, the company's emblem; these coins came to be known as "guineas".
2. Forts looking out to sea were operated on the African coast in order to protect British interests from onslaughts by other European vessels, thus facilitating the embarkation of enslaved Africans onto British ships. Maintenance costs for these forts were high and, to make matters worse, the R.A.C. was often accused of mismanagement.

1 per cent of Britain's total slave trade while in its glory days in the 1680s it had secured over 85 per cent of the trade as other companies operated illegally.[1] The R.A.C. was dissolved by parliamentary act in 1821 but by the 1720s it had already reached its nadir.

Interestingly, the battle between the R.A.C. and its private opponents was first and foremost waged in Parliament with the R.A.C. launching the first attack in 1690 in order to have its monopoly guaranteed by law. This move initiated protracted parliamentary debates on the organisation of the slave trade which were to last for nearly twenty-five years. In 1690 a committee of the House of Commons was appointed to look into the organisation of the African trade and decide whether it could be deregulated. Both camps engaged in a fair amount of petitioning and pamphleteering in order to win MPs over to their cause. Daniel Defoe, for instance, wrote in defence of the R.A.C. Separate traders did their utmost to convince Parliament that statutory protection for the R.A.C. would not serve the interests of the nation and pushed for unregulated trade to Africa instead. They also used the press in an effort to persuade public opinion to back their endeavours to liberalise the British transatlantic trade. Critics argued that the R.A.C. lacked efficiency as, among other things, it failed to meet the growing demand for enslaved Africans in the British Americas; the same sort of criticism Adam Smith later levelled at the very principle of monopoly which he dismissed as "a great enemy to good management".[2] Supporters of the R.A.C. countered that the maintenance of forts on the African coast was bound to be a drain on their finances but added that it was the only way of protecting the African trade from foreign intrusion. They also claimed that public interest was best served by a joint-stock company while separate traders would only advance their own interests.[3]

1. For more details on the Royal African Company, see William Pettigrew, "Parliament and the Escalation of the Slave Trade 1690-1714" in *The British Slave Trade: Abolition, Parliament and People*, ed. by Stephen Farrell, Melanie Uwin and James Walvin (Edinburgh: Edinburgh University Press, 2007) pp.12-26; Kenneth Morgan, ed. *The British Transatlantic Trade*. Vol.2: *The Royal African Company* (London: Pickering & Chatto, 2003), pp.XI-XXI.
2. Adam Smith, *An Inquiry into the Nature and Causes of the Wealth of Nations* (1776), 5th ed., 1789 (Harmondsworth: Penguin, 1979) Book I, chapter 11, p.251.
3. The author of an anonymous pamphlet in support of the R.A.C., for example, insists that "Trade and Commerce cannot be maintained or increased without Government, Order and regular Discipline; for in all confused Traffique it must necessarily happen, that while every single person pursued his own particular Interest, the Publique is deserted by All, and consequently must fall to Ruine. For which reason, the Crowne has Erected and Established Fraternities or Companies of Merchants, with Grant of Privileges exclusive to all others, as his Majesties Ancestors and Himself by their Royal Charters have been graciously pleased to do to the Royal African, East-India, Turkey, Hamburgh, Eastland and Muscovia Companies". *Certain Considerations Relating to the Royal African Company of England. In which, the Original Growth, and National Advantages of the Guiney Trade, are Demonstrated: As Also That the Same Trade cannot be*

Thus, less than a century before it debated the abolition of the slave trade, Parliament became a forum for discussion as to how the trade should be organised. The *modus operandi* was much the same as it would be in the 1780s; there was active lobbying from both sides with petitions circulating at Westminster and a considerable amount of propaganda, even if public opinion was not whipped up to the extent it would be when an abolitionist like Thomas Clarkson toured Britain in order to collect signatures for petitions to be presented to the House of Commons. The major difference between the way the slave trade was debated in the 1690s and in the 1780s concerns the nature of the debates themselves. In the late seventeenth century the transatlantic trade was taken for granted as it was said to generate profits which, it was assumed, were conducive to England's prosperity and grandeur in the face of international competition. The parliamentary debates did not seize the moral high ground as was the case some hundred years later but revolved around financial arguments such as how England would best benefit from the slave trade. Over the seventeenth century and well into the next century state institutions—Parliament and monarchs alike—had a vested interest in promoting the British transatlantic trade, a fact which is particularly revealing of the mercantilist approach to economic issues prevalent in those days.

The British transatlantic trade and mercantilist economics

The fact that the British transatlantic trade was gradually opened up to separate traders is seen by some historians as a spin-off of the government's efforts to provide it with external protection. Thus, Parliament passed a host of Navigation Acts between 1651 and 1696 in an attempt to regulate English trade, especially shipping, and preclude foreign interference with English commerce.[1] These were clearly protectionist barriers aimed at defending national interest. The first Navigation Act, which came into force in 1651, was especially targeted at the Netherlands, the then leading commercial power in Europe. It provided that:

> No goods or commodities whatsoever of the growth, production or manufacture of Asia, Africa or any part thereof; or of any islands belonging to them, [...] shall be imported or brought into this Commonwealth of England, or into Ireland, or any other lands, islands, plantations, or territories to this Commonwealth belonging, or in their possession, in any other ship or ships,

carried on, but by a Company and Joint Stock (London, 1680) published in Kenneth Morgan ed., *The British Transatlantic Slave Trade.* Vol.2: *The Royal African Company, op.cit.*, pp.5-14. One of the arguments put forward in support of the R.A.C. was that royal patronage legitimised its very existence.

1. Scotland had trade laws of its own passed by the Scottish Parliament. Not until the 1707 Act of Union, in fact, did Scotland enjoy commercial access to English colonies.

> vessel or vessels whatsoever, but only in such as do truly and without fraud belong only to the people of this Commonwealth, or of the plantations thereof, as the proprietors or right owners thereof.[1]

By and large, the 1651 Navigation Act failed to achieve its intended aim, for it was often circumvented; nevertheless it initiated similar pieces of legislation which helped to consolidate English trade.

The 1660 Navigation Act was passed after the Restoration but it re-enacted the 1651 act as it included the same provisions while adding to it significantly. Thus, it required that vessels should be manned by overwhelmingly British crews and it enumerated commodities produced in English colonies which could only be shipped to England or English possessions. For instance, sugar produced in the West Indies thanks to slave labour was to be transported in English ships to an English port from where it could be re-exported to other European countries. The 1663 Staple Act provided that all goods bound for English colonies had to go through an English port. As a result, the Dutch were eliminated from the English carrying trade and London soon overtook Amsterdam as Europe's largest warehouse. By the 1670s, with the help of protectionist legislation, England had secured a leading commercial position which it retained throughout the eighteenth century, and the slave trade was provided with a legislative framework that allowed it to thrive. Another three acts, respectively passed in 1673, 1696 and 1733, complemented the series of Navigation Acts and further codified trade. In addition to regulatory measures, the 1696 act included a provision for the establishment of a Board of Trade to enforce the law. The 1733 Molasses Act significantly placed heavy duties on molasses and sugar shipped from the French West Indies to British colonies in North America in support of the British sugar trade. The Navigation Acts were renewed and extended in 1786 and persisted well into the age of abolitionism, as they were not repealed until 1849. Since whole sectors of the British economy came to depend on overseas trade, it was felt that a battery of laws was needed to preserve the national interest.[2]

1. Reproduced in Samuel Gardiner, ed. *The Constitutional Documents of the Puritan Revolution 1625-1660* (Oxford: Clarendon Press, 1906) p.468. Other reasons than purely commercial concerns seem to have prompted the government to come up with the Navigation Act. The act was first passed in retaliation for the refusal of the Dutch government to negotiate an alliance with England, a move which the English regarded as an affront. Domestic and international events therefore resulted in the passing of the 1651 Navigation Act.
2. For further information on the Navigation Acts, see Nuala Zahedieh, "Overseas Expansion and Trade in the Seventeenth Century" in Nicholas Canny, ed. *The Origins of Empire, Oxford History of the British Empire, op.cit.*, pp.405-7; David Ormrod, *The Rise of Commercial Empires. England and the Netherlands in the Age of Mercantilism, 1650-1770* (Cambridge: Cambridge University Press, 2003) pp.31-37, 44-48, 309-311.

It is no accident that British trade, of which the transatlantic trade was a pillar, should have been thus regulated even when existing monopoly companies were dying out. State interference with overseas trade, which expressed itself through protectionist laws, was dictated by a mercantilist approach to the economy which had developed since the late sixteenth century and prevailed in the seventeenth century. The label "mercantilism" was used in retrospect to refer to those economic policies pursued by European nations, especially Britain and France, from the sixteenth to the nineteenth century. It was thought then that a nation's prosperity depended on the wealth it was able to accumulate; thus, in an effort to achieve a favourable balance of trade, the British government sought to produce wealth by promoting exports and limiting imports. Commercial policies were implemented which made it possible for Britain to produce a favourable balance of trade and thereby amass bullion: colonies became exclusive markets for their mother countries, trade monopolies were set up, Navigation Acts were passed, customs duties were levied on foreign goods entering British territory, whether on the mainland or in the colonies. All these measures contributed to Britain developing a competitive edge over its European rivals in international trade.[1] The mercantile system was meant to favour the interests of British merchants and producers against foreign competition but soon came under fierce criticism from such prominent thinkers as Adam Smith who, in his *Inquiry into the Nature and Causes of the Wealth of Nations*, debunked it point by point.[2]

The British transatlantic trade clearly fed into the British economy. Historians, however, disagree as to how much money the slave trade generated, who really benefited from it and to what extent it stimulated the British economy in the eighteenth century. Some scholars argue that it

1. It should be noted that Britain imported a great many commodities from overseas, either from its colonies or from other countries; for the latter, customs duties were levied. Besides, a significant number of goods entering Britain were re-exported to foreign markets. The profits derived from trade were channelled into an ever-expanding economy, with manufactured goods churned out both for the domestic market and for export.
2. The mercantile system remained the driving force behind British colonial trade until at least the beginning of the nineteenth century. By the mid-nineteenth century, though, laissez-faire economics, as advocated by Adam Smith, had taken hold of foreign exchanges. The repeal of the Corn Laws in 1846 and of the Navigation Acts in 1849 completed the dismantling of the mercantile system at home and abroad. Some historians like Seymour Drescher in his *Econocide: British Slavery in the Era of Abolition* (Pittsburgh: Pittsburgh University Press, 1977) deny that there is a correlation between the abolition of slavery and the emergence of a new economic system. Drescher's intended aim was to refute a thesis propounded by Eric Williams in a groundbreaking book, *Capitalism and Slavery* (Chapel Hill: University of North Carolina Press, 1944). Williams's "decline" thesis had it that the abolition of slavery was linked to the economic decline of British Caribbean colonies and to the demise of the old mercantile system. A new economic system was coming into existence, Williams argued, which ultimately made the slave trade and slavery obsolete.

set off the Industrial Revolution and, as a result, altered Britain's economic landscape while others play down its alleged impact on the industrialisation process that was to transform Britain beyond recognition. Historians seem to have reached consensus on the fact that the expansion of colonial trade did impact the British economy, even if their estimates of the profits accruing from it vary considerably.[1] If the effect of slave trade profits on the British national income cannot be measured with uncontroversial precision, the transatlantic trade clearly contributed to the prosperity of British merchants, the rise of financial institutions and the growth of British ports from an early period onwards. Bills of exchange allowing planters to pay for slaves were used extensively from the 1670s; they were sometimes presented by traders to banks where they could be cashed in but could also be submitted to other middlemen like private brokers. Marine insurance companies also benefited from the trade.[2]

Above all, the transatlantic trade fostered the growth of ports. As soon as the trade took off London played a crucial role in the shipment of manufactured goods to Africa and the import of staple crops from English colonies in the Americas. England's capital city became Europe's leading commercial hub with a large number of re-exports to European countries originating on its docks. It retained its dominance until the mid-1720s but the London-based Royal African Company was in sharp decline by then and the transatlantic trade moved to Bristol whose private traders had been instrumental in bringing about the R.A.C.'s demise. Bristol prospered on the sugar trade with the West Indies from the 1720s to the 1740s at which time Liverpool took over as the leading slave-trading outport. Liverpool maintained its supremacy through to the end of the slave trade in 1807. Thus, almost half of all British slaving voyages departed from Liverpool, mostly in the eighteenth century. It was not just British ports that thrived on the slave trade but the hinterland also reaped significant benefits. A case in point is Manchester whose cotton industry experienced dramatic growth in less than twenty years with most of its items exported to Africa via Liverpool and exchanged for slaves.[3] It is no accident therefore that Bristol

1. It is estimated that profit levels in the slave trade were no higher than 7.5 per cent in the latter half of the eighteenth century; source material is lacking to calculate profit levels prior to 1750 with any acceptable degree of accuracy. For a detailed presentation of the debates on the profits of the slave trade see Kenneth Morgan, *Slavery, Atlantic Trade and the British Economy, 1600-1800, op.cit.*, pp.24-48.
2. See Kenneth Morgan, *Slavery, Atlantic Trade and the British Economy, 1600-1800, op.cit.*, pp.74-79.
3. With its port making money from the tobacco and sugar trades Glasgow also became a great commercial city in the course of the eighteenth century, on a par with Bristol and Liverpool; yet, it did not participate directly in the slave trade the way its English counterparts did. For further information on the contribution of the slave trade to the economic activity of British ports, see Kenneth Morgan, *Slavery and the British Empire from Africa to America, op.cit.*, pp.61-66;

and Liverpool MPs should have been at the forefront of the opposition to the abolition of the slave trade when the issue was raised and debated in the British Parliament. They felt that the economic interests of their constituencies were at stake and that abolition would inevitably entail a severe crisis.

From Hawkins's exploratory slaving voyages to Liverpool's commitment to the slave trade, nearly two centuries elapsed during which the British transatlantic trade rose to dizzy heights. From a fledgling practice the slave trade turned into a flourishing business which buttressed Britain's commercial empire. From an organisational perspective, it was once a state-sponsored activity with monopoly companies trading on behalf of the monarch but it gradually became an arena for free internal competition, which attracted private merchants hankering after money. Almost from the outset, it was often high on the British political agenda, although in a more subdued way than when the abolition issue moved centre stage. Thus, it attracted attention on a number of occasions, especially when its organisation gave rise to heated debates in Parliament and when British governments adopted protectionist measures in an effort to outshine European rivals.

The economics of the transatlantic trade are a vexed issue. Arguably, the slave trade was central to the economic development of British colonies in the Americas and to the growing prosperity of their slave-holding plantocracy. Besides, it provided a significant impetus to the economic and financial activities most closely associated with it—the merchant corporation itself but also the banking and insurance sectors as well as the shipbuilding industry and a few other manufacturing industries. Ports like Bristol and Liverpool greatly benefited from it. Whether the slave trade had far-reaching repercussions on the British economy as a whole cannot be ascertained. To the anti-abolitionists of the late eighteenth century, however, there was not the least doubt about this, hence their repeated claims that abolition would not only bring about a slump in the economy of the West-Indies but would also damage Britain's economic activity, as this extract from an anonymous trade pamphlet testifies:

> That this [the slave trade] is as lucrative a branch of Commerce as any our Merchants are engaged in, the Wealth of Liverpool, Bristol, etc; whose principal Merchants are embarked in that Trade will confirm. [...] With Respect to our Country, it will not be difficult to point out the numerous Evils which

Kenneth Morgan, *Atlantic Trade and the British Economy, 1600-1800*, *op.cit.*, pp.84-93; Hugh Thomas, *The Slave trade*, *op.cit.*, pp.243-250; www.discoveringbristol.org.uk.

> must arise to our Commerce, from the Annihilation of Trade so peculiarly Advantageous to it and our Colonies.[1]

The author's vindication of the slave trade rests on the assumption that in the eighteenth century Britain's economic strength went hand in hand with its colonial empire, which it had taken one century and a half to build. This may explain why many years of passionate debates were needed before the British transatlantic trade eventually became a thing of the past.

Bibliography

Beckles, Hillary, "The 'Hub of Empire': The Caribbean and Britain in the Seventeenth Century", in Nicholas Canny ed., *The Oxford History of the British Empire.* Vol.I: *The Origins of Empire,* Oxford: Oxford University Press, 1998.

Clarkson, Thomas, *History of the Rise, Progress and Accomplishment of the Abolition of the African Slave Trade, by the British Parliament*, London, 1808.

Morgan, Kenneth, Law Robin, Oldfield, John, Ryden, David eds., *The British Transatlantic Trade*, 4 vols., London: Pickering and Chatto, 2003.

Morgan, Kenneth, *Slavery, Atlantic Trade and the British Economy, 1660-1800,* Cambridge: Cambridge University Press, 2000.

—, *Slavery and the British Empire from Africa to America*, Oxford: Oxford University Press, 2007.

Ormrod, David, *The Rise of Commercial Empires. England and the Netherlands in the Age of Mercantilism, 1650-1770,* Cambridge: Cambridge University Press, 2003.

Pestana, Carla Gardina, *The English Atlantic in an Age of Revolution, 1640-1661,* Cambridge, Mass. & London: Harvard University Press, 2004.

Pettigrew, William, "Parliament and the Escalation of the Slave Trade, 1690-1714", in Stephen Farrell, Melanie Uwin and James Walvin eds., *The British Slave Trade: Abolition, Parliament and People,* Edinburgh: Edinburgh University Press, 2007.

Richardson, David, "The British Empire and the Transatlantic Slave Trade, 1660-1807", in P.J. Marshall, *Oxford History of the British Empire.* Vol.II: *The Eighteenth Century,* Oxford: Oxford University Press, 1998.

Thomas, Hugh, *The Slave Trade. The History of the Transatlantic Slave Trade, 1440-1870,* New York: Simon & Schuster; London: Picador, 1997.

1. *Commercial Reasons for the Non-Abolition of the Slave Trade in the West-Indian Islands* (London: W. Lane, 1789) in David Ryden ed., *The British Transatlantic Trade.* Vol.4: *The Abolitionist Struggle; Promoters of the Slave Trade* (London: Pickering and Chatto, 2003) p.10.

Le discours des antiabolitionnistes britanniques de 1787 à 1833

Éric Molina

Introduction

Au sein du discours esclavagiste qui s'est développé au Siècle des Lumières dans les nations colonisatrices européennes, on constate que le discours antiabolitionniste anglais présente une réelle originalité de par la multiplicité des références employées par les auteurs de textes esclavagistes britanniques afin de faire évoluer leur argumentation au cours de la campagne pour l'abolition qui débuta dans les années 1770 et se termina en 1833 avec la promulgation de l'Émancipation finale des esclaves dans les colonies anglaises des Caraïbes.

Pour bien comprendre cette spécificité du discours antiabolitionniste anglais et son impact sur la société britannique et les sociétés créoles de l'époque, il paraît intéressant de se pencher sur les différents arguments qu'ont pu adopter les partisans de l'institution pour maintenir l'esclavage. On remarque que les antiabolitionnistes anglais ont en réalité combiné plusieurs modèles pour étayer leur défense du système, qu'il s'agisse de modèles pseudo-scientifiques fondés sur les nouvelles théories raciales concernant la gradation des espèces et les hypothèses polygénistes initiées par les naturalistes, de références religieuses empruntées à la Bible ou encore de modèles politiques et juridiques directement inspirés des civilisations antiques gréco-romaines. Le recours à ces modèles divers a permis aux antiabolitionnistes de moderniser et d'inclure de façon permanente dans leur discours le postulat de l'infériorité de la race noire, afin de pouvoir continuer d'utiliser à leur profit le statut de « bien meuble » des esclaves en se retranchant derrière la protection du droit à la propriété dans son interprétation juridique la plus stricte. D'autre part, l'analyse des arguments antiabolitionnistes anglais permet aussi de comprendre dans quelle mesure l'attitude inflexible des propriétaires a pu contribuer à favoriser l'éclosion des nouveaux courants réformateurs philosophiques et religieux qui se sont développés à l'époque du débat sur l'abolition.

Parmi les nombreux textes esclavagistes publiés au début des années 1770, ceux du chroniqueur jamaïcain Edward Long[1] permettaient déjà de

1. Ayant vécu de nombreuses années à la Jamaïque, qu'il dut quitter pour se retirer en Angleterre en raison de problèmes de santé, Edward Long écrivit plusieurs textes défendant le principe de l'infériorité de la race noire et justifiant l'esclavage, qui eurent un immense retentissement dans les cercles de pensée anglais au moment où le débat sur l'abolition commençait à prendre

mesurer l'influence considérable des théories raciales pré-darwiniennes sur le contenu de l'argumentation du discours antiabolitionniste anglais. En établissant une hiérarchie scientifique des races humaines qui plaçait systématiquement la race noire au bas de l'échelle par le biais de la gradation des espèces, puis en tentant de prouver de façon scientifique l'hypothèse du polygénisme, c'est-à-dire la non appartenance des Noirs à l'espèce humaine, les premiers naturalistes avaient en effet largement contribué à donner un fondement scientifique au postulat de l'infériorité de la race noire déjà présent dans le discours esclavagiste depuis les débuts de l'institution. Pour illustrer les diverses facettes et l'évolution particulière du discours négrier anglais jusqu'à l'Émancipation, on se référera à quelques auteurs représentatifs du point de vue des planteurs, William Beckford Jr et Bryan Edwards, à l'époque de l'Abolition de la Traite et trois auteurs négrier anglais représentant la position antiabolitionniste en métropole, Harris, Holroyd et Cobbett. Puis nous étudierons les transformations du discours des planteurs après 1807 à travers l'argumentation du pseudo « Révérent Hampden », mise en place pour tenter d'empêcher à tout prix la promulgation de l'Émancipation.

de l'ampleur. Ses écrits reflétaient parfaitement les inquiétudes et les préjugés sexuels et raciaux qui hantaient les partisans de l'esclavage colonial, que ceux-ci soient directement ou non partie prenante du système, comme on peut l'observer dans le pamphlet intitulé *Candid Reflexions Upon the Judgement lately awarded by the Court of King's Bench... On what is commonly called the Negroe Cause* que Long publia en 1772. Ce texte mettait en exergue les grandes peurs d'une pensée raciste anglaise naissante, pour qui la « race » blanche ne devait en aucun cas être contaminée par des unions mixtes qui auraient pu provoquer une dégénérescence et un appauvrissement. On peut noter que Long n'hésitait pas à ranger les Portugais et les Maures dans la même catégorie des « races » inférieures que les Noirs, et à qualifier le mélange des « races » de « contamination ». L'*Histoire de la Jamaïque* fut cependant le plus influent et le plus respecté des textes de Long, du fait de son expérience personnelle de la réalité du système esclavagiste pratiqué aux Antilles, qui lui assurait une caution morale auprès du public et des autres penseurs. Cet ouvrage, qui traitait d'une grande variété de sujets, est principalement connu pour ses descriptions très tendancieuses des populations noires africaines. Il contient également une description sévère du comportement des planteurs et des gouverneurs coloniaux et une critique des brutalités de l'esclavage qui furent utilisées par William Wilberforce dans ses discours au Parlement contre la traite négrière. Dans la partie du texte consacrée aux Noirs africains, Long affirmait que les Noirs étaient une espèce totalement distincte de la « race » blanche et faisaient donc partie d'un groupe racial intermédiaire entre l'humanité et les singes les plus évolués, en particulier les orangs-outangs, considérés par Linné et d'autres naturalistes comme la plus basse forme d'humanité. Long divisa par conséquent le genre humain en trois espèces différentes : les « Européens » et races similaires, les « Nègres » et les « Orangs-outangs », fournissant une justification pseudo-scientifique et prétendument vérifiée de façon empirique au principe d'infériorité de la « race » noire. Long, en énonçant ainsi les premières théories « polygénistes » sur les « races », semble avoir clairement influencé le naturaliste Charles White dans ses études sur les variations de l'espèce humaine. Son obtination à se cantonner le plus souvent dans son raisonnement négrier aux principes pseudo-scientifiques de « race » élaborés par les premiers naturalistes, au contraire de son homologue Kames ou d'autres écrivains esclavagistes de son siècle, a conduit certains chercheurs à le considerer comme le véritable « père » du concept discriminatoire de « *otherness* », fondement central du racisme anglais moderne.

William Beckford Jr

William Beckford Jr proposait une interprétation très particulière des réalités de l'institution esclavagiste pratiquée dans les colonies anglaises des Antilles et de ses bienfaits supposés sur les travailleurs serviles déportés du continent africain. On est loin de ressentir dans son discours presque « humaniste » la haine viscérale du Noir et les anxiétés racistes et xénophobes qui transparaissaient dans les textes du planteur Edward Long ou plus tard dans les écrits du chroniqueur politique William Cobbett. Cousin de l'auteur du célèbre roman gothique *Vathek*, William Beckford avait hérité des plantations de son père en Jamaïque, où il vécut pendant treize ans avant de rentrer en Angleterre pour s'installer à Somerley Hall, dans le Suffolk. « Beckford de Somerley », comme on le nommait, se trouva bientôt ruiné : il fut donc forcé de passer plusieurs années, emprisonné pour dettes à la prison de la Fleet, d'où il ne cessait d'envoyer des courriers et suppliques pour quémander de l'aide de son célèbre cousin romancier et de riches membres de sa famille. C'est pendant son séjour dans cette prison qu'il écrivit aussi ses *Remarks upon the Situation of Negroes in Jamaica*[1] et les dédicaça à Sir William Parsons, devenu depuis peu le directeur de l'Orchestre de musique royal, dont il recherchait probablement le soutien.

Dans son texte, Beckford défendait bien évidemment la position esclavagiste la plus courante, adoptée par les partisans du maintien de l'institution dès l'émergence du débat dans la seconde moitié du XVIIIe siècle : ceux-ci se prétendaient en effet investis, au nom de la « Civilisation » et en tant que planteurs, d'une obligation d'évangéliser et de « civiliser » leurs esclaves d'origine africaine.

> *I am not an advocate for the liberation of the slave. I am an advocate for all that can make him comfortable, I am an advocate for all that can make him happy; I am an advocate for his removal from his natal soil, that he may taste the comforts of protection, the fruits of humanity, and the blessings of religion.*[2]

Dans la première partie de ses *Remarks* il débutait en décrivant des exemples de mauvais traitements et d'abus infligés aux esclaves par certains propriétaires ; il plaidait aussi pour un réaménagement de l'institution, qu'il ne remettait pas en cause et considérait comme allant de soi. Ses propositions sur ce point concernaient donc essentiellement la nécessité

1. William Beckford Jr, *Remarks upon the Situation of Negroes in Jamaica, Impartially Made from Local Experience of Nearly Thirteen Years in that Island,* London, 1788. (reprint *Slavery, Abolition and Emancipation,* vol. 2, *The Abolition Debate*) pp. 253-280.
2. Beckford, *op. cit.* p. 252.

d'une plus grande sévérité des lois coloniales envers les propriétaires abusifs :

> *To wretches of this description, whose cruelty rises in proportion to the weakness of the object, no excuse should be made, no protection given; they should be deprived of the powers of punishment, hooted through the world as dishonourers of nature; should find no companion but shame, no rest but in death; and this completion of human punishment should be as painful as ignominious.*[1]

Beckford poursuivait son essai en décrivant à sa manière les réalités quotidiennes de la vie des esclaves, et même s'il semblait manifester une certaine compassion à leur égard, il ne leur accordait qu'un statut intermédiaire entre l'humain et l'animal domestique. Il se démarquait ensuite nettement de la position de la plupart des autres auteurs esclavagistes de l'époque par des propositions quelque peu utopiques pour améliorer un système auquel il croyait cependant profondément. Le chroniqueur s'extasiait par exemple sur les moments de loisirs du travailleur servile, qui était censé ne travailler que quelques heures par jour et passer le reste du temps à s'amuser et à discuter pendant la préparation du repas, le soir ou au cours du repos dominical. Le planteur tentait ainsi à sa manière de donner une perception positive de l'institution.

À l'examen de ses écrits, on a l'impression d'une description idyllique des rapports entre maîtres et esclaves, dans un monde où chacun est finalement satisfait dans son rôle social. Beckford allait même jusqu'à remercier les esclaves pour leur participation à la prospérité économique des colonies sucrières anglaises (et donc à celle de leurs maîtres) : « *I will defend where I can, and applaud where I ought, those unhappy creatures, who labouring under oppression are entitled to mercy, and as instruments of wealth deserve our gratitude*[2]. » Selon lui, les travailleurs serviles étaient même reconnaissants de leur condition envers leur maître s'il les traitaient avec bonté : « *Make a Negro estimable in his own eyes, and he will be faithful and just in yours*[3] ».

L'originalité du discours de Beckford réside donc dans sa vision idéaliste de l'institution servile coloniale, que l'on pourrait qualifier d'esclavagisme « *soft* », et qu'il tentait de faire partager à ses lecteurs en se réclamant, dans le titre de son essai, de son expérience de planteur dans les colonies pour légitimer sa défense de l'esclavage. D'autre part, même si le planteur semblait convaincu de l'infériorité naturelle des Noirs africains et des bienfaits que leur apportait l'esclavage, on peut noter qu'il est l'un des rares

1. Beckford, *op. cit.* p. 254.
2. Beckford, *op. cit.* p. 265.
3. Beckford, *op. cit.* pp. 255-56.

auteurs esclavagistes anglais à n'avoir pas tenté d'utiliser des références scientifiques ou religieuses pour étayer son argumentation. Dans son étude, Beckford se concentrait beaucoup plus sur l'étude de la relation maître-esclave que sur les aspects économiques de l'institution, mais il ne remettait cependant jamais en question la légitimité de l'esclavage et semblait considérer la condition servile comme parfaitement adaptée aux Africains. Plutôt qu'un utopiste, il semble donc que William Beckford Jr était avant tout un pragmatique, qui laissait de côté science et religion et se plaçait d'emblée dans une logique de la régulation du système. Même si on peut considérer que Beckford montrait dans ses considérations une foi illusoire en la possibilité de faire fonctionner le système de façon plus « humaine », on ne peut nier qu'il se plaçait malgré tout au cœur de la réalité de son contexte socio-culturel.

Bryan Edwards

À la fin du XVIIIe siècle, l'autorité d'Edwards en matière de questions coloniales lui valait le respect de ses pairs ; il devint l'un des plus actifs défenseurs de la cause esclavagiste au Parlement, face à William Wiberforce, promoteur de l'abolition. Son ouvrage le plus important reste *L'Histoire civile et commerciale des colonies britanniques aux Caraïbes*, publié en 1793[1]. Dans sa réponse aux propositions faites par William Wilberforce pour parvenir à l'abolition de la traite négrière, Edwards se défendait tout d'abord d'être un partisan de l'esclavage sous quelque forme que ce fût : « *I am no friend to slavery in any shape, or under any modification*[2]. » Il se référait ensuite à l'Antiquité et comparait le statut des esclaves de l'époque, qui n'avaient pas de droits, avec les avantages de l'esclavage codifié par la législation anglaise : « *On these principles, they raised their African slaves to a better condition, than was enjoyed by Slaves of Greece and Rome*[3]. » Edwards expliquait également dans son argumentation que l'institution esclavagiste était un phénomène propre à la nature humaine depuis des temps immémoriaux et que les planteurs coloniaux anglais avaient établi leur législation en se référant aux lois existant dans les sociétés antiques qui pratiquaient l'esclavage, tout en « adoucissant » les rigueurs de la législation romaine : « ... *Their conduct as legislators was comparatively mild, temperate, and exemplary*[4]. » Edwards allait

1. Bryan Edwards, *History, Civil and Commercial, of the British Colonies in the West Indies*, London: B. Crosby, 1788.
2. Edwards, *A Speech delivered at a Free Conference between the Honourable Council and Assembly of Jamaica... On the subject of Mr Wilberforce's Propositions in the House of Commons, Concerning the Slave Trade*, (Kingston, Jamaica, 1789 ; London, 1790) ; reprint *Slavery, Abolition and Emancipation*, vol. 2, *The Abolition Debate*, pp. 327-347.
3. Edwards, *A Speech Delivered at a Free Conference...*, *op. cit.*, p. 327.
4. Edwards, *op. cit.* p. 328.

même plus loin en soutenant que les planteurs avaient essentiellement élaboré leurs lois pour protéger les esclaves d'abus possibles de leurs maîtres envers eux :

> *I say then, Sir, that under this impression, they must have regarded the several limitations and restrictions which they created by law, not as giving energy to the rights of their Slaves (among the ancients the Slaves had no rights) but as so many limitations and abridgements of their own legal authority over them.*[1]

Le planteur soulignait qu'il était un adversaire de l'esclavage sous toutes ses formes : il était en effet parfaitement conscient que l'institution esclavagiste pouvait corrompre autant le maître que l'esclave : « *So degrading is the nature of slavery, that fortitude of mind is lost as free agency is restrained*[2]. » En Jamaïque, il œuvra pour rendre les règles qui codifiaient l'esclavage plus humaines, afin de réduire la mortalité des esclaves et de pouvoir parvenir en définitive à éliminer la nécessité pour les colonies d'importer des Africains. L'une de ses propositions les plus étonnantes préconisait de rattacher les esclaves au sol sur lequel ils travaillaient, à la manière du servage européen, afin d'empêcher leur vente et leur déplacement hors de leur lieu de travail d'origine. Il s'opposa fermement à la loi anglaise qui permettait aux créanciers de faire procéder à la vente des esclaves afin de recouvrer la dette de leur maître et cela même sur des marchés étrangers. Bien que d'après lui cet « exécrable statut » ait apporté une vie misérable à des milliers d'esclaves, Edwards faisait observer que les abolitionnistes étaient toujours demeurés muets sur le sujet : « *They are men of the world, and with all their philantropy, probably consider no rights so sacred as those of creditors*[3]. » Ce fut d'ailleurs Edwards lui-même qui obtint finalement l'abrogation de cette loi[4]. Il avait cependant la conviction profonde que toute émancipation précipitée entraînerait la ruine économique et des affrontements constants entre les « races ».

Edwards admettait aussi qu'il lui était arrivé de souhaiter que l'Angleterre abolît la traite négrière, donnant en cela un exemple d'humanité aux autres nations. Ses études sur le sujet l'avaient toutefois convaincu qu'un tel bouleversement provoquerait pour les esclaves des souffrances considérables : les marchands d'esclaves étrangers se seraient en effet précipités pour acheter les Noirs abandonnés par les Britanniques, et le reste des captifs auraient été massacrés par leurs ravisseurs africains pour éviter

1. Edwards, *op. cit.* p. 330.
2. Edwards, *op. cit.* p. 331.
3. Edwards, *op. cit.* p. 335.
4. Lowell J. Ragatz, *The Fall of the Planter Class in the British Caribbean 1763-1833*, New York, 1928, p. 272.

les dépenses nécessaires à leur entretien et à leur nourriture. Il rejoignait en cela les idées de l'*absentee* J.B. Holroyd et de la majorité des auteurs esclavagistes, qui se déclaraient convaincus que les esclaves étaient mieux traités sous la législation anglaise que dans les autres colonies des Antilles. Dans les Caraïbes, où le nombre de femmes noires se révélait insuffisant pour empêcher le nombre d'esclaves de décliner, chaque esclave aurait eu à faire face à une charge de travail beaucoup plus lourde. Pour éviter ces problèmes, Edwards pensait que la traite avait besoin d'être réformée plutôt que d'être abolie. Dans tous les cas, Edwards soulignait avec force que les Noirs étaient bien plus heureux aux Amériques qu'en Afrique : même si quelques Européens sans scrupules exploitaient les penchants naturels pour la violence des natifs africains envers leurs frères, leurs victimes se trouvaient ensuite libérées de la barbarie par les colons caribéens.

D'un point de vue moderne, Edwards peut semble-t-il être considéré comme un défenseur convaincu de la « suprématie blanche » : il affirmait que les esclaves étaient enclins naturellement à la soumission et étaient incapables d'éprouver des sentiments d'amour raffiné, mais préféraient la promiscuité sexuelle et les changements fréquents de partenaires. Il évoquait également « l'odeur déplaisante » des Noirs, et Edwards doutait même de leurs capacités à comprendre la musique, mais ne paraissait pas réellement considérer les Noirs comme une race inférieure : ils étaient simplement pour lui des « sauvages » qui provenaient d'un « continent barbare ». Dans un poème faisant allusion à sa maîtresse noire, Edwards admettait clairement que des planteurs jamaïcains pussent avoir des relations sexuelles avec des esclaves africaines, bien qu'il affirmât que la descendance issue de ces unions constituait un « fardeau de reproche » pour la société coloniale : « *A sable queen of love / [whose] skin excell'd the raven plume / Her breath the fragrant orange bloom / Her eye the tropic beam*[1]. » Bien que représentatif de la « plantocratie éclairée », Edwards montrait aussi dans ses écrits sa haine profonde des abolitionnistes : il percevait en effet les attaques extérieures contre l'esclavage colonial comme une conspiration contre le système de la propriété esclavagiste. Edwards incarne donc, à l'aube du XIXe siècle, un discours antiabolitionniste plutôt réformateur, en même temps qu'il se révèle un farouche défenseur de l'institution servile coloniale.

1. Edwards, *History Civil and Commercial*, *op. cit.*, pp. 363-68.

J.B. Holroyd, Comte de Sheffield

Le discours des propriétaires d'esclaves résidant en Grande-Bretagne, qui tiraient profit de l'esclavage colonial mais n'avaient qu'une vague idée des réalités de l'institution, est aussi très différent de celui des chroniqueurs esclavagistes qui résidaient dans les colonies, tout en conservant malgré tout des arguments communs. Les écrits de J.B. Holroyd, comte de Sheffield, qui résidait en Angleterre, sont donc représentatifs d'un discours esclavagiste qui ne connaissait pas la réalité quotidienne de l'esclavage, au contraire de planteurs tels que Edwards ou Beckford. John Baker Holroyd, premier comte de Sheffield, fut l'une des autorités majeures de son temps en matière de commerce et d'agriculture. Il était député à la Chambre des Communes depuis 1780 et fut nommé par la Couronne Pair d'Irlande et baron Sheffield de Dunmore en 1781. En plus de sa qualité de Pair d'Irlande, il siégea également aux Communes comme député de Bristol, succédant en cela à Edmund Burke, et prit une part active à la défense des intérêts de la cité de Bristol dans la traite esclavagiste. Il occupa un rôle de premier plan dans l'opposition à la première proposition d'abolition de la traite présentée par Wilberforce au Parlement en 1791. Il fut plus tard élevé à la fonction de Pair du Royaume-Uni, en 1802, et fut finalement fait comte de Sheffield en 1812. Holroyd était aussi un ami intime de l'écrivain Edward Gibbon, dont il édita les œuvres après sa mort.

Faisant partie des « *absentee* » anglais bénéficiaires de l'esclavage, Holroyd était, comme tous les partisans de l'institution, convaincu que les Africains étaient destinés dès leur naissance à devenir des esclaves et insistait dans son texte sur les avantages pour ces esclaves-nés de bénéficier de la législation anglaise pour mieux vivre leur condition inévitable, comme il l'expliquait dans un essai publié en 1790 et intitulé *Observations on the Project for Abolishing the Slave Trade and on the Reasonableness of Attempting some Practicable Mode of Relieving the Negroes*[1]. Dans son exposé, Holroyd proposait essentiellement des dispositions pour améliorer les conditions de transport des esclaves à bord des vaisseaux négriers, mais, comme tous les défenseurs de l'institution, il ne remettait jamais en question le principe du système esclavagiste appliqué dans les colonies. Comme beaucoup de partisans de l'esclavage, il affirmait au contraire qu'il était préférable pour les esclaves de vivre sous la législation anglaise, qui, seule pouvait les mettre à l'abri du destin misérable qui les attendait en Afrique : « *It can hardly be expected that any proposition will be offered for bettering the situation*

1. Holroyd, *Observations on the Project for Abolishing the Slave Trade and on the Reasonableness of Attempting some Practicable Mode of Relieving the Negroes*, London, 1790; reprint *Slavery, Abolition and Emancipation*, vol. 2, *The Abolition Debate*, pp. 357-363.

of the negroes in their own country; it is only while on board British ships that the British Legislature can afford them any relief[1]. » Reprenant un argument souvent utilisé par les antiabolitionnistes de tout bord, Holroyd insistait sur les dommages économiques considérables que provoquerait l'abolition de la traite et il expliquait qu'en prenant la responsabilité de cette décision le gouvernement anglais ne ferait que causer la ruine des planteurs coloniaux, des négociants et des autres intervenants impliqués dans le système esclavagiste, sans améliorer en quoi que ce fût la condition des esclaves.

> *It is admitted that British Laws may, in a great degree, turn the slave trade into another channel; but if it is inexpedient to pass laws that may be resisted, or denied, and at best be ineffectual;"if British laws cannot render the situation of the Negroes in Africa and in the West Indies better, even by the sacrifice of the sugar plantations, of policy, manufactures, shipping, property, and peace; and if the mode proposed for relieving negroes is impracticable, would it not be advisable to turn our mind from a ridiculous bubble towards some probable means of amending their situation, and take some advantage of an opportunity extremely favourable for relieving them, as far as circumstances will allow?*[2]

Plutôt qu'une suppression de la traite imposée de force par le pouvoir central, Holroyd proposait que les assemblées coloniales fussent autorisées à prélever une taxe sur chaque esclave importé, taxe dont le montant serait reversé aux planteurs pour chaque esclave né et élevé dans les colonies.

> *The great object of procuring the best treatment for the Negroes in the West Indies, and of encouraging their population, and a gradual cessation of the importation of slaves, must be attained through the several assemblies of those islands. By their imposing a duty on the import of Negroes from Africa, and giving that duty as a bounty on every Negro reared within the island, the importation of African slaves would, in the course of a few years, become less necessary, and in due time it would cease of course.*[3]

Sur le plan des conséquences politiques possibles envisagées par les partisans de l'esclavage en cas d'abolition, il est intéressant de comparer la position de l'Anglais Holroyd avec celle du planteur jamaïcain Bryan Edwards, à propos de l'indépendance législative des assemblées des colonies anglaises dans les Caraïbes. De façon étonnante, Holroyd semblait en effet partager les opinions du planteur jamaïcain, dont les positions paraissaient clairement influencées par la récente indépendance des États-Unis, sur les conséquences possibles de l'abolition. L'extrait du texte de Holroyd commençait en effet par une allusion aux causes de cette indépendance des États-Unis, qui avait représenté un coup très dur

1. Holroyd, *op. cit.* p. 356.
2. Holroyd, *op. cit.* p. 354.
3. Holroyd, *op. cit.* p. 363.

pour l'Empire britannique, d'un point de vue politique et économique. Il continuait sa déclaration au Parlement en affirmant que la promulgation de l'abolition aux Antilles et le non-respect par la métropole du droit de propriété des planteurs risquaient de forcer les assemblées législatives coloniales à suivre l'exemple américain.

> *It may be observed, greatly to the praise of the British subjects in the West-Indies, that they have conducted themselves with temper. They have not yet followed the examples which stare them in the face: but if we proceed, we shall force them to declare their rights.*[1]

On remarque ainsi que l'exemple des États-Unis a influencé de façon significative le contenu du discours antiabolitionniste anglais métropolitain : les revendications pour une plus grande autonomie législative des assemblées coloniales en matière d'esclavage, associées à la menace explicite d'une sécession éventuelle des colonies antillaises d'avec la métropole, faisaient désormais partie intégrante des considérations développées par les esclavagistes pour tenter de reculer l'échéance de l'abolition de la traite et du système servile colonial.

Raymund Harris

Au début des années 1780, divers écrivains esclavagistes avaient tenté d'associer la lutte contre l'esclavage avec les nouvelles perspectives religieuses qui mêlaient hétérodoxie, fanatisme religieux et innovation, jouant sur les préjugés de l'opinion contre les Quakers et les autres mouvements évangélistes, que l'on soupçonnait de vouloir saper l'autorité de l'Église et de l'État par leur remise en question de l'institution esclavagiste. Granville Sharp et ses amis abolitionnistes furent accusés d'omettre dans leur réflexion sur l'esclavage d'importants passages de la Bible, et d'en placer d'autres hors de leur contexte. L'un des arguments les plus habiles du discours antiabolitionniste anglais, qui devait plus tard être souvent repris par les esclavagistes du Sud des États-Unis, fut de dire que l'agitation antiesclavagiste empêchait de plus en plus les maîtres de traiter leurs esclaves avec charité chrétienne[2]. En général, toutefois, les antiesclavagistes se cantonnèrent à un silence prudent, comptant sur leurs députés auprès du Parlement pour renforcer leur position par la voie politique. Au début de l'année 1788, alors que le Privy Council de la Chambre des Lords commençait ses auditions et ses investigations sur la traite négrière, un nouveau pamphlet circula parmi les riches notables de Londres et de Liverpool. Écrit par un certain Révérend Raymond Harris, il était intitulé :

1. Holroyd, *op. cit.* p. 361.
2. Brion Davis, *The Problem of Slavery in the Age of Revolution*, pp. 541-542.

Scriptural Researches on the Licitness of the Slave Trade, Shewing its Conformity with the Principles of Natural and Revealed Religion, Delineated in the Sacred Writings of the Word of God[1]. Ce texte résumait parfaitement les arguments religieux du discours antiabolitionniste anglais jusqu'à l'abolition de la traite. Il exprimait aussi l'opposition croissante des bénéficiaires de l'esclavage colonial aux réformes proposées par Sir William Dolben pour restreindre le nombre d'esclaves qu'un navire négrier pourrait transporter, et leur colère face aux enquêtes menées par le Privy Council à propos des conditions de la traite esclavagiste.

Les arguments de Harris pour expliquer et justifier la légitimité religieuse de l'institution servile se répartissaient en trois sections : dans le livre premier, il tentait de démontrer la conformité de la traite esclavagiste avec les lois de la Nature en utilisant l'Ancien Testament depuis la Genèse jusqu'à la « dispersion mosaïque » ; la deuxième partie de son essai se rapportait aux Dix Commandements, et la troisième se référait au Nouveau Testament. Harris commençait par désarmer ses opposants éventuels en concédant que l'oppression ne pouvait en aucun cas être justifiée par la tradition ou la nécessité d'expansion. La question principale, selon lui, était de savoir en quoi la traite esclavagiste était intrinsèquement illicite, quelles que fussent les circonstances. Bien évidemment, il existait des abus et des mauvais traitements au sein de l'institution esclavagiste, comme dans beaucoup d'autres applications de la Loi, mais cela ne prouvait pas que cette institution fût mauvaise en soi. Les problèmes liés à son application et à sa légitimité devaient donc être traités séparément. Mais comment, en ce cas, les hommes pouvaient-ils savoir si une pratique était ou non contraire à la loi divine ? Pour Harris, qui s'adressait à un auditoire protestant, la Bible était le seul guide possible. Les traditions, les habitudes, « les sens ou la raison humaine », tout cela était faillible. Quiconque possédait « quelque prétention à la religion » devait se soumettre à l'autorité finale des Saintes Écritures ; et toute personne qui prétendait accepter la Bible comme la parole incontestable de Dieu devait donner son assentiment à chaque affirmation contenue dans les Écritures, sans réserve et sans jamais remettre en question les impénétables voies du Seigneur.

1. Harris, *Scriptural Researches on the Licitness of the Slave Trade, Shewing its Conformity with the Principles of Natural and Revealed Religion, Delineated in the Sacred Writings of the Word of God*, (reprint *Slavery, Abolition & Emancipation*, vol. 2, *The Abolition Debate*, pp. 283-322). Raymundo Harris était un jésuite espagnol résidant à Liverpool qui utilisait le nom de plume de Révérent Raymund (ou Raymond) Harris. Harris avait été expulsé d'Espagne en 1767, et après avoir vécu dans différents pays d'Europe, il s'était finalement installé à Liverpool où il avait fondé une école pour les jeunes garçons issus de l'aristocratie ou de la grande bourgeoisie anglaise. S'étant querellé avec l'archevêque catholique de Liverpool, il fut suspendu de ses fonctions de prêtre.

Le texte de Harris synthétisait parfaitement l'argumentation utilisée par le discours antiabolitionniste pour justifier la légitimité religieuse de l'esclavage. Dans un premier temps, il utilisa les nombreuses références à cette institution présentées dans l'Ancien Testament pour montrer que les textes fondateurs de la religion chrétienne ne condamnaient en aucun cas la servitude, mais se contentaient de la réglementer, comme si cette institution faisait naturellement partie de la loi Divine.

It is singular enough, that the very first Law, or Judgement, in the Scripture language, enacted by God himself immediately after he had delivered the Ten Commandments to his people, should be respecting the Slave Trade...[1]

Harris utilisa l'exemple de l'esclavage pratiqué par les Hébreux et codifié dans l'Exode pour démontrer que ce système avait reçu l'approbation divine et pouvait être appliqué sans que soient transgressés les commandements de la religion chrétienne.

Here, it is evident in the first place, that, however limited the time was of the slavery of an Hebrew, he was yet in the strictest sense of the word a true and real slave for the time. [...] But, were the Slave Trade, or the purchasing of those of our own species, and dealing in human flesh, a pursuit of that heinous and crying nature, as to be essentially unlawful, essentially incompatible with the principles of reason, nature, and true Religion, would God, Justice and Sanctity itself, have authorized the practice of it with so positive, so manifest, so explicit a sanction?[2]

Harris rassurait ici les personnes et institutions impliquées dans la traite négrière quant à la légalité religieuse de leur commerce. Il parvint même à donner une justification religieuse au principe de l'esclavage héréditaire en qualité de bien meuble qui caractérisait l'institution esclavagiste coloniale.

The Words of this Law, and they are the words of God, do expressly declare, that Slaves thus purchased from the Heathen and Sojourners among them, shall be the POSSESSION; that is, the real and lawful property, of the purchasers: a property so strictly their own, that they shall bequeath it to their Children at their death, as a part of their paternal estate, an estate for ever, for they shall be your bondmen for ever, says the Law [...] from this most decisive, most explicit, and irrefragable authority of the Written Word of God visibly encouraging the prosecution of the Slave Trade, and declaring in the most categorical language [...] that a Slave is the real, indisputable, and lawful property of the purchaser.[3]

1. Harris, *op. cit.*, Livre II p. 2.
2. Harris, *op. cit.* p. 3.
3. Harris, *op. cit.* p. 4.

Harris s'appuya également sur la théorie des peuples maudits par Dieu selon la malédiction de Cham et voués éternellement à l'esclavage afin d'expier les péchés de leurs pères pour mieux légitimer l'institution servile.

> *It being therefore evident from the uniform tenour of the Sacred Writings, that neither the reduction of the Gibeonites then living, nor that of their guiltiest descendants, yet unborn, to perpetual Slavery, was ever condemned by any mark or intimation whatever of God's displeasure, but manifestly ratified in the sequel by several undoubted assurances of his divine approbation; it is easy to conclude, whether the reducing of the innocent as well as the guilty part of our fellow creatures to the condition of Slaves, or even to hereditary bondage or Slavery, be in its own nature licit or illicit, criminal or unjust.*[1]

Dans le livre trois de son essai, Harris procéda à la partie la plus difficile et la plus habile de sa démonstration en s'appuyant sur l'absence totale de références à l'esclavage dans le Nouveau Testament : il publiait en effet son pamphlet en Angleterre, et s'adressait donc en priorité à un public chrétien, mais non catholique. D'après lui, le fait que les rédacteurs du Nouveau Testament n'aient pas jugé utile d'en parler suffisait largement à prouver qu'ils avaient considéré au vu des premières Écritures que cette institution avait l'approbation divine et ne nécessitait de ce fait aucune condamnation de leur part.

> *From this undeniable position it follows necessary, that, as the Writings of both the Testaments have the same weight of Authority, essentially incapable of contradicting itself [...] whatever is declared in the One to be intrinsically good or bad, just or unjust, licit or illicit, must inevitably be so according to the principles of the Other [...] if therefore the Slave Trade appears as, I trust, it does, from the preceding train of Scriptural arguments, in perfect harmony with the principles and decisions of the Word of God, registred in the Sacred Writings of the Old Testament, respecting the intrinsic nature of that Trade.*[2]

Tout au long de la dernière partie de son essai, Harris s'employa habilement à combattre les abolitionnistes, et en particulier les Quakers, sur leur propre terrain, pour démontrer que le Nouveau Testament ne pouvait en aucun cas contredire les Premières Écritures, qui, d'après lui, avaient toujours considéré l'esclavage comme faisant partie de l'ordre naturel des choses.

> *In effect, this constant and uniform silence of the Sacred Writers of the New Testament is a matter of such public notoriety; I mean their never disapproving the practice of the Trade, in which the rights of Christian justice and humanity*

1. Harris, *op. cit.* p. 2.
2. Harris, *op. cit.* Livre III, p. 5.

are said to be so materially injured ought to attract the particular attention of every impartial inquirer into the merits of the present Controversy.[1]

Harris concluait enfin son plaidoyer pour le maintien de l'esclavage en résumant l'ensemble de sa réflexion dans des « *Corollaires* » placés à la fin de son essai.

Since no abuse or malpractices whatever, though of the greatest magnitude, committed in former times in the prosecution of the Slave Trade, ever inducted to the Almighty to prohibit or abolish that Trade, but only to check by wholesome and coercive Laws the violence of unnatural masters, and to punish the transgressors with great severity; there appears no reason whatever why the abuses and malpractices said to be perpetrated in our days in the prosecution of the same Trade, evidently subject to the control of the Legislature, should be deemed a powerful inducement to proceed to the abolition of it.[2]

Le City Council de Liverpool remercia chaudement Harris (qui lui avait dédicacé son ouvrage) pour sa contribution à la cause antiabolitionniste et lui alloua la somme de cent livres sterling (environ sept mille livres actuelles) pour le récompenser de ses efforts[3]. Les abolitionnistes prirent très au sérieux le pamphlet de Harris et, en juillet 1788, le Comité pour l'Abolition accueillit avec soulagement la parution d'un texte publié sous le pseudonyme de Roscoe, qui réfutait point par point les affirmations de Harris en faveur de la légalité religieuse du système esclavagiste. Le Comité accepta de payer les frais d'impression et de publication de deux mille exemplaires supplémentaires. De plus, au moins six réponses au texte de Harris furent publiées dans le courant de cette même année 1788. Le fait qu'il soit parvenu à associer Ancien et Nouveau Testament généra aussi l'inquiétude et le doute dans les rangs abolitionnistes : James Ramsay lui-même fut obligé d'admettre en privé qu'il ne se sentait pas le droit de mettre en doute la sincérité de Harris sur le plan de ses convictions, mais exprima sa crainte que : « quelques personnes sérieuses pouvaient lire ce pamphlet sans pour cela voir leur croyance envers la parole du Créateur choquée, et leur bienveillance envers leurs frères affectée[4]. »

1. Harris, *op. cit*. p. 6.
2. Harris, *op. cit., Corollaries*, p. 4.
3. Brion Davis, *The Problem of Slavery in the Age of Revolution*, ch. XI : "The Good Book", p. 543.
4. James Ramsay, MS *Remarks on Harris*, Ramsay papers, Phillipps MS 17780, fols.29-32, Rhodes House, Oxford; Ramsay, *Examination of the Reverend Mr Harris's "Scriptural Researches on the Licitness of the Slave Trade"* (London 1788).

William Cobbett

Au début du XIXe siècle, les réflexions du journaliste politique William Cobbett en faveur du maintien de l'institution esclavagiste dans les colonies anglaises constituaient aussi une excellente illustration du contenu du discours antiabolitionniste anglais, juste avant la promulgation de l'abolition de la traite négrière par le Parlement britannique. Cobbett fut sans conteste l'un des plus influents commentateurs politiques de son temps. À partir de 1802, il débuta la rédaction hebdomadaire de son *Political Register,* connu aussi sous l'appellation *Annual Register,* qu'il continua à publier jusqu'à sa mort, en 1835. Au plus fort de sa diffusion, son *Political Register* atteignait 50 000 exemplaires, qui étaient lus à haute voix dans les tavernes et les *Coffee Houses*, ce qui multipliait encore leur audience. Dans l'article intitulé « *Slave Trade* » de l'un de ses premiers *Political Registers,* publié en 1802, Cobbett reproduisit une lettre qu'il avait écrite à l'archevêque de Rochester en 1796, où il attaquait les allégations des abolitionnistes sur les horreurs de la traite négrière et prenait clairement le parti des antiabolitionnistes, dressant un véritable catalogue des justifications de l'esclavage.

> *[…] It is impossible you should consent to the preamble of the bill about to be sent to you, which, should it ever pass into a law, holds up the West Indian planters, and the merchants of the kingdom, to the detestation and abhorrence of their countrymen, as person supporting a traffic contrary to humanity and justice, although such an assertion arraigns the wisdom and goodness of the Deity who authorized it, and by means whereof he was heretofore pleased to preserve a great and powerful nation, and the ancestors of his chosen people from famine and destruction.*[1]

Il mettait en avant non seulement la légitimité historique, mais également juridique et religieuse de l'institution servile coloniale :

> *The planters have a right, my lord upon every principle of law and justice, to carry on that trade, in order to be supplied with negroes to cultivate their lands; […] but, my lord, our cause does not rest solely on human laws. If the doctrine taught by your lordship, and the other prelates and ministers of the Christian church, be true, the slave trade is sanctioned by the divine law […] I need not to your lordship observe, that although the word for 'slave' in the Greek sacred scripture, and the corresponding term in the Hebrew, are translated 'servant', they signify 'unconditional slaves', over whom the lord had the supreme authority, and the power of life and death; and in several passages those words are translated 'bond men' and 'bond maids'.*[2]

1. William Cobbett, *Summary of Politics*, from *Cobbett's Political Register* (12 June 1802), reprint *Slavery, Abolition and Emancipation*, vol. 8, *Theories of Race*, pp. 267-268 ; Cobbett, *Political Register: Slave Trade*, lettre écrite en 1796 à l'archevêque de Rochester, publiée en 1802. Reprint *Slavery, Abolition and Emancipation*, vol. 2, *The Abolition Debate*, pp. 373-377.
2. Cobbett, *op. cit.* p. 376.

Cobbett soutenait que la traite esclavagiste avait reçu l'approbation indiscutable des Saintes Écritures.

That the sacred Scriptures of the Old and New testament authorize a slave trade, your lordship dares not deny: nay, my lord, you must allow they do more. Under the law, the slave trade is in a manner commanded by God Almighty, and under the Gospel dispensation, the holding in slavery persons purchased as slaves, is not only mentioned by our blessed Saviour and his apostles, without censure or disapprobation, but rules are given by St Paul and St Peter, how slaves ought to demean themselves to their masters.[1]

Cobbett concluait sa lettre en soutenant que le maintien de la traite était indispensable à la prospérité du commerce britannique et de ses colonies des Caraïbes.

[...] and the abolition of which will most certainly involve the fortunes of the West Indian planters and merchants, and in all human probability, the greater part of the commerce, navigation, and manufactures of Great Britain, in one common ruin.[2]

Cobbett affirmait également tout au long de ses écrits sa profonde croyance en l'infériorité naturelle des Africains. Après 1808, il modéra toutefois quelque peu ses positions sur l'esclavage. Il est aussi intéressant de noter qu'il ne consommait jamais de rhum, sucre ou café, car c'étaient des produits de l'institution servile coloniale[3]. Bien qu'ayant d'abord soutenu la politique conservatrice du gouvernement Pitt contre la Révolution française, Cobbett était devenu par la suite un radical, partisan d'une réforme complète du Parlement. Malgré cela, il demeura toujours un partisan de l'esclavage et de la traite négrière, contrairement au conservateur Wilberforce, qui demeura l'un des plus fervents défenseurs de l'abolition. Les écrits de Cobbett sont très symptomatiques de l'attitude de défiance envers les Noirs africains qui prévalait à cette époque dans les opinions esclavagistes européennes, et révélent les peurs et les complexes que ceux-ci inspiraient aux tenants de la supériorité de la « race » blanche :

And, are we to be called upon to grant money, are our countrymen to be sent to Sierra Leone, to cultivate the acquaintance of this black, and brutal, and bloody race? [...] Are they to officiate in our churches and marry our daughters? [...] and that some means should be taken to put a stop to the increase of Blacks in this country, at any rate, where they have made no little progress in changing the colour of the inhabitants. [...] It is truly shocking to see the number of English women, who are married to Negroes: our streets

1. Cobbett, *op. cit.* p. 376.
2. Cobbett, *op. cit.* p. 377.
3. Peter J. Kitson, *Slavery, Abolition and Emancipation*, vol. 8, biographie Cobbett, p. 371.

> *and public walks are continually disgraced with the disgusting spectacle; and whom are we to blame but ourselves for foolishly yielding to the importunities of those who have the address to make us pay for the genteel education of these sable intruders?*[1]

Cobbett mettait aussi l'accent sur l'inquiétude de l'opinion publique anglaise à propos des révoltes d'esclaves dans les colonies des Antilles et de l'utilisation de soldats noirs au sein de l'armée britannique dans les colonies.

> *The news from Dominica is of a most melancholy nature. A letter from Roseau, printed in the Barbados papers, states, that the black corps had revolted, and killed their officers […] It is hardly fair for those, who have silently seen the establishment of the black corps, now to find fault with that establishment; but, for us, who have uniformly insisted, that negroes never ought to be thus put upon a level with white men, even as musicians or drummers, we may with great propriety, cite the events in Dominica in confirmation of our opinion. The introduction of negroes into the army, the clothing of them in regimentals, necessarily degrades the profession of the soldier. […] We hope that those corps will be disbanded with all convenient speed, and that the peace and security of our colonies will be committed exclusively to the arms of Britain.*[2]

Il critiquait aussi la mode grandissante de ce qu'il appelait la « négromania ». Cobbett, en employant ce terme, se référait sans doute à l'engouement populaire pour les Noirs africains apparu en Angleterre à la fin du XVIIIe siècle, car ils représentaient l'image même de l'exotisme, et leur possession constituait souvent un élément de prestige dans les classes privilégiées de la métropole. Les nouvelles tendances religieuses qui avaient pris naissance à la même époque prônaient également le principe de l'égalité des Noirs et des Blancs. Les mariages interraciaux qui s'étaient multipliés du fait de cette nouvelle perception de l'image du Noir par le public étaient en particulier une grande source d'inquiétude pour les défenseurs de la « pureté » et de la suprématie incontestable de la « race » blanche. L'inquiétude exprimée par Cobbett sur ces différents sujets coïncidait donc parfaitement avec les idées d'Edward Long exposées dans son *History of Jamaica*, à propos des dangers du mélange des sangs pouvant provoquer la dégénérescence de la race blanche, et qui se retrouvent fréquemment dans la littérature pro-esclavagiste de l'époque. Les attaques de Cobbett contre les adversaires de l'esclavage lui offraient en même temps l'opportunité de critiquer les mouvements religieux et les hommes politiques favorables à l'abolition, et en particulier d'attaquer

1. Cobbett, *op. cit.* p. 271.
2. Cobbett, *op. cit.* p. 272.

Wilberforce et Clarkson, leaders du mouvement abolitionniste et membres de la secte Évangéliste de Clapham.

> *Is it for the benefice of wretches like these, that an academy is to be supported at Clapham? […] It is time the nation should be roused from its philanthropic dream; that it should see this matter in the true light.' […] The notable discovery of the inhumanity and injustice of the slave trade, has never been made until the present an era of anarchy and confusion, wherein impious men have presumed to set up their own ideas of humanity and justice (in contradiction to the laws of God) as the standard of perfection.*[1]

Cobbett n'hésitait pas à attaquer les abolitionnistes, et en particulier les politiques, en ironisant sur leurs préoccupations humanitaires envers les esclaves africains qui vivaient dans les colonies des Caraïbes, tout en insistant sur leur total manque de considération pour les effroyables conditions de vie imposées aux couches populaires les plus défavorisées en Grande-Bretagne.

> *Your lordship, by referring to that evidence, will learn, that the labour of the slaves in the sugar colonies is lighter than that of the British peasantry; and that they are better provided for, in sickness and in health, in infancy and in old age, than the labouring poor in any part of Europe.*[2]

Cet argument avait auparavant été utilisé par Beckford, qui se fondait déjà sur la comparaison de la condition des esclaves des colonies avec celle des classes les plus misérables de la population métropolitaine pour affirmer que les travailleurs serviles employés dans les colonies vivaient en réalité bien mieux que les pauvres anglais.

Le discours esclavagiste avant l'Émancipation de 1833

En 1824, le leader de la Chambre des Communes George Canning exprimait la position contrastée des instances politiques anglaises sur l'abolition de l'esclavage. Les propositions contenues dans le discours qu'il prononça en 1824 devant la Chambre des Communes[3] illustrent clairement la manière dont le gouvernement britannique envisageait les conditions possibles de l'émancipation et les problèmes auxquels il se trouvait confronté pour la réaliser. Canning proposait à la Société contre l'esclavage et à ses adversaires antiabolitionnistes une approche modérée de l'émancipation afin de favoriser la mise en place des propositions du

1. Cobbett, *op. cit.* p. 269.
2. Cobbett, *op. cit.* p. 373.
3. George Canning, *The Speech of the Rt. Hon. George Canning, in the House of Commons, on the 16th Day of March, 1824, on Laying before the House the 'Papers in Explanation of the Measures Adopted by His Majesty's Government, for the Amelioration of the Condition of the Slave Population in His Majesty's Dominions in the West Indies* (London, 1824). Reprint *Slavery, Abolition & Emancipation*, vol. 3, *The Emancipation Debate*, pp. 231-243.

London West Indian Committee, dirigé par l'un de ses amis, Charles Ellis. Ce comité proposait d'apporter diverses modifications de l'institution servile coloniale, dans le but de contrer les attaques du Parlement, susceptible de pouvoir céder à la pression politique des partisans de l'émancipation des esclaves. Toutefois, il n'était absolument pas question pour les planteurs d'envisager la disparition du système, ni même d'autoriser les esclaves à acheter leur liberté à un prix convenable.

C'est peu de temps après que fut publié à Londres en 1824, sous le nom d'auteur de **Reverend John Hampden**, un pamphlet intitulé *A Commentary on Mr Clarkson's Pamphlet, Entitled 'Thoughts on the Necessity of Improving the Condition of the Slaves in the British Colonies, with a View to their Ultimate Emancipation*[1]. Dans ce texte, l'auteur exposait la position des planteurs et des autres partisans du maintien de l'esclavage dans les colonies, que représentait le *London West Indian Committee*, sur le sujet de l'émancipation et sur ses dangers éventuels pour l'économie et l'unité politique de l'Empire britannique. Il faut préciser que Clarkson incarnait l'adversaire principal des esclavagistes : à cette époque, il venait en effet d'effectuer une tournée de réunions publiques dans tout le Royaume-Uni, afin de redonner un souffle au mouvement national en faveur de l'émancipation des esclaves et de favoriser la création de nouvelles associations qui viendraient grossir les rangs du mouvement abolitionniste. Cette tournée politique nationale de Clarkson, ajoutée à la publication de son pamphlet, avait déclenché la réaction des antiabolitionnistes, qui s'étaient sentis très menacés par la portée considérable de ses déclarations : que ce soit dans ses déclarations publiques ou dans son pamphlet, Clarkson mettait l'accent sur le fait que l'esclavage était illégal au regard de la loi anglaise, et il expliquait aussi que laisser les législatures coloniales édicter leurs propres lois pour améliorer soi-disant la condition des esclaves n'apporterait aucun progrès réel.

L'influence considérable de Clarkson et son prestige auprès des populations de l'Empire britannique étaient donc une grande source d'inquiétude pour les membres du West Indian Committee, qui se devaient de réagir pour contrer absolument la progression des abolitionnistes. Hampden, en sa qualité supposée de propriétaire colonial, défendait donc essentiellement les intérêts des planteurs contre les accusations de Clarkson. Au début de son pamphlet, Hampden se défendait d'attaquer celui-ci personnellement, mais au fur et à mesure que l'on progresse dans le texte, son discours révèle clairement combien les planteurs se sentaient menacés par la logique et la force d'argumentation de l'éminent abolitionniste. Cette peur reposait

1. Rev. John Hampden, *A Commentary on Mr Clarkson's Pamphlet, Entitled 'Thoughts on the Necessity of Improving the Condition of the Slaves in the British Colonies, with a View to their Ultimate Emancipation*, (London, 1824). Reprint *Slavery, Abolition & Emancipation*, vol. 3, pp. 147-215.

sur le fait que tous les écrits et déclarations de Clarkson étaient repris quotidiennement par la presse et la communauté littéraire britanniques, deux puissantes forces de propagation du courant abolitionniste auprès du public.

Se posant en « témoin oculaire » de la réalité de l'esclavage colonial, Hampden s'opposait aux déclarations de Clarkson, qui affirmait que la condition des esclaves dans les colonies n'avait subi aucune amélioration depuis l'abolition de la traite. Usant d'une logique parfois teintée d'un certain racisme, qui reste même à cette époque l'une des composantes caractéristiques du discours pro-esclavagiste des propriétaires coloniaux, Hampden rétorquait à Clarkson que les esclaves étaient mieux traités depuis l'abolition de la traite, car ceux qui étaient nés et vivaient dans les colonies étaient à présent mieux « civilisés », du fait de la cessation des importations quotidiennes de nouveaux esclaves africains, qu'il appelait « barbares ».

> *It is almost as needless as it is tiresome to repeat [...] that the general condition of the slaves, and the established system of treatment have been considerably improved within the last few years; which is no doubt, in a great measure, the effect of the abolition, but by no means resulting so much from calculations of policy, as the necessary consequence of progressive civilization amongst the slaves, since the era when the natural progress has ceased to be interrupted by the constant accession of barbarian.*[1]

Le 10 juin 1823, au cours d'une rencontre avec les membres de la Société contre l'esclavage, Canning, quant à lui, avait déjà suggéré deux méthodes possibles pour parvenir enfin à l'abolition de l'esclavage : la première consistait à autoriser les esclaves à acheter leur liberté, la seconde était d'accorder le statut d'homme libre à tous les enfants d'esclaves nés après une date convenue. Toutefois, il se refusait à adopter l'une ou l'autre de ces méthodes avant d'avoir acquis plus d'éléments de réflexion. Dans son discours au Parlement du 16 mai 1824, plutôt que de défendre sans réserve l'émancipation des esclaves, comme il l'avait fait pour l'abolition de la traite, Canning prit soin de protéger les intérêts des planteurs en persuadant les abolitionnistes d'accepter en partie les propositions du West Indian Committee, avec qui il possédait de solides affinités. Il allait toutefois plus loin en préconisant l'émancipation graduelle et contrôlée de la population servile des colonies, et il affirmait que cette approche constituait la meilleure façon d'amener les esclaves à la « liberté ». Canning commençait son discours en expliquant tout d'abord que la question de l'émancipation était le sujet le plus délicat auquel avait jamais été confronté

1. Hampden, *op. cit.* pp. 152-53.

le Parlement britannique. Il insistait dans son discours sur la nécessité pour la Grande-Bretagne de procéder à l'émancipation « graduellement et avec prudence ».

> *Do we, in the ardour of our nascent reformation, forget that during the ages for which this system has existed, no preceding generation of legislators has ventured to touch it with a reforming hand? And have we the vanity to flatter ourselves that we can annihilate it at a blow?*[1]

Il opérait ensuite une distinction entre l'esclavage en tant que concept abstrait et en tant que nécessité économique. Peu de gens, expliquait-il, osaient défendre la légitimité de l'esclavage, mais les réalités économiques faisaient que le gouvernement devait protéger les droits et possessions des planteurs. Canning affirmait par conséquent qu'il ne s'agissait pas de choisir entre la servitude perpétuelle et l'émancipation immédiate et non préparée, mais qu'il convenait de se poser un certain nombre de questions.

> *I hope I shall not be considered as misrepresenting the collective sense of Parliament, and the general feeling of the Country, when I describe that sense and feeling to have been an unequivocal abhorrence of Slavery in the abstract; an acknowledgment of the almost hopeless difficulty of curing all its horrors; [...] But the repeated sanctions of the Legislature, the settled rights of inheritance, and the various ramifications of property and of interest growing out of them, create impediments which the House are not prepared to sweep at once away, in order that we may have a clear stage for the exhibition of theoretical experiments. [...] If I'm asked, whether I am for the permanent existence of Slavery in our Colonies, I say, No. But if I'm asked, whether I'm favourable to its immediate abolition, I say, No [...] happily, however, we are not driven to either of these extremes. Between the two, there is an open debatable ground.*[2]

Dans son pamphlet négrier, Hampden reprenait également cette idée chère aux défenseurs de l'institution servile coloniale, selon laquelle il était absolument nécessaire de séparer le raisonnement abstrait sur l'esclavage de la réalité de ses applications dans les Caraïbes et son influence considérable sur l'économie coloniale, et par conséquent celle de la Nation toute entière : les planteurs coloniaux avaient en effet toujours soutenu que les partisans de l'émancipation des esclaves, dans leur discours, représentaient l'esclavage comme une notion abstraite et utilisaient ses aspects les plus négatifs, sans tenir aucun compte des réalités concrètes que recouvrait ce système. Selon ce raisonnement, que critiquaient les esclavagistes, l'esclavage se réduisait alors à une simple hypothèse théorique susceptible

1. Canning, *op. cit.* p. 231
2. Canning, *op. cit.* p. 242

d'être débattue sans que fussent pris en compte le système des plantations dans les îles des Antilles et la grande diversité des situations.

> *The planter's vindication, happily for him, does not require a justification of slavery in the abstract; nor are his rights of so subtle and unsubstantial a nature that they can be successfully assailed, or need to be defended by the skill of the casuist: he grounds his vindication on universal principles of reason and common sense, on constitutional maxims; and on this fundamental law of civilized society—that the rights of property are sacred—that private property, however vested, claims the protection of that government by which it has been sanctioned, and to which it pays tribute and allegiance.*[1]

Canning, pour sa part, distinguait dans sa réflexion les colonies qui observaient strictement les directives de la Couronne, telles que Trinidad, et les îles comme la Jamaïque, qui préféraient suivre la politique de leurs propres assemblées législatives coloniales et manifestaient clairement des velléités d'autonomie vis-à-vis de la métropole. Il exprimait ainsi une vérité connue de tous les membres du Parlement britannique : il était bien plus facile d'imposer une réforme législative en vue de l'émancipation des esclaves aux colonies directement affiliées à la Couronne qu'à celles qui possédaient leur propre assemblée législative.

> *Gentlemen are aware that the Colonies are divided into two classes; one of which (the smaller number) are governed by the Crown, without the intervention of local Legislative Assemblies; the other and larger class have Legislative Assemblies framed in miniature after the model of those of the Mother Country. As such assemblies are not a little jealous of the rights and privileges, by the possession of which they resemble the institutions of the parent State, the Colonies of the first class are much the more easily manageable. Experiments may therefore be tried with greater facility in the Colonies wholly governed by the Crown.*[2]

À ce propos, Hampden prenait la défense des assemblées coloniales et de leurs législations sur l'esclavage en expliquant qu'elles avaient contribué à améliorer de façon importante la condition de leur population servile, contrairement à ce que disait Clarkson. Il allait même plus loin en affirmant que la plupart des esclaves étaient réellement et profondément attachés à leurs maîtres.

> *The only effectual mode of refuting these calumnies would be, by establishing the contrary positions; by shewing that the system of slave laws, though still very imperfect, has lately undergone essential improvements; that the members of the Legislatures have voluntarily set bounds to their individual authority as masters. [...] It is a truth illuminated by positive facts, that the domestic government or rule of the master, is in general mild and indulgent; that on the*

1. Hampden, *op. cit.* p. 159.
2. Canning, *op. cit.* p. 228.

part of the slave, there is commonly a very strong attachment to the person and protection of his master, a fondness for home, and even no aversion to his humble lot, which would be quite impossible if that lot were so intolerable as it has been represented.[1]

Pour appuyer ses idées sur l'émancipation progressive des esclaves, Canning utilisa l'exemple des propositions faites par l'Assemblée de Trinidad (Trinidad Order of Council) qu'il résumait en quelques points. Canning préconisait tout d'abord la suppression du fouet pour les femmes esclaves, ainsi que comme stimulant pour le travail. Il demandait aussi la mise en place de l'instruction religieuse pour tous les esclaves, l'abolition du travail et des marchés le dimanche, l'encouragement au mariage et le maintien de l'unité familiale. Il suggérait également d'accorder à tous les esclaves le droit d'acheter leur liberté et d'accéder à la propriété. Enfin, Canning demandait que les preuves produites par un esclave en cas de litige avec son maître fussent admises devant un tribunal. Hampden, pour sa part, ironisait sur le fait que la colonie de Trinidad, citée en exemple de progrès et d'avancées pour la condition des esclaves, avait le plus fort taux de mortalité de toutes les colonies antillaises.

A still more satisfactory proof of the justness of this remark is furnished by the labours of the abolitionists themselves; from whom we learn, that in the Colony of Trinidad, the institutions of which are the most favourable to the happiness of the slave, the waste of Negro life proceeding from excessive toil, surpasses every thing that had been known in the annals of West Indian plantership.[2]

Dans la dernière partie de son argumentation contre la suppression du système esclavagiste colonial, Hampden en appelait au respect de la notion de droit de propriété, et à son application aux esclaves comme à la terre ; l'émancipation ne pouvait selon lui qu'entraîner le déclin de la nation britannique.

[Emancipation] would inevitably be the ruin of a numerous class of our fellow subjects; the sacrifice of an important branch of territory; the sunset of British light, and influence in these regions of the western hemisphere, and the protracted reign of darkness, vice, and barbarism.[3]

Pour conclure son discours au Parlement, Canning concédait quant à lui que ses propositions allaient bien au-delà de celles faites par les planteurs tout en restant en deçà des espérances de la Société antiesclavagiste : il refusait de prendre parti plus avant sur le sujet de l'émancipation. Ces exemples de la transformation notable du discours sur l'abolition en

1. Hampden, *op. cit.* p. 155.
2. Hampden, *op. cit.* p. 156.
3. Hampden, *op. cit.* p. 154.

Angleterre dans les années 1820 nous permettent de nous représenter l'état de l'opinion anglaise sur l'esclavage à cette époque : le pamphlet de Hampden est une illustration des arguments du discours antiabolitionniste peu avant l'Émancipation ; plus précisément, il reflète la position des planteurs issus des colonies possédant une Assemblée législative, par opposition à Canning, qui privilégiait dans son texte les colonies dites « de la Couronne ». Le discours esclavagiste des planteurs après l'abolition de la traite revendiquait essentiellement la prise en compte des implications économiques de l'esclavage colonial et réclamait une application du droit de propriété qui l'emportait sur les considérations philosophiques à propos de la légitimité de l'institution servile. Ce discours intégrait aussi presque systématiquement des revendications pour une autonomie législative accrue des Assemblées coloniales vis-à-vis de la métropole, revendications qui s'apparentaient à celles des planteurs français, eux aussi influencés par l'exemple de la Révolution américaine. Le fait que Canning n'ait repris qu'une partie de leurs propositions de « réforme » du système et qu'il continuait d'envisager l'émancipation des esclaves comme la finalité du débat qui se déroulait sur la scène politique anglaise avait déçu les planteurs du West Indian Committee.

D'autre part, Canning exprimait sa préférence envers les colonies « de la Couronne » et proposait qu'elles fussent le terrain d'expérimentation d'une émancipation graduelle. En reprenant les dispositions législatives du 'Trinidad Order of Council', Canning avait ainsi provoqué une réaction virulente des planteurs issus des colonies possédant des Assemblées législatives semi-autonomes du pouvoir central, qui lui répondaient directement, ainsi qu'à Clarkson et au Premier ministre Pitt le jeune, par le truchement du pamphlet de Hampden :

> *The Colonial Legislatures must be called on, says Mr Clarkson, to send their respective code to Parliament for revision; an unconstitutional invasion of their rights, of which he seems fully sensible, but which he attempts to justify by the authority of Mr Pitt, Mr Canning, and Lord Holland.*[1]

Les propositions très nuancées de Canning sur l'émancipation montrent clairement que les politiques et l'opinion publique ne voulaient plus continuer à privilégier le droit de propriété des planteurs contre les intérêts économiques et moraux de la nation anglaise. La nécessité de prendre en compte tous les paramètres économiques et politiques qu'impliquait une émancipation devenue de plus en plus nécessaire aux yeux de l'opinion publique britannique força donc le gouvernement britannique à adopter une position intermédiaire, pour parvenir finalement à la suppression complète

1. Hampden, *op. cit.* p. 185.

de l'esclavage dans les colonies anglaises, qui fut promulguée en 1833, mais ne devint effective qu'après une période « d'apprentissage » de cinq ans et une indemnisation économique des planteurs par la métropole.

Bibliographie

Beckford Jr., William, *Remarks upon the Situation of Negroes in Jamaica, Impartially Made from Local Experience of Nearly Thirteen Years in that Island*, Londres, 1788.

Cobbett, William, *'Summary of Politics'*, from *Cobbett's Political Register*, Londres, juin 1802.

—, *Political Register: Slave Trade, Lettre écrite en 1796 à l'archevêque de Rochester* publiée en 1802.

Edwards, Bryan, *A Speech delivered at a Free Conference between the Honourable Council and Assembly of Jamaica… On the Subject of Mr Wilberforce's Propositions in the House of Commons, Concerning the Slave Trade*, Kingston, Jamaica, 1789 ; Londres, 1790.

—, *History Civil and Commercial*, (3 vols.), Londres, 1793-1801.

Hampden, Rev. John, *A Commentary on Mr Clarkson's Pamphlet, Entitled 'Thoughts on the Necessity of Improving the Condition of the Slaves in the British Colonies, with a View to their Ultimate Emancipation*, Londres, 1824.

Harris, Raymund, *Scriptural Researches on the Licitness of the Slave Trade, Shewing its Conformity with the Principles of Natural and Revealed Religion, Delineated in the Sacred Writings of the Word of God*, Liverpool: H. Hodgson, 1788.

Holroyd, J.B., Earl of Sheffield, *Observations on the Project for Abolishing the Slave Trade and on the Reasonableness of Attempting some Practicable Mode of Relieving the Negroes*, Londres, 1790.

Kitson, J. Peter , Lee Debbie, *Slavery, Abolition and Emancipation, Writings in the Romantic Period* (8 Vol.), Londres: Pickering & Chato, 1999.

Une vision du Noir à l'époque de la traite : la petite note de David Hume

Michel Prum

NEGRO, Homo pelli nigra, *a name given to a variety of the human species, who are entirely black, and are found in the Torrid zone, especially in that part of Africa which lies within the tropics. [...] Vices the most notorious seem to be the portion of this unhappy race: idleness, treachery, revenge, cruelty, impudence, stealing, lying, profanity, debauchery, nastiness and intemperance, are said to have extinguished the principles of natural law, and to have silenced the reproofs of conscience. They are strangers to every sentiment of compassion, and are an awful example of the corruption of man when left to himself.*

Encyclopædia Britannica (1798), entrée « *Negro* »

Introduction : esclavage moderne, esclavage antique

L'esclavage britannique, à l'époque moderne[1], a peu de choses à voir avec l'esclavage tel qu'il se pratiquait et se concevait à l'époque antique. À Rome, l'esclave était avant tout une prise de guerre, un vaincu qui n'avait pas eu le courage de mourir. Son statut n'était pas associé à la couleur de sa peau, à la nature de ses cheveux ni à quelque autre caractéristique phénotypique. Il pouvait d'ailleurs racheter sa liberté et redevenir ainsi un homme libre parmi les autres. Il n'y avait donc pas, pourrait-on dire, d'essentialisation de l'esclave. La condition servile était un *état* — parfois transitoire, parfois pérenne — mais un état et non une *nature*. Cela ne veut pas dire que sa condition était moins douloureuse : il était durement traité, pouvait être massacré ou mutilé, mais cette oppression n'était pas imposée au nom de la race, car ce concept, au sens où nous l'entendons aujourd'hui, n'existait pas.

Certes toute pensée essentialiste de l'esclave n'était pas totalement absente, en particulier en Grèce. Ainsi, par exemple, Aristote écrit-il, dans le premier livre de *Politiques* :

> Le même rapport se retrouve entre l'homme et les autres animaux. D'une part les animaux domestiques sont d'une nature meilleure que les animaux sauvages, d'autre part, le meilleur pour tous est d'être gouvernés par l'homme car ils y trouvent leur sauvegarde. De même, le rapport entre mâle et femelle

1. L'historiographie française découpe l'histoire en quatre périodes : antique, médiévale, moderne et contemporaine. C'est dans ce sens qu'est employé ici le terme « moderne », pour désigner les trois siècles qui vont de la découverte du Nouveau Monde (1492) à la Révolution française (1792).

> est par nature un rapport entre plus fort et plus faible, c'est-à-dire entre commandant et commandé. Il en est nécessairement de même chez tous les hommes. Ceux qui sont aussi éloignés des hommes libres que le corps l'est de l'âme, ou la bête de l'homme (et sont ainsi faits ceux dont l'activité consiste à se servir de leur corps, et dont c'est le meilleur parti qu'on puisse tirer), *ceux-là sont par nature des esclaves* ; et pour eux, être commandés par un maître est une bonne chose, si ce que nous avons dit plus haut est vrai. Est en effet esclave par nature celui qui est destiné à être à un autre (et c'est pourquoi il est à un autre) et qui n'a la raison en partage que dans la mesure où il la perçoit chez les autres mais ne la possède pas lui-même[1].

Mais cette nature d'esclave n'était pas liée à une appartenance ethnique. Celui qui est « destiné à être à un autre » ne l'est pas parce que lui-même est noir et l'autre blanc, mais parce qu'il a l'esprit faible. L'humanité est perçue comme diverse mais la suprématie blanche n'est pas encore posée en principe. « Les hommes diffèrent par leur savoir, écrit Cicéron, mais sont tous égaux par leur aptitude au savoir : il n'est pas de race qui, guidée par la raison, ne puisse parvenir à la vérité[2]. »

Dans les débats qui nous intéressent ici, sur l'abolition de l'esclavage, les adversaires de cette abolition se réfèrent de façon récurrente à la Bible, et en particulier à la malédiction de Cham (en anglais « *the curse of Ham* ») dans la Genèse. On se rappelle que Noé avait trois fils : Japhet, Sem et Cham.

> Ayant bu du vin, [Noé] fut enivré et se dénuda à l'intérieur de sa tente. Cham, père de Canaan, vit la nudité de son père et avertit ses deux frères au dehors. Mais Sem et Japhet prirent le manteau, le mirent tous deux sur leurs épaules et, marchant à reculons, couvrirent la nudité de leur père ; leurs visages étaient tournés en arrière et ils ne virent pas la nudité de leur père. Lorsque Noé se réveilla de son ivresse, il apprit ce que lui avait fait son fils le plus jeune. Et il dit « Maudit soit Canaan ! Qu'il soit pour ses frères le dernier des esclaves[3] ! »

Cette malédiction (« Qu'il soit pour ses frères le dernier des esclaves ! ») est utilisée par les antiabolitionnistes anglais comme preuve que l'esclavage était légitimé par les Saintes Écritures. Or le texte qui vient d'être cité ne précise pas que Cham est noir. Ce n'est qu'au début de l'époque moderne, à la fin du XVe siècle, que Cham est progressivement ethnicisé. Le Portugais Gomes Eanes de Zurara (1410-1474) semble être le premier à relier la traite des Noirs à la malédiction de Cham (les Portugais sont aussi les premiers à mettre en place la traite des Noirs, à partir de 1444, et incidemment les derniers des grandes puissances européennes à l'abolir, aussi tard

1. Aristote, *Politiques*, L.1, ch. 5, traduction de Pierre Pellegrin, Paris, Nathan, Les intégrales de philo, 2004, p. 35. C'est nous qui soulignons.
2. Cité par Léon Poliakov, *Le Racisme*, Paris, Seghers, 1976, p. 41.
3. La Genèse, 10, 18-25 (Bible de Jérusalem).

que 1869). Selon Léon Poliakov, grand spécialiste du racisme, l'érudit allemand Georg Horn (1620-1670) est le premier (en 1666), à l'université de Leyde (Pays-Bas), à proposer une division de l'humanité en fonction de la postérité de Noé[1]. Les Blancs descendraient de Japhet, les Asiatiques de Sem (d'où le mot sémite) et les Noirs de Cham. La Bible, autrefois *colour-blind*, sert désormais à justifier la traite négrière[2].

Essor de la traite et racialisation

Cette nouvelle pensée raciste[3], qui commence avec la traite portugaise et se développe surtout avec l'essor du commerce triangulaire, en particulier anglais et français, semble donc servir de légitimation intellectuelle d'une pratique inique. Comment transporter des êtres humains entassés à fond de cale comme des marchandises (le « bois d'ébène »), comment les vendre et les maltraiter tout en conservant l'estime de soi et se considérer toujours comme de bons chrétiens ? Si je veux tuer mon chien, je dis qu'il a la rage. L'Occident chrétien doit donc relire ses mythes fondateurs, comme la Genèse, et inventer une hiérarchisation des races ou, mieux encore (si l'on peut dire), chasser les Noirs de l'humanité, en faire des intermédiaires entre l'homme et l'orang-outan, comme le font par exemple l'Écossais Lord Monboddo (1714-1799), dans *Of the Origin and Progress of Language* (1773-1792) ou, avant lui, l'Anglais Edward Tyson (1650-1708).

D'où aussi le succès des thèses polygénistes, qui se mettent en place aux XVIe et XVIIe siècles, et qui brisent l'unité du genre humain et posent que tous les hommes ne descendent pas des mêmes ancêtres, Adam et Eve, mais que certains hommes (les Noirs par exemple) sont issus de tribus pré-adamites[4]. Caïn ne dit-il pas à Yahvé, qui le punit de bannissement après le meurtre d'Abel : « Le premier venu me tuera[5] ». Il y a donc d'autres hommes sur terre. En Angleterre, Matthew Hale, auteur de *The Primitive*

1. Léon Poliakov, *op. cit.*, p. 57.
2. Certains ont voulu voir dans le « Je suis noire *mais* belle » du Cantique des cantiques un exemple, certes unique, de racisme biblique. Il s'agit en fait d'une mauvaise traduction du grec *melain eimi kai kalè*, où la conjonction *kai*, très polysémique, peut signifier tout aussi bien « et » : « Je suis noire *et* belle ».
3. Le mot « raciste » est bien sûr anachronique ici : il n'apparaît qu'au XXe siècle. Nous nous autoriserons malgré tout, par commodité, à l'employer, comme on peut parler du « féminisme » de Wollstonecraft ou de l'« eugénisme » de Platon.
4. On notera que la définition du « Nègre » de *l'Encyclopédie britannique*, citée en exergue de ce chapitre, malgré la violence de son racisme — qui peut surprendre dans une entrée d'encyclopédie dont on s'attendrait à ce qu'elle soit scientifique et objective — se rattache néanmoins clairement au monogénisme : le Noir appartient à l'espèce humaine dont il est une variété et sa déchéance est due non à sa nature mais à sa situation (« *an awful example of the corruption of man when left to himself* »).
5. Genèse, *op. cit.*, 3, 14.

Origination of Mankind, Considered and Examined to the Light of Nature (1677) et John Atkins (1685-1757) plaident la cause polygéniste[1].

Le débat sur l'esclavage qui fait rage dans la seconde moitié du XVIIIe siècle s'inscrit donc dans cet héritage d'une racialisation de l'humanité, voire, pour les auteurs polygénistes, d'une fragmentation du genre humain. Ce que l'on peut considérer comme un recul de la pensée se renforce paradoxalement à l'époque des Lumières. Le siècle de la Raison souffre le développement de thèses obscurantistes. En France Voltaire voit dans les Noirs des « animaux » d'une autre espèce[2]. De l'autre côté de la Manche, le meilleur exemple de racisme anti-Noir est le philosophe David Hume, qui est pourtant l'un des représentants les plus célèbres des Lumières écossaises.

De Ham à Hume

David Hume (1711-1776) est le défenseur de la tolérance et le pourfendeur des préjugés. Il croit en la sympathie entre les êtres, il défend les valeurs d'altérité. Enfin il professe un humanisme universaliste en écrivant dans son *Enquiry Concerning Human Understanding* (1748) :

> *It is universally acknowledged that there is a great uniformity among the actions of men, in all nations and ages, and that human nature remains still the same, in its principles and operations. The same motives always produce the same actions: the same events follow the same causes. Ambition, avarice, self-love, vanity, friendship, generosity, public spirit: these passions, mixed in various degrees, and distributed through society, have been, from the beginning of the world, and still are, the source of all the actions and enterprises, which have ever been observed among mankind. Would you know the sentiments, inclinations, and course of life of the Greeks and Romans? Study well the temper and actions of the French and English.*[3]

Et pourtant en 1753, Hume révise son essai *Of National Characters* (1748) en y ajoutant une note infrapaginale ouvertement raciste. Cette note a été largement reprise en Grande-Bretagne par les partisans de l'esclavage, qui y ont vu un encouragement en faveur de la suprématie des Blancs. Du point de vue de la recherche universitaire, toute une littérature a été consacrée à ces quelques lignes. Aucune note de bas de page, dans toute l'histoire, n'a sans doute fait couler plus d'encre que celle-ci. Nous nous référerons

1. Les polygénistes les plus connus sont Giordano Bruno (1548-1600) en Italie et, en France, Isaac de La Peyrère (1596-1676), dont l'ouvrage *Prae-Adamitae* (1655) est brûlé en place publique. Voltaire sera aussi polygéniste.
2. Voltaire, *Essai sur les mœurs et l'esprit des nations* (1756), chap. II, « Des différentes races d'homme », Paris, Lefèvre, 1829, p. 7.
3. David Hume, *Enquiry Concerning Human Understanding*, Tom L. Beauchamp (ed.), Oxford: Oxford University Press, 2000, p. 64.

en particulier à l'article de John Immerwahr : « Hume's Revised Racism » (1992)[1] et à celui, plus récent, d'Emmanuel Chukwudi Eze : « Hume, Race and Human Nature » (2000)[2].

Qu'a donc écrit Hume dans cette note ?

> *I am apt to suspect the negroes and in general all other species of men (for there are four or five different kinds) to be naturally inferior to the whites. There never was a civilised nation of any other complexion than white, nor even any individual eminent either in action or speculation. No ingenious manufactures amongst them, no arts, no sciences. On the other hand, the most rude and barbarous of the whites, such as the ancient GERMANS, the present TARTARS, have still something eminent about them, in their valour, form of government, or some other particular. Such a uniform and constant difference could not happen, in so many countries and ages, if nature had not made an original distinction betwixt these breeds of men. Not to mention our colonies, there are NEGROE slaves dispersed all over EUROPE, of which none ever discovered any symptoms of ingenuity; tho' low people, without education, will start up amongst us, and distinguish themselves in every profession. In JAMAICA, indeed, they talk of one negroe as a man of parts and learning; but 'tis likely he is admired for very slender accomplishments, like a parrot, who speaks a few words plainly.*[3]

Cette note est maintenue en l'état dans les nombreuses éditions que Hume révise, y compris la dernière édition parue de son vivant, celle de 1770. Pourtant, dans la toute dernière édition de 1777, donc posthume, que Hume avait révisée peu de temps avant sa mort, la note est modifiée. Toute la fin demeure. Seul est amendé le début.

> *I am apt to suspect the negroes ~~and in general all other species of men (for there are four or five different kinds)~~ to be naturally inferior to the whites. There ~~never~~ scarcely ever was a civilised nation of ~~any other~~ that complexion ~~than white~~, nor even any individual eminent either in action or speculation.*

Malheureusement, les éditeurs de Hume du XIXe siècle, Thomas Hill Green et Thomas Hodge Grose, n'ont pas tenu compte de cette révision et la correction n'a pas été apportée avant 1985 (par Eugene F. Miller). Donc la plus grande partie de la littérature consacrée à la note de Hume est fondée sur la première version de celle-ci.

1. John Immerwahr, "Hume's Revised Racism", *Journal of the History of Ideas*, vol. 53, n° 3, juillet-septembre 1992, pp. 481-486.
2. Emmanuel Chukwudi Eze, « Hume, Race and Human Nature », *Journal of the History of Ideas*, vol. 61, n° 4, octobre 2000, pp. 691-698.
3. David Hume, *Essays, Moral, Political and Literary*, Eugene F. Miller (ed.), Indianapolis, Liberty Fund, 1987, Part I, chap. 21, 17, note 10.

La polémique Hume / Beattie

Il semble que la décision tardive de Hume vienne d'une réaction aux critiques de James Beattie (1735-1805), autre universitaire écossais (Aberdeen) — celui qui a fait connaître Hume à Kant. En 1770, Beattie publie *An Essay on the Nature and Immutability of Truth in Opposition to Sophistry and Scepticism*[1]. Dans l'avant-dernier chapitre de cet ouvrage, Beattie s'attaque à la note de Hume. Il conteste le fait qu'il n'y ait jamais eu de nation ou d'individu non-blanc civilisé. Il note : « *Of the facts here asserted [by Hume], no man could have sufficient evidence, except from a personal acquaintance with all the negroes that now are, or ever were, on the face of the earth. Those people write no histories*[2]. » C'est sans doute en réponse à cette critique que Hume transforme son *never* en *scarcely ever*.

Par ailleurs, Beattie démonte les arguments de Hume en se fondant essentiellement sur les sociétés pré-colombiennes (Pérou, Mexique). Des Noirs, Beattie ne dit pas grand chose, sinon que les esclaves noirs ont montré « *symptoms of ingenuity, notwithstanding their unhappy circumstances*[3] ». Ils font « d'excellents artisans » et « musiciens ». Les critiques racistes de Beattie reprochent avant tout à Beattie d'utiliser les réalisations culturelles des sociétés pré-colombiennes pour réfuter la notion d'infériorité des Noirs défendue par Hume.

Hume utilise cette faiblesse de l'argumentation de Beattie dans la révision de sa note. Il concentre son attaque contre les seuls Noirs, rendant ainsi inopérantes les références aux civilisations pré-colombiennes. Du coup, Hume renforce son racisme anti-Noir, plutôt qu'il ne l'atténue.

Par ailleurs la révision de Hume correspond à l'abandon de la thèse polygéniste. Il abandonne complètement les références à la polygénèse de la première version (« *and in general all other species of men (for there are four or five different kinds* »). Abandon ou clarification : peut-être la première version était-elle simplement ambiguë et « *species* » était-il employé de façon non scientifique.

Mais par ailleurs la révision de Hume montre à quel point il tenait à l'essentiel de son discours anti-Noir, contrairement à ce qu'écrivait en 1980 Richard H. Popkin dans son article « *Hume's Racism*[4] » (qui ne connaissait pas à cette date la révision — puisqu'elle n'apparaît qu'en 1985) et voyait dans la note infrapaginale peut-être « *a casual addition* », alors qu'elle est

1. Réédité en 2004 chez Kessinger Publishing (Whitefish, MT).
2. Cité par Immerwahr, *op. cit.*, p. 484.
3. *Ibid.*
4. Richard H.Popkin, "Hume's Racism", *in* Richard A.Watson & James E. Force (eds.), *The High Road to Pyrrhonism*, San Diego: Austin Hill, 1980.

bien délibérée, voire opiniâtre. Popkin était influencé, dans son jugement, par le fait qu'il voyait Hume comme un opposant de l'esclavage. Mais on peut être antiesclavagiste et raciste (l'inverse est également possible). Par ailleurs nous reviendrons à la fin de ce chapitre sur l'antiesclavagisme de Hume.

Henry Louis Gates a montré en 1987 qu'il existait des intellectuels noirs dans des cercles que Hume connaissait[1]. En particulier, l'« homme très talentueux » (« *man of parts* ») vivant en Jamaïque que Hume mentionne dans sa note (« *In JAMAICA, indeed, they talk of one negroe as a man of parts and learning* »), a pu être identifié par Gates. C'était Francis Williams, né en 1700, diplômé de l'Université de Cambridge, qui enseigna le latin et les mathématiques et publia de la poésie latine. Williams protesta vivement et publiquement contre la note de Hume, mais Hume ne lui répondit jamais[2].

Eric Morton, dans un article de 2002, « Race and Racism in the Works of David Hume », paru dans *Journal on African Philosophy*[3], note aussi les nombreux événements récents où les Noirs avaient fait preuve de courage (*valour*), et que Hume ne pouvait pas ignorer : soulèvements d'esclaves au Brésil, Surinam, Haïti, Tobago, Montserrat, etc. À la Jamaïque, les Noirs, par leur résistance, arrivent même à imposer un rapport de force aboutissant à la signature d'un Traité (1739) leur garantissant la liberté et le droit de propriété « *for ever* » sur un petit territoire de l'île.

Racisme et empirisme

Eze, dans un article de 2000, s'emploie à relier le racisme de Hume à sa philosophie de la connaissance. Pour Hume, l'esprit est une collection de perceptions « *united together by certain relations*[4] ». L'infériorité du Noir, pour Hume, vient de l'incapacité supposée de celui-ci à disposer de cette capacité organisatrice et unificatrice des perceptions. Hume distingue les fonctions passives et actives du raisonnement. Raisonner, c'est comparer. Si l'on compare deux objets présents, la comparaison est un acte passif

1. Henry Louis Gates, *Figures in Black: Words, Signs and the "Racial" Self*, Oxford: Oxford University Press, 1987.
2. Né à Kingston, Jamaïque, en 1702, de parents noirs non esclaves, Williams fut remarqué, en raison de sa vive intelligence, par le duc de Montagu, qui lui permit d'aller faire ses études à Cambridge. En lisant une de ses odes, le révérend Robert Boucher Nicholls, Doyen de Middleham, se serait exclamé : « *I have never heard an orang-utan has composed an ode. Among the defenders of slavery we do not find one half of the literary merit of Francis Williams.* » http://209.85.135.104/search?q=cache:P8ejjSKwPgAJ:www.100greatblackbritons.com/bios/francis_williams.htm+%22francis+williams%22&hl=fr&ct=clnk&cd=1&gl=fr
3. Eric Morton, « Race and Racism in the Works of David Hume », *Journal on African Philosophy*, I, 2002, pp. 1-27.
4. Emmanuel Chukwudi Eze, *op. cit.*, p. 693.

entre deux « perceptions », sans exercice de la pensée. En revanche, si l'un des objets, voire les deux sont absents, l'association est un processus actif qui relève du raisonnement. Quand Hume affirme « *no Negro is capable of eminent* [...] *action or speculation* », c'est à cette activité mentale qu'il se réfère. Il ne dénie pas au Noir les fonctions mentales et cognitives, mais leur attribue, parmi ces fonctions, le seul niveau passif (et donc inférieur) des sensations, de la réception des impressions. Si l'objet disparaît des sens, le Noir, selon Hume, perd la capacité d'inférer de façon abstraite des relations entre objets. Pour Hume, l'esprit du Noir est comme celui d'un enfant, mais d'un enfant qui resterait toujours enfant. Pour Eze, le discours de Hume permet de justifier le fait que le Noir, comme le cheval, peut être vendu. Il apporterait donc sa contribution aux partisans de l'esclavage colonial.

> *If the mental capacity of the Negro—which is to say the level of humanity—is more nearly animal than white, is there any reason why the Negro could not be sold like a horse or, to stay with Hume's example, a dog? Is it possible that Hume added this footnote to the essay "Of National Character" as a statement of principled philosophical position on the debate current at the time in England and America about whether or not the Negro is a legitimate "article of trade"?*[1]

David Livingston, dans son livre de 1998 sur Hume[2], explique que le but de ses révisions est essentiellement d'adapter ses écrits à l'actualité (« *to address the issues of that period* »), donc aux débats sur l'esclavage, et Eze, en s'appuyant sur Livingstone, voit la note infrapaginale comme un argument en faveur du *chattel slavery*.

> *If Negroes lack naturally and permanently the capacity for self—and social—constitution through the arts and the sciences and through related projects of culture, government, and civilization, then slavery and subsequently colonialism might indeed have been viewed by Hume as forms of containment in defense of civilization, rather than the usually asserted "educational" value of slavery (Hegel) or the "mission to civilize" (Lugard).*[3]

Eric Morton conclut lui aussi que la méthodologie empirique de David Hume est entachée par ses *a priori* idéologiques. Son discours, lorsqu'il aborde la question des Noirs, n'est pas scientifique, mais apologétique, au service de l'esclavage. « *I argue that the purpose of his racist law was not one of knowledge, but one of justification for power and dominion by some over others*[4]. »

1. *Ibid.*, p. 696.
2. *Philosophical Melancholy and Delirium: Essays in the Philosophy of David Hume*, Chicago: University of Chicago Press, 1998, p. 281.
3. Emmanuel Chukwudi Eze, *op. cit.*, p. 696.
4. Eric Morton, *op. cit.*, p. 6.

Pourtant Hume est sans doute plus complexe, ou ambigu, que ce qu'en disent Eze et Morton. S'il s'attaque à « l'esclavage » politique, c'est-à-dire à l'arbitraire du prince, il rejette aussi « l'esclavage réel », « l'esclavage domestique ». Dans le chapitre XI de la deuxième partie de son *Enquiry Concerning Human Understanding*, intitulé « Of the Populousness of Ancient Nations », dans lequel il s'intéresse avant tout à l'effet de l'esclavage sur la croissance démographique, Hume écrit : « *The remains which are found of domestic slavery, in the American colonies* [...], *would never surely create a desire of rendering it more universal*[1]. » Ce que Hume semble surtout reprocher à cet esclavage, c'est d'altérer l'humanité des maîtres, habitués à commander dès leur plus jeune âge. « *The little humanity, commonly observed in persons, accustomed, from their infancy, to exercise so great authority over their fellow-creatures, and to trample upon human nature, were sufficient alone to disgust us with that unbounded dominion*[2]. » Ce passage semble rattacher Hume au monogénisme plus qu'au polygénisme puisque les esclaves sont appelés « *fellow-creatures* », doués d'une « nature humaine ». On sait que Hume a plus « joué[3] » avec le concept de polygénisme qu'il ne l'a vraiment soutenu, puisqu'il s'en est débarrassé lors de la révision de l'édition de 1777. Mais le chapitre « Of the Populousness of Ancient Nations » reste ambigu, car il s'oppose plus à l'universalisation de l'esclavage qu'à son existence même et déplore les conséquences de cette institution sur les maîtres plus que sur les travailleurs asservis.

Conclusion : Lumières et esclavage

Si la « petite note » de David Hume a servi de référence intellectuelle aux adversaires de l'abolition de l'esclavage, on voit donc que cette filiation n'est pas sans poser problème. Ceci étant dit, il n'en demeure pas moins que Hume, au travers de cette note, exprime un mépris viscéral des Noirs, qu'il tient à conserver malgré toutes les critiques, nous l'avons vu, jusqu'à sa mort. Si la note de 1753 a fait couler tant d'encre, on notera que, dans le corps même de l'essai « *Of National Characters* », écrit dès 1748, dans un passage qui, lui, n'a jamais été révisé, il décrit les Noirs comme des ivrognes prêts à tout pour assouvir leurs penchants alcooliques, y compris à vendre enfants et femmes.

> *You may obtain any thing of the NEGROES by offering them strong drink; and may easily prevail with them to sell, not only their children, but their wives and mistresses, for a cask of brandy.*[4]

1. David Hume, *Essays, op. cit.*, Part II, chap. 11, p. 6.
2. *Ibid.*
3. Immerwahr parle de « *flirtation with polygenesis* », *op. cit.*, p. 485.
4. David Hume, *Essays, op. cit.*, Part I, chap. 21, 32.

Cette remarque raciste sur l'alcoolisme des Noirs n'a pas suscité autant de commentaires que la note de 1753[1]. Il est vrai que, pour violente que soit la charge, elle est moins forte que la terrible affirmation de la note, selon laquelle les Noirs n'ont jamais été capables de la moindre réalisation intellectuelle, et que leurs maigres productions littéraires relèvent du psittacisme.

L'exemple de David Hume montre donc la complexité du paysage intellectuel au XVIIIe siècle : le combat pour l'abolition de l'esclavage n'a pas toujours opposé les tenants des Lumières aux forces obscurantistes, mais certains philosophes des Lumières eux-mêmes ont pu, sinon défendre directement l'esclavage, du moins contribuer à renforcer les bases idéologiques de la suprématie blanche[2].

Bibliographie

Eze, Emmanuel Chukwudi, « Hume, Race and Human Nature », *Journal of the History of Ideas*, vol. 61, n° 4, octobre 2000, pp. 691-698.

Gates, Henry Louis, *Figures in Black: Words, Signs and the "Racial" Self*, Oxford: Oxford University Press, 1987.

Hume, David, *Essays, Moral, Political and Literary*, Eugene F. Miller (ed.), Indianapolis: Liberty Fund, 1987.

Immerwahr, John, "Hume's Revised Racism", *Journal of the History of Ideas*, vol. 53, n° 3, juillet-septembre 1992, pp. 481-486.

Morton, Eric, « Race and Racism in the Works of David Hume », *Journal on African Philosophy*, I, 2002, pp. 1-27.

Poliakov, Léon, *Le Racisme*, Paris, Seghers, 1976.

Popkin, Richard H., "Hume's Racism", *in* Richard A.Watson & James E. Force (eds.), *The High Road to Pyrrhonism*, San Diego: Austin Hill, 1980.

1. Notons cependant Eric Morton, *op. cit.*, p. 11 ; également Andrew Valls, *Race and Racism in Modern Philosophy*, Ithaca: Cornell University Press, 2005, p. 146, note 32.
2. Au siècle précédent John Locke (1632-1704), autre représentant des Lumières britanniques, a investi de grosses sommes dans la Traite négrière, au travers de la Royal African Company. Locke est le co-auteur, en tant que secrétaire du comte de Shaftesbury, de la constitution de Caroline (*Fundamental Constitutions of Carolina*, 1669), dont une clause précise : « *Every free man of Carolina shall have absolute power and authority over his negro slave of what opinion or religion soever.* »

Le contexte nord-américain de l'antiesclavagisme britannique : le débat atlantique sur l'esclavage et l'abolition (1688-1787)

Marie-Jeanne Rossignol

The British antislavery movement that began in the late 1780s was, therefore, a late-born sibling in the family of Anglo-American antislavery campaigns.

Christopher Leslie Brown, *Moral Capital. Foundations of British Abolitionism*. 2006.

Comme l'indique Christopher Brown, on ne peut bien comprendre la campagne antiesclavagiste britannique qui s'enclenche vraiment en 1787 sans connaître et comprendre le mouvement antiesclavagiste qui l'a précédée en Amérique du Nord, dans les colonies britanniques tout d'abord, avant la guerre d'Indépendance, puis dans les nouveaux États américains, après 1776. La première partie de cet article présente brièvement les colonies britanniques d'Amérique du Nord (les futurs États-Unis) et leur implication dans la traite et l'esclavage, et ce, dans le cadre de l'Empire britannique en Amérique. Puis on aborde les débuts du mouvement antiesclavagiste nord-américain, de 1688 à 1776, sous ses diverses facettes : il s'agit d'un mouvement atlantique (les colonies sont impliquées mais la métropole l'est également par le biais de la circulation des hommes et des idées), où les convictions des Quakers et les idées du Grand réveil religieux jouent un rôle moteur. En troisième partie, est examinée la guerre d'indépendance américaine (1775-1783), qui constitue un tournant pour le mouvement antiesclavagiste nord-américain, mais également britannique : si les Britanniques libèrent des esclaves dans le cadre des opérations militaires, il n'en reste pas moins que seuls les Américains procèdent à de réelles émancipations de masse, immédiates et graduelles, tout en inscrivant les droits naturels au cœur de leurs nouvelles institutions, et en s'attaquant à la traite. Ces avancées américaines vont constituer un élément déterminant dans l'ouverture du débat britannique après 1783 : elles remettent effectivement en cause la position de la Grande-Bretagne comme première nation des libertés. Présents en Angleterre à la fin de la guerre d'Indépendance, les Quakers nord-américains prennent part à la naissance d'un engagement plus net de la communauté britannique contre la traite et l'esclavage : ce point est examiné en quatrième partie. L'historiographie de la question est très importante aux États-Unis, même si elle ne rivalise pas encore avec celle du mouvement abolitionniste des années 1830 à la Guerre de sécession : il n'est cependant pas question ici d'en faire une recension exhaustive. Il est pourtant indispensable de signaler, parmi d'autres grands historiens tels Sylvia Frey, les noms de David Brion Davis et de Christopher Brown, qui, des années 1960 à aujourd'hui, ont apporté à l'étude de ce mouvement atlantique l'acuité d'esprits précis et érudits : leurs idées sont examinées en détail dans ce travail.

1. L'Empire britannique atlantique et l'esclavage 1607-1756 : l'Amérique du Nord et les Antilles

a) Un seul Empire britannique dans les Amériques : le développement précoce des Antilles, fondées sur le « sucre et les esclaves »

Comme le rappelle Richard S. Dunn dans son livre *Sugar and Slaves. The Rise of the Planter Class in the English West Indies, 1624-1713*, on a tendance à oublier que les pionniers de l'agriculture de plantation britanniques en Amérique (Amérique du Nord et Caraïbes) firent partie d'une seule et même vague d'émigration impériale atlantique, des années 1600 à 1630[1]. Si nombre de ces colonies britanniques se tournent d'abord vers le tabac, que ce soit en Amérique du Nord ou dans les Antilles, les colonies antillaises (la Barbade puis toutes les autres) développent à compter des années 1640 la monoculture sucrière, un type d'économie qui requiert un grand nombre de travailleurs, voués à d'éprouvantes conditions de travail. Après s'être brièvement tournés vers les domestiques blancs recrutés en Angleterre ou en Irlande, les planteurs des Caraïbes font appel à l'esclavage de masse : les Africains, entre autres qualités, sont mieux adaptés au climat et forment bientôt la majorité des résidents[2]. La traite britannique est gérée dans un premier temps par la *Company of Royal Adventurers into Africa* (1663) par la *English Royal African Company* (1672-1713), qui détient un monopole sur ce commerce jusqu'en 1698, mais elle s'ouvre ensuite à la concurrence des intérêts privés[3]. Quant aux planteurs caribéens, dès fortune faite, ils sont le plus souvent absents et restent en Angleterre, près du pouvoir, afin de défendre leurs intérêts[4] ; et les propriétés de ces grands planteurs

1. Richard S. Dunn, *Sugar and Slaves. The Rise of the Planter Class in the English West Indies, 1624-1713,* (1972). New York: Norton, 1973), p.XIII. Le premier groupe de colons s'installe en Virginie en 1607, St. Christophe reçoit ses pionniers en 1624, la Barbade en 1627, Nevis en 1628, Montserrat et Antigua dans les années 1630 et la Jamaïque en 1655, alors que les Pères pèlerins débarquent à Plymouth en 1620 (Nouvelle-Angleterre), suivis par de plus larges contingents de Puritains à compter de 1630.
2. Dunn, *op. cit.*, pp. 19, 67-74. Peter H. Wood, *Black Majority. Negroes in Colonial South Carolina from 1670 through the Stono Rebellion* (1974), New York: Norton, 1975, p. 8.
3. Herbert S. Klein, *The Atlantic Slave Trade*, New York: Cambridge University Press, p. 80. Dunn, *Sugar and Slaves*, pp. 20, 46.
4. Dunn, *op. cit.*, pp. 101-102. Voir également le chapitre "British Sojourners" pp. 3-34, in Andrew Jackson O'Shaughnessy, *An Empire Divided. The American Revolution and the British Caribbean*, Philadelphie: University of Pennsylvania Press, 2000.

à la richesse indécente sont gérées par des contremaîtres qui viennent pour s'enrichir et non s'établir, d'où peut-être des relations d'une brutalité inouïe entre dominés et dominants[1]. Chez les colons blancs, le climat et les maladies ne permettent pas la constitution de familles et de générations stables[2]. Ces petites colonies ont une valeur inestimable aux yeux de Londres, puisqu'à la fin du XVIIe siècle, les exportations de sucre de la Barbade ont plus de valeur à elles seules que toutes les exportations des colonies d'Amérique du Nord réunies[3].

b) L'évolution des colonies d'Amérique du Nord du XVIIe au XVIIIe siècle : sociétés esclavagistes et sociétés avec esclaves

Parallèlement, les colonies d'Amérique du Nord connaissent une évolution variée : certaines, comme la Virginie, le Maryland, le Delaware, les Carolines, deviennent également des colonies de plantations, dont le tabac est la principale ressource, suivie par le riz et l'indigo (mais le coton ne s'implantera vraiment qu'à partir du début du XIXe siècle). Des planteurs de la Barbade émigrent en particulier vers les Carolines, au développement desquelles ils vont imprimer leur marque à compter de 1663 : dès le début, les Noirs représentent entre un quart et un tiers des nouveaux arrivants[4]. Comme dans les colonies britanniques des Antilles, toutes les colonies du sud qui s'adonnent à la monoculture ont rapidement recours aux esclaves pour leurs qualités d'agriculteurs et leur résistance aux maladies et au climat, même si leurs importations d'Africains restent bien plus limitées au XVIIe siècle[5]. Mais les planteurs nord-américains restent sur place, et les engagés blancs, s'ils survivent au climat délétère, cherchent à devenir propriétaires à leur tour une fois leur contrat rempli envers un planteur : la terre ne manque pas, contrairement aux Antilles. Les premiers esclaves étaient arrivés en 1619 en Virginie et une certaine ambiguïté demeure quant à leur statut lors des premières décennies, alors qu'aux Antilles, les esclaves sont immédiatement considérés comme des êtres inférieurs.

1. Voir l'ouvrage de Trevor Burnard, *Mastery, Tyranny and Desire. Thomas Thistlewood and his Slaves in the Anglo-Jamaican World*, Chapel Hill and London: The University of North Carolina Press, 2004. Basé sur le journal du contremaître, puis propriétaire Thomas Thistlewood, ce livre détaille de manière parfois dérangeante les traitements auxquels étaient soumis les esclaves sous le contrôle de Thistlewood.
2. Dunn, *op. cit.*, p. 77.
3. Dunn, *op. cit.*, p. 85.
4. Peter H. Wood, *Black Majority. Negroes in Colonial South Carolina from 1670 through the Stono Rebellion*, New York: Norton, 1975, pp. 9, 25.
5. Pour Richard S. Dunn, « *The initial difference between slavery in the two sectors of English America is that the island colonists plunged into the slaveholding business and mainland colonists inched into it. [...] By 1660 [...] there were about twenty thousand blacks in Barbados, two thousand in the Leewards, and five hundred in Jamaica—as against a thousand in Virginia.* » p. 226. À cette époque, les colonies nord-américaines ne reçoivent d'ailleurs que les esclaves qui n'ont pas été vendus aux Antilles.

Dans les deux types de colonies, ce n'est pourtant qu'à la fin du siècle que l'esclavage devient une institution codifiée. Comme aux Antilles, les colonies d'Amérique du Nord créent cette législation dans un complet vide juridique anglais, de même qu'ils organisent les relations raciales entre les groupes sans bénéficier de précédent métropolitain[1]. Face à un manque de main-d'œuvre en provenance des îles britanniques, les planteurs importent davantage d'esclaves venus d'Afrique, et progressivement, ces colonies se transforment en « *slave societies* », sociétés esclavagistes où l'esclavage constitue le socle économique et social de la communauté[2].

Mais les esclaves africains sont également importés dans les colonies du centre (« *middle colonies* »), comme la Pennsylvanie, New York, le New Jersey, où ils viennent travailler sur les grandes fermes des colons blancs. En Nouvelle-Angleterre (aujourd'hui Maine, New Hampshire, Vermont, Massachusetts, Rhode Island, Connecticut), les colons s'adjoignent également des esclaves, pour les aider dans des tâches domestiques, en particulier. Il ne s'agit plus vraiment de colonies de plantations, au sens où l'on peut l'entendre dans les Antilles, même si les esclaves d'origine africaine sont vraiment nombreux dans certaines colonies comme New York ou le New Jersey. Ce sont des sociétés avec esclaves (« *societies with slaves* »), où les Africains-Américains ne constituent pas la majorité (ce qui est le cas aux Antilles), et représentent parfois un très faible pourcentage de la population, comme dans le Massachusetts. Cependant, les grands ports du nord de la côte sont également impliqués dans la traite autrement que par l'importation et l'utilisation d'esclaves : les armateurs de Boston, New York, Newport et Providence (Rhode Island) sont partie intégrante de l'économie mondiale de la traite et de l'esclavage. Ils affrètent des bateaux, vendent aux colonies des Antilles les provisions nécessaires aux esclaves dans une économie de monoculture, importent les molasses antillaises qu'ils transforment en rhum[3].

Au fil du XVIIIe siècle, les colonies du nord de l'Amérique continentale s'engagent davantage dans une économie esclavagiste : alors qu'ils transitaient auparavant par les Caraïbes, les esclaves sont importés directement d'Afrique et leur nombre croissant permet de faire face à l'insuffisance de la main-d'œuvre européenne, que retiennent les nombreuses guerres impériales du début de la première moitié du siècle. Les esclaves sont

1. Dunn, *op. cit.*, pp. 223-227.
2. Ira Berlin, *Many Thousands Gone: The First Two Centuries of Slavery in North America*, Cambridge, Ma.: Belknap Press of Harvard University Press, 1998, p. 96.
3. Au milieu du XVIIIe siècle, c'est surtout dans le Rhode Island, à Newport, et dans une moindre mesure à Providence, que s'organisait la flotte américaine de la traite atlantique : voir Charles Rappleye, dans *Sons of Providence. The Brown Brothers, the Slave Trade, and the American Revolution*, New York: Simon and Schuster, 2006, p. 54.

plus nombreux dans les ports, de Boston à Philadelphie, où les élites ont également davantage recours à des domestiques esclaves. L'expansion de l'esclavage est encore plus notable dans les campagnes de la Pennsylvanie, du New Jersey et de New York. Plus largement implantée, l'institution de l'esclavage se renforce sur le plan juridique : l'émancipation devient plus difficile ; les Noirs libres sont victimes de discrimination et les lois sur les esclaves se durcissent[1].

Au sud, le développement de l'esclavage est encore plus net : au début du XVIIIe siècle, la Chesapeake (Virginie, Delaware, Maryland), écrit Ira Berlin, « remplace brièvement la Jamaïque comme marché d'esclaves le plus rentable » : tout en maintenant un contrôle strict des esclaves, les planteurs exercent également une autorité paternaliste qui vise à atténuer la possibilité des conflits, et rassemblent autour d'eux les petits propriétaires dans un consensus racial[2]. Plus au sud, la Géorgie s'engage sur la voie de l'esclavage (alors que ses fondateurs en avaient banni l'institution à l'origine) tandis que la Caroline du Sud parvient à une « majorité noire » au milieu du siècle[3]. Un tel portrait des colonies continentales laisse penser qu'à la veille de la Guerre de Sept Ans (1754), qui va déchirer l'Amérique du Nord, leurs habitants sont aussi insensibles au sort des esclaves que leurs compatriotes des îles britanniques des Caraïbes. Pourtant, en dépit des chiffres des importations d'esclaves et du succès de l'institution au milieu du XVIIIe siècle, la nature spécifique des colonies britanniques d'Amérique du Nord permet l'expression et le développement d'une critique de l'esclavage : au moment de la Guerre de Sept Ans, le premier mouvement antiesclavagiste anglo-américain y prend son essor.

2. Les débuts du mouvement antiesclavagiste dans les colonies britanniques d'Amérique du Nord 1688-1776 : réseaux quakers transatlantiques, Grand réveil anglo-américain, premières revendications noires

a) L'action des réseaux quakers transatlantiques

Le fondateur de la secte des Amis, George Fox, visite en 1671 la Barbade, la plus prospère des colonies britanniques des Caraïbes. Il encourage alors ses auditeurs à convertir les esclaves, à bien les traiter, puis à les libérer[4].

1. Berlin, *op. cit.*, pp. 176-188.
2. C'est la thèse d'Edmund Sears Morgan dans le classique *American Slavery, American Freedom: The Ordeal of Colonial Virginia*, New York: Norton, 1975.
3. Berlin, *op. cit.*, pp. 109-176.
4. Voici la citation exacte, tirée du *Journal de George Fox* (1694) : » *Respecting their negroes: I desired them to endeavor to train them up in the fear of God, not only those that were bought with their money, but also those that were born into their families, that all might come to the knowledge of the Lord; that*

À la suite de cette visite, les Quakers installés aux Antilles britanniques cherchèrent bien à convertir les esclaves ; mais la portée de leur action était réduite de par la discrimination dont ils faisaient l'objet de la part du clergé anglican et des élites locales ; d'autre part, ils ne rejetèrent pas l'esclavage[1]. Pour David Brion Davis, pionnier et autorité des études sur l'antiesclavagisme atlantique, ces sectaires pourtant si anticonformistes (tolérance, tutoiement de rigueur, peu de respect pour les hiérarchies traditionnelles, souci de l'égalité sociale, toutes valeurs qui leur valent ultérieurement un grand succès auprès des philosophes français[2]), partageaient avec les autres occidentaux une vision du monde où l'on pouvait réconcilier liberté et esclavage, conversion et asservissement[3]. En Angleterre comme aux colonies, il est établi entre la fin du XVIIe siècle et le début du XVIIIe que le baptême ne libère pas l'esclave, pas plus que son introduction sur le sol anglais d'ailleurs[4]. Les Quakers s'installent aux Antilles, mais surtout en Amérique du Nord continentale, où William Penn fonde la Pennsylvanie, qui leur est dédiée. On trouve aussi des communautés importantes de Quakers dans le Rhode Island, dans le New Jersey, mais également dans les colonies du sud, en Virginie, dans les Carolines, dans le Maryland : ils sont propriétaires d'esclaves, ou impliqués dans la traite, comme les non-Quakers.

Comme l'explique Davis, la communauté quaker, qui admet difficilement le compromis spirituel, est cependant probablement mieux armée que d'autres pour embrasser la question de l'esclavage et dénoncer l'incompatibilité de cette institution avec les principes de la religion chrétienne (tous les hommes sont égaux devant Dieu, disent les Quakers)[5]. En 1688, des Quakers de Germantown, près de Philadelphie, rédigent une pétition (qui a d'ailleurs peu d'effet sur les autorités quakers) : leur texte dénonce la traite, et l'esclavage plus généralement. De telles pratiques ne sont pas chrétiennes, et nul ne voudrait subir ce que l'on fait subir aux Africains, en raison simplement de leur couleur de peau[6]. Dès 1696, les Quakers de Pennsylvanie recommandent aux membres de la secte de ne pas s'impliquer

so, with Joshua, every master of a family might say, "as for me and my house, we will serve the Lord." I desired also, that they would cause their overseers to deal mildly and gently with their negroes, and not use cruelty towards them, as the manner of some has been and is; and that after certain years of servitude they should make them free. »
http://www.hallvworthington.com/wjournal/gfjournal8b.html

1. Dunn, *op. cit.*, pp. 104-105.
2. Jeanne-Henriette Louis et Jean-Olivier Héron, *William Penn et les quakers : Ils inventèrent le nouveau monde*, Paris, Gallimard, Découvertes Gallimard, 1990, pp. 154-159.
3. David Brion Davis, *The Problem of Slavery in Western Culture*, New York: Oxford University Press, 1966, pp. 303-306.
4. Davis, *op. cit.*, pp. 208-211.
5. Davis, *op. cit.*, p. 308.
6. Texte de la pétition : http://www.quakerinfo.org/history/slavery.html.

dans la traite, et cherchent l'appui de leurs frères de Londres, qui, eux aussi, en 1727, s'expriment contre le trafic d'être humains à travers l'Atlantique : mais il ne s'agit pourtant pas encore de prévoir des sanctions contre ceux qui s'y engageraient, et les Quakers, d'une rive à l'autre de l'Atlantique, se confinent tout d'abord à une position de compromis prudente, dans la mesure où les intérêts commerciaux de nombre d'entre eux sont liés à la traite et à l'esclavage[1].

Les premiers militants antiesclavagistes de la communauté livrent donc leur bataille aux marges de celle-ci, au risque d'en être chassés : Ralph Sandiford, puis Benjamin Lay subissent dans les années 1730 l'ire des autorités quakers, mais cherchent, à travers le rejet de l'esclavage qu'ils assimilent au péché et au diable, le retour à la pureté primitive de leur foi[2]. La Guerre de Sept Ans fournit le contexte d'un réexamen plus collectif des pratiques esclavagistes de la secte : pour les pacifistes que sont les Quakers, la guerre et ses violences sont le signe du péché, et il faut travailler à davantage de pureté ; leur refus de participer aux hostilités les isole également du reste des colons et conduit la secte à se regrouper sur elle-même et donc à raviver la discipline interne. Nul mieux que John Woolman n'incarne les idéaux de la communauté des Quakers au milieu du XVIIIe siècle : dans son journal spirituel, ce tailleur petit propriétaire rapporte les étapes de son combat contre l'esclavage auprès des Amis américains, qu'il convainc en arpentant les colonies, du New Jersey à la Caroline du nord et en rédigeant des pamphlets antiesclavagistes[3]. La communauté quaker reste une communauté atlantique, alliant les deux rives de l'Océan, et Woolman meurt d'ailleurs en Angleterre en 1772[4].

La vie de militant antiesclavagiste de Woolman correspond aux années où, brusquement, de part et d'autre de l'Atlantique, les Quakers aboutissent à des décisions fermes envers la traite, puis l'esclavage, en ce qui concerne les membres de la secte : dans ce mouvement, les Quakers américains sont à l'avant-garde. Loin d'être marginalisé comme ses prédécesseurs, John Woolman s'impose progressivement comme le héraut des idées nouvelles en Amérique du Nord. En 1757 et 1758, les Quakers londoniens s'inquiètent du rôle joué par leurs co-religionnaires dans la traite ; mais ce sont les

1. Davis, *op. cit.*, pp. 314-316.
2. Davis, *op. cit.*, pp. 320-326.
3. *Some Considerations on Keeping Negroes* (1759) et *Some Considerations on Keeping Negroes*, part 2 (1762).
4. Comme d'autres Quakers nord-américains, Woolman rend visite aux Amis britanniques et meurt à York le 7 octobre, sans jamais cesser de considérer la traite comme un abominable péché d'avarice qu'il dénonce jusqu'à son dernier souffle : voir sa dernière lettre p. 191 dans *The Journal and Major Essays of John Woolman*, ed. by Phillips P. Moulton, Richmond, IN.: Friends United Press, 1971. Pour une version en ligne du journal (publié pour la première fois en 1774), voir http://etext.lib.virginia.edu/toc/modeng/public/Woojour.html.

Quakers de Pennsylvanie qui prennent une mesure concrète dès 1758 en interdisant aux membres de la secte de participer au commerce d'esclaves[1]. En 1760, les Quakers de Nouvelle-Angleterre considèrent que l'importation d'esclaves mérite sanction et, en 1761, le *London Yearly Meeting* décrète que les Quakers se livrant à la traite s'exposent à un désaveu : cependant en 1766, les Quakers londoniens prônent à nouveau la prudence sur le sujet[2]. En 1759, le Quaker philadelphien Anthony Bénézet publie son premier ouvrage antiesclavagiste *Observations on the Inslaving, Importing and Purchasing the Negroes* ; cet ouvrage est suivi d'autres appels à la responsabilité collective des sujets de l'empire face à la traite et l'esclavage, tel *A Caution to Great Britain and Her Colonies Of the Calamitous State of the Enslaved Negroes in the British Dominions*, publié en 1766[3]. En 1763, Bénezet interpelle les Quakers londoniens, puis à nouveau en 1773 : il faut mettre un terme à la traite des esclaves[4].

Si les Quakers britanniques soutiennent pour le moment les efforts des Américains sans enthousiasme, tel n'est pas le cas de Granville Sharp, qui est sensibilisé au sort des Noirs des colonies que leurs maîtres amènent à Londres : ses écrits le signalent à Bénezet, qui entame une correspondance avec lui[5]. Sharp, qui n'est pas Quaker, connaît en 1772 une victoire fondamentale devant les tribunaux britanniques lors de l'arrêt Somerset, qui protège les Noirs esclaves en Angleterre sans récuser l'esclavage aux colonies ; reste aux Quakers nord-américains l'apanage de l'engagement sur la voie de l'antiesclavagisme par des mesures concrètes, puisqu'en 1774, à la veille de l'indépendance américaine, *le Philadelphia Yearly Meeting* exige de ses membres Quakers qu'ils émancipent leurs esclaves aussi vite que possible, et qu'ils s'abstiennent de tout commerce d'esclaves sous peine de désaveu[6]. En 1776, le *Philadelphia Yearly Meeting* interdit aux Quakers de posséder des esclaves, une décision qui est progressivement reprise par les autres communautés de la secte en Amérique du Nord.

1. Davis, *op. cit.*, p. 330.
2. David Brion Davis, *The Problem of Slavery in the Age of Revolution 1770-1823*, Ithaca, NY.: Cornell University Press, 1975, p. 215.
3. Une citation de ce dernier ouvrage montre bien l'ampleur de la réflexion de Bénezet, qui ne se limite pas aux colonies d'Amérique du Nord : « *How the* British *nation first came to be concerned in a practice, by which the rights and liberties of mankind are so violently infringed, and which is so opposite to the apprehensions* Englishmen *have always had of what natural justice requires, is indeed surprising.* » In *A Caution* [...], Philadelphia: Miller, 1766, p. 36.
4. Judith Jennings, *The Business of Abolishing the Slave Trade*, London: Frank Cass, 1997, p. 22.
5. Christopher Leslie Brown, *Moral Capital. Foundations of British Abolitionism*, Chapel Hill, N.C.: The Omohundro Institute of Early American History and Culture, University of North Carolina Press, 2006, p. 99.
6. Jean Soderlund, *Quakers and Slavery. A Divided Spirit*, Princeton New Jersey: Princeton University Press, 1985, p. 4 ; et Davis, *Slavery in the Age of Revolution*, p. 215. Ce « *yearly meeting* » regroupait également les Quakers du New Jersey, d'une partie du Delaware et du Maryland.

Cette décision n'affecte en apparence qu'une communauté religieuse, mais les Quakers sont encore très influents en Pennsylvanie (où ils représentent une large part de la population), même s'ils ne dirigent plus cette colonie depuis la Guerre de Sept Ans ; et ils appartiennent partout en Amérique du Nord à des groupes sociaux puissants, marchands ou fermiers prospères. En 1774, le *New England Yearly Meeting* décide de militer pour des lois « tendant à l'abolition de l'esclavage[1] ». Bien que leur pacifisme les désigne à la méfiance populaire en temps de guerre, l'exemple des Quakers ne peut qu'avoir un impact non négligeable sur les Nord-Américains qu'ils fréquentent dans leurs affaires, sur les ports ou dans les assemblées locales, tels Benjamin Franklin, propriétaire d'esclaves à Philadelphie, puis à la fin de sa vie président de la *Pennsylvania Abolition Society*[2]. Les écrits de John Woolman, Anthony Bénézet, et plus généralement l'action des Quakers, ont d'ailleurs une influence internationale, dans le monde anglo-américain mais également en France, où cette secte égalitaire continue de plaire aux philosophes et publicistes de la fin de l'Ancien Régime, tels l'Abbé Raynal ou Jacques-Pierre Brissot, en dépit de quelques controverses[3].

b) Grand réveil et Lumières, revendications noires

L'impact des initiatives quakers est d'autant plus fort qu'au milieu du siècle, le Grand réveil religieux anglo-américain contribue également à rappeler l'égalité des hommes et à sensibiliser les colons d'Amérique du Nord au sort de leurs esclaves. C'est au fond de son cœur que chaque évangélique trouve Dieu, dans une rencontre émotionnelle tout autant que spirituelle : ainsi le Réveil, mouvement transatlantique, favorise-t-il l'indignation morale. Les souffrances des esclaves paraissent intolérables[4] et John Wesley, fondateur du méthodisme, rédige en 1774 un pamphlet antiesclavagiste[5]. Un autre évangélique, Samuel Hopkins, disciple du prédicateur Jonathan Edwards, personnalité emblématique du Grand

1. Rappleye, *op. cit.*, p. 169.
2. Dans *Runaway America. Benjamin Franklin, Slavery and the American Revolution*, David Waldstreicher, New York: Hill and Wang, 2004, rappelle que Benjamin Franklin fut étroitement impliqué dans la question de l'esclavage : imprimeur des pamphlets de Benjamin Lay en 1737, il profita pourtant de l'esclavage et posséda des esclaves. Il promouvait également un « empire blanc » en Amérique du Nord. Il ne devint un antiesclavagiste militant qu'après son retour de France, en 1784, et surtout en 1790, l'année de sa mort. Mais entretemps, lors de la controverse entre les Treize colonies et la métropole, il avait adopté le point de vue des Quakers dans une série d'écrits antiesclavagistes anonymes ou privés, surtout afin d'incriminer la métropole, initiatrice de la traite. Son opposition à l'esclavage, au final, relève plutôt des arguments économiques développés en 1776 par Adam Smith contre un système de travail jugé archaïque, que des considérations philanthropiques, religieuses et philosophiques qui étaient répandues à l'époque.
3. Edith Phillips, *The Good Quaker in French Legend*, Philadelphia: University of Philadelphia Press, 1932, pp. 100, 118-119.
4. Davis, *op. cit.*, pp. 386-389.
5. Davis, *op. cit.*, p. 382.

réveil nord-américain, publie en 1776 *A Dialogue Concerning the Slavery of the Africans.*

Tout le protestantisme anglo-américain s'ouvre d'un côté à une émotion humaniste en cette deuxième moitié du siècle, et il trouve d'un autre côté un terrain d'entente avec la philosophie des Lumières pour qui l'Amérique du Nord constitue un lieu d'élection dans la deuxième moitié du XVIIIe siècle. L'égalité des hommes et la liberté, valeurs prêchées par les philosophes, sont mises en avant par les débats de la Révolution américaine, dans la décennie qui commence en 1765. Quoique l'émancipation des esclaves ne constitue pas l'objectif prioritaire des révolutionnaires, l'utilisation des concepts politiques d'« esclavage » et d'« esclaves » dans le discours des révolutionnaires conduit progressivement ceux-ci à envisager fin de la traite et émancipation (un point qui sera développé dans la partie suivante). Ce même discours révolutionnaire trouve un écho notable auprès des Noirs qui, dans les colonies du nord, commencent à appliquer ces principes à leur propre cas, en particulier à la suite de la décision Somerset[1]. Dès 1773, des esclaves de Boston déposent des pétitions pour obtenir leur liberté auprès de la « *general court* » (assemblée et cour suprême) du Massachusetts et du gouverneur de la colonie[2]. Le milieu du siècle a vu de nombreuses révoltes, dans les colonies des Caraïbes, mais aussi en Amérique du Nord (*Stono Rebellion* en Caroline du sud en 1739, et conspiration de New York en 1741), qui indiquent assez bien le mécontentement des esclaves face à un régime disciplinaire accru : ils ne peuvent que prêter une oreille intéressée aux idées nouvelles d'égalité et de liberté qui se répandent dans la deuxième moitié du siècle.

L'évolution des colonies nord-américaines sur le sujet se concrétise par la fondation, en 1775, de ce qui deviendra la *Pennsylvania Abolition Society*, alors nommée *Society for the Relief of Free Negroes Unlawfully Held in Bondage*, par un groupe qui ne se limite pas aux Quakers ; elle témoigne de l'engagement concret des Nord-Américains envers l'antiesclavagisme[3].

1. Brown, *Moral Capital*, p. 99
2. Sylvia Frey, *Water from the Rock. Black Resistance in a Revolutionary Age*, Princeton: Princeton University Press, 1991, p. 53.
3. Comme l'indique le nom de cette société, il s'agissait dans un premier temps, alors que de nombreux esclaves avaient été libérés par leurs maîtres quakers, de les protéger dans un environnement hostile face à des tentatives de capture et de déportation vers des colonies moins éclairées. Pour Jean R. Soderlund, les Quakers voulaient bien davantage débarrasser leur communauté religieuse du « péché » que constituait l'esclavage pour lui redonner sa cohérence religieuse originelle, que libérer vraiment tous les asservis. Il n'empêche que cet exemple collectif d'émancipation, émanant d'un groupe religieux et social alors puissant, et implanté des deux côtés de l'Atlantique, donna une dimension concrète aux condamnations des Lumières et de l'évangélisme et eut une véritable force d'entraînement. Voir Soderlund, *Quakers and Slavery. A Divided Spirit*, Princeton, N.J.: Princeton University Press, 1985, pp. 173-187.

Deux ans auparavant, en 1773, un non-quaker militant révolutionnaire, Benjamin Rush, médecin presbytérien à Philadelphie, et futur signataire de la Déclaration d'indépendance, avait publié un document de 85 pages entièrement consacré à la dénonciation de l'esclavage des Africains-Américains : le sujet n'était plus noyé dans d'autres considérations antibritanniques comme cela avait été le cas auparavant dans le pamphlet de James Otis, qui est pourtant toujours cité en exemple. Comme Otis, Rush reprenait l'argumentation de Montesquieu, mais il balayait aussi tous les autres arguments possibles : les esclaves jouissaient d'une intelligence et d'une moralité égales ; le christianisme ne pouvait tolérer l'esclavage ; les esclaves étaient soumis à d'intolérables cruautés, physiques et mentales ; la traite entretenait la guerre en Afrique, et bien d'autres encore. Rush terminait par un vibrant appel aux révolutionnaires américains qui doivent donner l'exemple en détruisant l'esclavage. Son texte est nourri de la philosophie des droits naturels ; on y trouve aussi des influences quakers (comme dans l'expression « *bear testimony* ») et la sensibilité philanthropique typique de l'époque (« *universal tie of benevolence* ») :

> *Ye Men of SENSE and VIRTUE—Ye ADVOCATES for American Liberty, rouse up and espouse the cause of Humanity and general Liberty. Bear a testimony against a vice which degrades human nature, and dissolves that universal tie of benevolence which should connect all the children of men together in one great Family.—The plant of liberty is so tender a Nature, that it cannot thrive long in the neighbourhood of slavery. Remember the eyes of all Europe are fixed upon you, to preserve an asylum for freedom in this country, after the last pillars of it are fallen in every quarter of the Globe.*[1]

Plus tard, Jacques-Pierre Brissot de Warville, fondateur de la Société des Amis des Noirs, puis révolutionnaire français, n'aura pas de mots assez chaleureux pour chanter les Quakers et les Treize colonies, où le mouvement antiesclavagiste a véritablement commencé avec la Révolution, selon lui : ce texte en est bien l'illustration[2].

1. Benjamin Rush, *An Address to the Inhabitants of the British Settlements on the Slavery of the Negroes in America (The Second Ed.) To Which is added, A Vindication of the Address, in Answer to a Pamphlet Entitled "Slavery not forbidden in Scripture; or, A Defence of the West India Planters [Fifteen Lines of Verse, Signed Proteus]*, Philadelphia, 1773. Eighteenth Century Collections Online, Gale Group. James Otis, *The Rights of the British Colonies Asserted and Proved*, Boston, 1764. In Bernard Bailyn ed. *Pamphlets of the American Revolution, 1750-1776*, vol. 1 1750-1765, Cambridge, Ma.: The Belknap Press of Harvard University Press, 1965, p. 477.
2. Voir *Mémoire sur les Noirs de l'Amérique septentrionale. Lu à l'assemblée de la Société des Amis des Noirs*, le 9 février 1789, Paris : Bailly, 1789. Le nom de la société française « Société des Amis » indique bien l'influence quaker.

c) Quelques hypothèses sur l'apparition du mouvement antiesclavagiste dans les colonies britanniques d'Amérique du Nord : une opinion blanche éclairée, nombreuse, au contact quotidien des esclaves

On terminera cette assez longue deuxième partie en émettant quelques hypothèses (parmi d'autres) sur l'apparition de ce mouvement antiesclavagiste organisé : pourquoi en Amérique du Nord, et dans les Treize colonies, et non dans les autres colonies britanniques d'Amérique (les Antilles) ou en Angleterre même, siège de l'Empire, puisque ne s'y crée un groupe organisé de militants antiesclavagistes qu'en 1783[1] ? S'ils sont largement impliqués dans l'économie esclavagiste et dans la traite, les colons nord-américains, à la différence de leurs compatriotes des Antilles, forment une majorité blanche face aux esclaves (sauf en Caroline du Sud) : on considère d'ordinaire que les colons des Antilles, dominés numériquement par les asservis, étaient de ce fait particulièrement résistants à toute idée antiesclavagiste[2]. En outre, les plus riches et les cultivés vivaient en Grande-Bretagne et quant aux autres, on n'envisage pas suffisamment le fait qu'ils étaient isolés sur de petites îles, la plupart du temps, et pouvaient difficilement constituer, s'ils l'avaient voulu, une opinion antiesclavagiste, active, nombreuse et organisée. À l'inverse, les colonies nord-américaines demeurent, du XVIIe au XVIIIe siècle, des espaces de peuplement vers lesquels se dirigent essentiellement des sujets de Sa Majesté, mais aussi des groupes d'Européens parfois persécutés, tels les Huguenots français ou les Piétistes allemands. Les conditions de vie et le climat y sont meilleurs (au centre et au nord) qu'en Europe : les colons ont de grandes familles, et les enfants survivent davantage qu'en Europe. La population qui augmente reste rurale ; mais elle s'organise également autour de villes à l'importance croissante, telles New York, Philadelphie et Boston[3], où se développent universités, bibliothèques, et loges maçonniques au fil du XVIIIe siècle : on ne note pas une telle évolution aux Antilles britanniques, et les fils des colons des Antilles se dirigent toujours vers l'Angleterre pour y étudier. En

1. Judith Jennings, *The Business of Abolishing the Slave Trade*, Frank Cass: Londres, 1997, pp. 22-33.
2. « By the early eighteenth century, then, Africans formed in most of the British and French islands the great majority of the population. The Europeans had become a small garrison among the slaves." J.H. Parry, Philip Sherlock, Anthony Maingot, *A Short History of the West Indies*, New York: St. Martin's Press, 1987, p. 67.
3. Gary B. Nash, *The Urban Crucible. The Northern Seaports and the Origins of the American Revolution*, Cambridge, Ma.: Harvard University Press, 1986. O'Shaughnessy (« Black Majorities », pp. 35-57) explique qu'au moment où l'armée représente la tyrannie britannique pour les Nord-Américains (début des années 1770), leurs compatriotes des îles des Antilles réclament de nouvelles garnisons et davantage de soldats, en raison de révoltes d'esclaves qui se multiplient depuis le milieu du siècle.

général plus prospère qu'en Europe, cette population inclut une large élite éclairée, avide de nouvelles du Vieux Continent, de journaux et d'ouvrages importés : le sujet de la traite et de l'esclavage est au cœur des débats des Lumières, depuis la condamnation de l'esclavage par Montesquieu, dont l'*Esprit des Lois* est largement diffusé dans toute l'Europe et le monde anglo-américain ; la publication de l'*Histoire philosophique des deux Indes* de l'Abbé Raynal en 1770, ouvrage très populaire, va faire connaître encore plus largement l'argumentaire antiesclavagiste des Lumières[1]. À la différence de leurs compatriotes des Îles britanniques, les colons, même s'ils ne possèdent pas d'esclaves personnellement, et quelle que soit la colonie (nord, centre ou sud), sont confrontés à la présence quotidienne des esclaves[2] ; et ceux-ci constituent une main-d'œuvre qui augmente au fil du siècle. Enfin, comme le rappelle Robin Blackburn, les colons du nord et du centre étaient pénétrés de la perspective d'une expansion blanche et anglo-saxonne à travers le continent : l'accroissement du nombre d'esclaves, « race » inférieure selon nombre d'entre eux, pouvait mettre en danger cette vision d'avenir. Certains rejetaient donc l'esclavage et la traite sous l'effet de ce que Blackburn appelle « *aversive notions of racial difference* », un racisme à peine déguisé[3].

Les conditions étaient donc réunies pour qu'en ces colonies, bien davantage qu'aux Antilles ou en Angleterre, se développe une opinion

1. La célèbre critique de l'esclavage de Montesquieu se trouve dans la 3e partie de *l'Esprit des lois* (1746), au livre XV : « Comment les lois de l'esclavage civil ont du rapport avec la nature du climat », qui comprend les chapitres V « De l'esclavage des nègres », VI « Véritable origine du droit de l'esclavage », VII « Autre origine du droit de l'esclavage », VIII « De l'inutilité de l'esclavage parmi nous », IX « Des nations chez lesquelles la liberté civile est généralement établie ». *L'Histoire philosophique et politique des établissemens et du commerce des Européens dans les deux Indes*, de l'abbé Raynal, fut publié tout d'abord en 1770 à Amsterdam, mais connut rapidement une carrière éditoriale exceptionnelle : de nombreuses rééditions, des traductions en allemand, espagnol et anglais (éditions en Écosse et à Londres et réimpressions, ce qui indique bien la large diffusion de l'ouvrage). Voir Olivier Pétré-Grenouilleau, *Les Traites négrières. Essai d'histoire globale*, Paris, Gallimard, 2004, p. 279.
2. Il y avait de nombreux esclaves à Londres et plus largement, dans les ports anglais dans la deuxième moitié du XVIIIe siècle : ils accompagnaient leurs maîtres, planteurs des Antilles, ou servaient comme marins, tels Olaudah Equiano. Mais le public britannique, même éclairé, les considérait, comme l'explique Christopher Brown dans *Moral Capital*, comme la conséquence inévitable et déplaisante d'un empire lointain, et non comme une question relevant de la philanthropie métropolitaine, au moins jusqu'en 1772. Voir *Moral Capital*, pp. 94-101.
3. Robin Blackburn, *The Making of New World Slavery: from the Baroque to the Modern 1492-1800*, London, New York: Verso, 1997, pp. 323-324. Blackburn met ainsi en garde contre une lecture hâtive d'un des premiers pamphlets antiesclavagistes nord-américains, *The Selling of Joseph*, publié par Samuel Sewall à Boston en 1700 : « *This work contained some reasonable arguments against the personal and social morality of slaveholding, but it also appealed to aversive notions of racial difference* ». Le même raisonnement s'applique au texte de Benjamin Franklin de 1751 « Observations Concerning the Increase of Mankind, Peopling of Countries, etc. », in *The Portable Benjamin Franklin*, éd. par Larzer Ziff, New York: Penguin Group, 2005, pp. 322-329, où la dénonciation de l'esclavage vise essentiellement à défendre le travail « blanc » et se conjugue à l'affirmation de la supériorité blanche et anglo-saxonne.

antiesclavagiste, suffisamment forte et nourrie pour se faire entendre. La guerre d'Indépendance, qui aboutit à la rupture du lien entre colonies nord-américaines et métropole, va permettre aux ex-colonies d'avancer sur la voie de l'abolition de la traite et de l'esclavage, bien avant la Grande-Bretagne, et de se positionner en pays de la liberté face aux Britanniques.

3. La guerre d'Indépendance : libérations britanniques, réactions africaines-américaines, débat britannique

a) Les libérations opérées par l'armée britannique pendant le conflit : stratégie militaire britannique, révolution noire réelle

Lorsqu'éclatent les hostilités entre la Grande-Bretagne et l'essentiel de ses colonies nord-américaines, au printemps 1775, les autorités métropolitaines sont bien conscientes que la partie la plus conséquente de leur Empire américain — en termes d'hommes, de biens, et de territoire — est en jeu. Il n'y a alors qu'environ 9 millions de Britanniques face à presque 3 millions de Nord-Américains dans les Treize colonies rebelles[1]. Dans ce groupe de coloniaux, 20 % sont des esclaves originaires d'Afrique, presque deux fois plus nombreux que les esclaves présents dans les colonies britanniques des Antilles, où l'on ne compte que 50 000 colons blancs environ[2]. Les Britanniques se sont battus contre la France tout au long du XVIIIe siècle, et en particulier lors de la récente Guerre de Sept Ans, pour préserver et étendre ces colonies et n'entendent évidemment pas les perdre. Les années de controverse impériale qui précèdent la guerre d'Indépendance (1765-1775) et leur cortège de violences (manifestations de rue, attaques contre les représentants du pouvoir britannique, répression de la part des troupes de Sa Majesté) ont suscité un fort ressentiment de part et d'autre, même si les Nord-Américains ne sont pas encore prêts à rompre avec la métropole. C'est plutôt dans ce contexte répressif qu'il faut comprendre la décision de novembre 1775 de Lord Dunmore, le gouverneur de Virginie, qui, par une proclamation, promet la liberté aux esclaves qui rejoindraient les troupes britanniques pour combattre[3]. En aucun cas cela n'indique que la Grande-Bretagne aurait alors décidé d'émanciper les esclaves de ses

1. Voir pour des estimations Edward Royle, *Modern Britain. A Social History 1750-1997*, 2e éd., London: Arnold, 1997 p. 43. Également H.T. Dickinson ed., *A Companion to Eighteenth Century Britain*, New York: Blackwell, 2002, pp. 452-453.
2. Voir David Brion Davis, pp. 161-162, *Western Culture* : en 1790, la population esclave de l'Amérique du Nord est supérieure à celles des autres colonies britanniques : 757 000 Noirs en Amérique du Nord (dont 92 % esclaves), soit presque 20 % de la population totale, 455 000 Noirs dans les Antilles britanniques, 86 % de la population totale.
3. Voir texte de la proclamation sur : http://www.pbs.org/wgbh/aia/part2/2h42t.html.

colonies[1], tout au plus que les officiers britanniques pensent ainsi affirmer la domination impériale en s'appropriant la propriété de colons rebelles[2]. Quand on apprend la nouvelle à Londres, il s'ensuit d'ailleurs un tollé d'indignation : marchands et hommes politiques accusent le ministère North d'encourager des pratiques barbares (armer les esclaves contre les maîtres) qui risquaient de se retourner contre les Britanniques en ébranlant tout le système esclavagiste[3].

Rétrospectivement, cette mesure constitue le premier acte d'émancipation de masse dans les colonies britanniques d'Amérique du Nord puisqu'elle aboutit au rassemblement de 800 esclaves en fuite auprès de Dunmore au cours de l'hiver 1775-1776 et à la création d'un « Régiment éthiopien » qui a pour blason « Liberté pour les esclaves[4] » ; mais il s'agit avant tout, on vient de le voir, d'une action opportuniste et assez mal contrôlée, qui vise à effrayer et déstabiliser les élites sudistes, très engagées dans la controverse révolutionnaire, en particulier en Virginie où l'on trouve certains des ténors de la rébellion, tels Patrick Henry ou Thomas Jefferson. Les autres gouverneurs reprennent la menace qui ne produit pas exactement l'effet escompté : les esclaves quittent effectivement les plantations, mais les maîtres se mobilisent encore davantage autour de la cause révolutionnaire, poussant à l'indépendance, car le pouvoir métropolitain a ainsi osé s'attaquer à une des valeurs phares de la Révolution : la propriété[5]. Du côté britannique, du début à la fin des hostilités, recueillir des esclaves ne s'apparente pas à une entreprise réfléchie et concertée : certains officiers voient en eux des malheureux qu'il convient d'aider ; d'autres les considèrent comme des prises de guerre ou les exploitent. Le théâtre des opérations militaires n'est pas le lieu d'une remise en question britannique, sinon sur le plan individuel pour certains officiers. En Géorgie, l'occupation britannique ne se traduit par aucune mesure de libération

1. Je vais ici résumer en partie un article de 2001, paru dans *Dix-huitième siècle* (n° 33, pp. 281-299) : « Esclavage et espace atlantique. Courants et contre-courants révolutionnaires, l'article 7 du traité anglo-américain de 1783 et ses conséquences jusqu'en 1794 ». Au printemps 1775, au moment du début des hostilités, le ministère North tente de faire passer une proposition aux Communes, qui aurait permis d'émanciper les esclaves pour s'en servir contre les colons ; cette mesure est rejetée mais fait son chemin chez les militaires. Sylvia R. Frey, *Water from the Rock. Black Resistance in a Revolutionary Age*, Princeton, NJ.: Princeton University Press, 1991, pp. 54-55.
2. Brown, *Moral Capital*, p. 254. Brown replace cette stratégie britannique dans le plus large contexte du centre métropolitain face aux droits des colons à la fin du dix-huitième siècle. La métropole pouvait s'ériger en protectrice des droits des faibles (les esclaves) face à des colons tyranniques et étroitement attachés à leurs intérêts.
3. Frey, *op. cit.*, pp. 69-73.
4. Simon Schama, dans *Rough Crossings. Britain, The Slaves and the American Revolution*, Londres: BBC Books, 2006, pp. 99-110, raconte l'échec de cette première mobilisation britannique.
5. Frey, *op. cit.*, pp. 56-65. S. Frey détaille les rumeurs d'insurrection, les fuites réelles et la mobilisation des colons, colonie du sud après colonie du sud.

générale : seuls les Noirs qui servent dans l'armée obtiennent la liberté, et pour le reste, les Britanniques cherchent plutôt à maintenir les esclaves sur la propriété de leurs partisans loyalistes ; mais un tiers des esclaves fuient[1]. En Caroline du Sud, les Britanniques aliènent les planteurs en promettant de protéger les esclaves qui fuiraient les rangs ennemis et les rejoindraient : mais l'armée ne peut faire face au flot de réfugiés car, au total, c'est un quart de la population esclave qui quitte les plantations[2]. À la fin de la guerre d'Indépendance, en 1783, les Britanniques ne restituent pas aux autorités américaines les esclaves qui s'étaient réfugiés auprès d'eux dans New York et Charleston occupées, alors qu'ils se sont engagés dans le cadre du traité de paix à restituer les esclaves saisis pendant les hostilités : mais il s'agit encore de rétorquer au mauvais traitement des loyalistes *tories* (pro-britanniques) par les nouveaux Américains, davantage que de protéger les esclaves réfugiés auprès de l'armée britannique. Lorsque les Britanniques rapatrient quelque 3 000 Noirs loyalistes en Nouvelle-Écosse après la guerre, cette colonie est d'ailleurs encore esclavagiste et les anciens esclaves y seront victimes de discrimination.

On pourrait reprendre pour tous les esclaves du sud cette phrase de Sylvia Frey :

> *Perhaps because the liberator seemed surprisingly like the master, many black Virginians consciously chose neutrality. [...] When division and confusion among whites improved their chances for success, when British prospects looked good, they took advantage of the opportunities offered and escaped in great numbers.*[3]

Effectivement, la déstabilisation de la société causée par le passage des troupes britanniques, en particulier au sud (et la guerre civile qui l'accompagne), permet à des dizaines de milliers d'esclaves de fuir leurs plantations dans cette région, et donc de résister, car la fuite est en Amérique du Nord la forme de résistance la plus répandue[4]. Face à une guerre d'indépendance blanche, menée par des planteurs esclavagistes, les Africains-Américains asservis réussissent à imposer leur propre révolution de liberté, même si cette lecture du rôle des Noirs dans le conflit et la naissance de la nation américaine s'avère réductrice. En effet, les Noirs américains vont aussi gagner leur liberté en patriotes à compter de 1777, dans l'Armée continentale dirigée par George Washington[5]. Ils réclament cette incorpo-

1. *Ibid*, pp. 81-107.
2. *Ibid*, pp. 108-142.
3. *Ibid*, p. 156.
4. Peter Kolchin, *Une Institution très particulière : l'esclavage aux États-Unis 1619-1877*, Paris, Belin, 1998, p. 169.
5. Frey, *op. cit.*, pp. 77-79 : on recruta tout d'abord les libres, puis à partir de 1777, des esclaves à qui on promettait la liberté en échange de leur engagement.

ration, envers laquelle les dirigeants de la nouvelle nation sont tout d'abord perplexes : mais les proclamations britanniques poussent les Américains à réagir en acceptant eux aussi les Noirs dans les rangs de l'armée. En participant aux combats, jusqu'à la victoire finale de Yorktown en 1781, ces soldats vont gagner l'estime de Washington et Lafayette et conduire ces deux hommes, et d'autres, sur la voie d'une volonté d'émancipation concrète au sortir de la guerre[1]. Reste que pour les Noirs effectivement libérés par l'armée britannique, et qui vont après la guerre trouver un refuge bien précaire en Nouvelle-Écosse, la liberté est « britannique », un thème appelé à connaître le succès plus tard[2].

b) L'exemple nord-américain et le débat britannique

Si les libérations effectuées par l'armée britannique n'indiquent pas un engagement véritable de la Grande-Bretagne envers l'antiesclavagisme, pourtant, dès le début de la controverse impériale, la notion d'« esclavage » est au cœur des débats politiques qui opposent les colons d'Amérique du Nord à la Couronne. Depuis John Locke et son *Second Treatise of Civil Governement* de 1690, ce terme signifie l'état dans lequel un gouvernement absolu maintient les sujets et appartient au vocabulaire de l'opposition britannique : dans les pamphlets des révolutionnaires américains, il réfère à l'oppression exercée selon eux par la Couronne à leur endroit[3]. Cependant, les colons savent bien que ce terme renvoie également à cette large population d'asservis qui réside en leur sein : étant donné le contexte favorable à l'antiesclavagisme en Amérique du Nord au milieu du siècle

1. Voir article de M.J. Rossignol « La Révolution américaine et l'abolition de l'esclavage 1765-1808 : d'une ambition des Lumières à l'échec constitutionnel fédéral », *Cahiers de Nantes* (à paraître) ; aussi Henry Wiencek, *An Imperfect God. George Washington, His Slaves and the Creation of America*, New York: Farrar, Strauss, Giroux, 2003 et Benjamin Quarles, *The Negro in the American Revolution*, Chapel Hill: The University of North Carolina Press, 1961.
2. Dans *Rough Crossings*, Simon Schama raconte l'histoire de ces anciens esclaves, de la Nouvelle-Écosse à la Sierra Leone : mais il précise : « *If there was a British Freedom, there was also a Dick Freedom—and a Jeffery Liberty—fighting in a Connecticut regiment on the American side.* », p. 17.
3. Pour la référence à John Locke, voir *The Second Treatise of Civil Government*, 1690, Chapter IV « Of Slavery » http://www.constitution.org/jl/2ndtreat.htm/. John Locke lui-même était un des investisseurs de la Royal African Company ; en tant que membre du Board of Trade, il était également un des pères de l'esclavage colonial ; mais il ne considérait pas les Africains comme des êtres inférieurs : voir Blackburn, *Making of New World Slavery*, p. 329, pour ces détails. Pour des exemples d'utilisation politique de "*slaves*" et "*slavery*" par les pamphlétaires les plus connus de la Révolution américaine, voir James Otis : « *The law of nature never invested them with a power of surrendering their own liberty; and the people certainly never entrusted any body of men with a power to surrender theirs in exchange for slavery.* » p. 477, *The Rights of the British Colonies Asserted and Proved*, Boston, 1764. In Bernard Bailyn ed. *Pamphlets of the American Revolution, 1750-1776*, vol. 1 1750-1765, Cambridge, Ma.: The Belknap Press of Harvard University Press, 1965 ; John Dickinson dans *Letters from a Farmer in Pennsylvania* : « *Those who are taxed without their consent, given by themselves or their representatives, are Slaves. We are taxed without our consent, expressed by ourselves or our representatives. We are therefore—I speak it here with grief—I speak it with Indignation—we are […] Slaves!* », p. 61, New York: John Holt, 1768; Eighteenth Century Collections Online. Gale Group. À la page 43 se trouve une autre utilisation du terme.

(évangélisme, Lumières, actions concrètes de la communauté quaker), ils ne peuvent longtemps résister à cette proximité idéologique, qui les expose à des critiques, voire des sarcasmes britanniques. Ainsi assiste-t-on à une vague de pétitions et d'actions antiesclavagistes dans les colonies britanniques d'Amérique du Nord à compter de 1765, qui visent plutôt l'arrêt de la traite, mais ont parfois une plus large portée selon la région[1].

Christopher Brown a étudié en détail cette apparition de la notion et de la réalité du concept d'esclavage dans le conflit anglo-américain, processus assez complexe et que je me contente ici de résumer de façon schématique. Au début des troubles impériaux, les Anglais critiquent les Américains, qui dénonceraient la « *tyranny* » britannique alors qu'ils détiennent eux-mêmes des esclaves. Taxés d'hypocrisie, les Américains réagissent en dénonçant à leur tour la Grande-Bretagne, dont le commerce et l'industrie s'appuient sur la traite et un empire esclavagiste : une attaque qui surprend les Britanniques, qui avaient jusque-là réussi à bien compartimenter l'empire et la nation. La nation reposait sur des valeurs de liberté, et l'empire avait ses propres codes, que l'on pouvait mépriser sans établir de liens directs entre les deux[2].

Les Américains prennent évidemment rapidement l'avantage sur le terrain de la cohérence idéologique : alors que les troubles impériaux s'aggravent, du nord au sud, les colons d'Amérique du Nord réclament l'arrêt de la traite, que refusent les gouverneurs britanniques et la Couronne. Le Virginien Thomas Jefferson, futur rédacteur de la Déclaration d'indépendance, utilise en 1774 cet argument dans le pamphlet *A Summary View of the Rights of British America* : désireux d'affranchir leurs esclaves, les colons veulent tout d'abord taxer ou interdire la traite, mais, se plaint-il, la Couronne s'y oppose et préfère laisser les « corsaires » (navires négriers) britanniques s'enrichir[3]. Le Premier congrès continental nord-américain interdit effectivement la traite cette même année. En juin 1776, alors que Thomas Jefferson rédige la Déclaration d'indépendance, il y insère un paragraphe d'opposition à la traite dans la liste des récriminations améri-

1. Brown, *Moral Capital*, pp. 105-110.
2. Brown, *op. cit.*, pp. 124-134.
3. Texte disponible sur http://www.yale.edu/lawweb/avalon/jeffsum.htm/ Thomas Jefferson, A Summary View of the Rights of British America, July 1774. Papers 1: 121-135. Le passage pertinent est le suivant : « *For the most trifling reasons, and sometimes for no conceivable reason at all, his majesty has rejected laws of the most salutary tendency. The abolition of has rejected laws of the most salutary tendency. The abolition of domestic slavery is the great object of desire in those colonies where it was unhappily introduced in their infant state. But previous to the infranchisement of the slaves we have, it is necessary to exclude all further importations from Africa. Yet our repeated attempts to effect this by prohibitions, and by imposing duties which might amount to a prohibition, have been hitherto defeated by his majesty's negative: thus preferring the immediate advantages of a few British corsairs to the lasting interests of the American states, and to the rights of human nature deeply wounded by this infamous practice.* »

caines envers le Roi : non seulement la traite britannique y est stigmatisée, mais Jefferson dénonce également l'appel de Lord Dunmore, qui vise selon lui, en armant les esclaves, à empêcher les Américains de conquérir la liberté qu'ils désirent (une argumentation bien contradictoire). Cette référence est de toute façon supprimée sous l'influence de la Caroline du sud et de la Géorgie, ce qui indique bien les difficultés auxquelles vont être confrontés les colons, une fois la guerre finie, dans la mise en œuvre concrète de leurs intentions antiesclavagistes[1]. Toujours en 1776, le Second congrès continental décide que « *no slaves be imported into any of the Thirteen United Colonies* », ce qui conduit divers États à interdire l'importation d'esclaves (le Delaware cette même année, la Virginie en 1778). Ces demandes d'arrêt de la traite, si nobles en apparence, ne sont d'ailleurs pas dépourvues d'ambiguïté : en freinant l'arrivée de nouveaux Africains dans cette période trouble, les Nord-Américains cherchent également à éviter davantage de rébellions ou de fuites vers l'ennemi. Et certains États, comme la Virginie, préfèrent vendre aux autres États situés plus au sud leur surplus d'esclaves. En outre, les proclamations britanniques ont frappé les esprits, même au nord ; et un opposant sincère de l'esclavage tel que le pasteur Samuel Hopkins, pour qui la guerre incarne la colère de Dieu face à l'asservissement des Africains, voit dans la libération des esclaves le moyen d'éviter une révolte servile[2].

Cependant, quelque complexes qu'en soient les motivations, l'engagement concret des Nord-Américains envers un arrêt de la traite, leurs nombreux plaidoyers contre l'esclavage, ébranlent la position britannique, et fournissent aux premiers antiesclavagistes d'outre-Atlantique un modèle et un appui de taille. Et n'oublions pas le texte même de la Déclaration d'indépendance de 1776 qui proclame que « *all men are created equal, that*

1. Voici le texte du passage http://www.loc.gov/exhibits/declara/ruffdrft.html/ From: *The Papers of Thomas Jefferson*. Vol. 1, 1760-1776. Ed. Julian P. Boyd. Princeton: Princeton University Press, 1950, pp. 243-247 : « *he has waged cruel war against human nature itself, violating it's most sacred rights of life & liberty in the persons of a distant people who never offended him, captivating & carrying them into slavery in another hemisphere, or to incur miserable death in their transportation thither. this piratical warfare, the opprobrium of* ***infidel*** *powers, is the warfare of the CHRISTIAN king of Great Britain. determined to keep open a market where MEN should be bought & sold, he has prostituted his negative for suppressing every legislative attempt to prohibit or to restrain this execrable commerce: and that this assemblage of horrors might want no fact of distinguished die, he is now exciting those very* ***people to rise in arms among us****, and to purchase that liberty of which he has deprived them, & murdering the people upon whom he also obtruded them; thus paying off former crimes committed against the* ***liberties*** *of one people, with crimes which he urges them to commit against the* ***lives*** *of another.* »
2. Davis, dans *Slavery in the Age of Revolution*, cite un passage du *Dialogue* de Hopkins bien révélateur des craintes qu'avaient suscitées les libérations britanniques, p. 295 : « *God is so ordering it in his Providence, that it seems absolutely necessary somthing should speedily be done with respect to the slaves among us, in order to our safety, and to prevent their turning against us in our present struggle, in order to get their liberty. Our oppressors have planned to get the blacks, and induce them to take up arms against us, by promising them liberty, on this condition.* »

they are endowed by their Creator with certain unalienable Rights, that among these are Life, Liberty and the pursuit of Happiness » : ces lignes sont bien comprises comme une invitation universelle à la jouissance de ces droits.

En 1776, Granville Sharp diffuse en Angleterre des pétitions antiesclavagistes de Virginie, du Maryland, et du New Jersey : la cause des patriotes américains lui paraît être également celle des droits des Africains[1]. Depuis 1775, il s'est mis en congé de son poste de fonctionnaire et occupe son temps à rédiger des pamphlets antiesclavagistes : les efforts des colons lui ont fait percevoir à la fois l'ampleur du problème de la traite et de l'esclavage, qui gangrène l'Empire et la nation britannique, et l'urgence qu'il y a à agir ; ils ont servi de déclencheurs[2].

Pendant la guerre d'Indépendance, les Nord-Américains poursuivent leur effort antiesclavagiste, après un bref affaiblissement en 1775 qui se traduit, entre autres, par l'interruption des réunions de la *Society for the Relief of Free Negroes Unlawfully Held in Bondage* à Philadelphie ; mais bien vite, les États du nord et du centre émancipent les esclaves, soit immédiatement comme le Vermont (1777) et le Massachusetts (1783), soit graduellement, comme la Pennsylvanie, qui passe une telle loi en 1780. Cette loi n'émancipe que les enfants des esclaves, et seulement lorsque ceux-ci auront atteint l'âge de 28 ans[3]. Il s'agit de protéger la propriété, valeur clé de la Révolution comme des Lumières en général. Dans le sud, les émancipations privées sont rendues plus faciles (loi de Virginie de 1782), même si elles restent très encadrées, pour que les esclaves libérés ne restent pas à la charge des communautés locales. Certains États, comme le Rhode Island et le Connecticut (1784), le New Jersey (1804) ou New York (1799), ne parviennent aux décisions d'émancipation graduelle que plus tard, après la guerre ; d'autres, comme la Virginie, refusent toute loi d'émancipation générale graduelle[4]. Aujourd'hui, les historiens font relativement peu de cas de cette grande vague d'émancipations : « *In practice, the Revolutionary generation set in motion only a gradual and 'grudging' emancipation* », écrit Christopher Brown, en reprenant les termes d'un historien américain radical, Al Young[5]. Mais comme le rappelle Ira Berlin, de quelques milliers avant le conflit impérial, le nombre d'esclaves libres atteignit presque deux

1. Brown, *Moral Capital*, pp. 166-171.
2. Brown, *op. cit.*, pp. 176-178.
3. Texte de la loi disponible sur http://www.yale.edu/lawweb/avalon/states/statutes/pennst01.htm/
4. Thomas Jefferson donne les détails de cet amendement qui ne fut jamais voté dans « Laws », *Notes on the State of Virginia*, (1787), New York: Norton, 1982, William Peden ed., pp. 137-138.
5. Brown, *op. cit.*, p. 109.

cent mille individus en 1810 aux États-Unis[1]. Et les contemporains ne s'y trompèrent pas : pour ceux qui considéraient la question de l'esclavage comme un des grands problèmes du temps, la nouvelle nation américaine s'érigeait ainsi en championne de la liberté, sur le plan des droits des colons blancs, mais également sur celui des droits des asservis. Tel fut le point de vue (excessivement enthousiaste) de Lafayette et de Brissot, futurs fondateurs de la Société des Amis des Noirs en France. En Grande-Bretagne, la victoire idéologique des colons — et leur victoire militaire tout court — contraignirent de nombreux membres de l'élite à admettre que le monopole de la liberté ne pouvait appartenir à une nation dont la prospérité coloniale reposait sur le travail des esclaves. Si la Grande-Bretagne voulait regagner sa place de première nation des libertés, et donner à nouveau l'exemple d'un pays vertueux, il faudrait que son empire tout entier soit régi selon un mode de fonctionnement plus adapté aux idées religieuses, morales, philosophiques et politiques du temps, à savoir les droits naturels, et l'égalité des hommes en particulier[2].

Pendant la durée des hostilités, le prosélytisme de Granville Sharp peut paraître peu efficace ; l'infatigable militant semble faire peu d'émules, même chez les « radicaux » anglais proches des idées de la Révolution américaine et critiques de la « corruption » gouvernementale britannique. Pourtant les années de la Révolution américaine correspondent en fait, comme l'a démontré Christopher Brown, à la parution de premiers plans d'émancipation britanniques, dont certains ne sont diffusés qu'après la guerre : ces auteurs cherchent des solutions à la crise de l'Empire ; l'émancipation des esclaves doit permettre la poursuite de la prospérité coloniale dans le respect des valeurs humanistes[3]. Ces plans sont peu viables car ils supposent que l'Empire britannique dispose de davantage d'autorité sur ses colonies qu'il n'en a en réalité. Après la guerre, la lutte contre la traite va apparaître comme un angle d'attaque plus réaliste que l'émancipation des asservis.

1. Ira Berlin, « The Revolution in Black Life », in *The American Revolution. Explorations in the History of American Radicalism*, DeKalb: Northern Illinois University Press, 1976, Alfred F. Young ed., p. 351.
2. Brown, *op. cit.*, pp. 202-206. Linda Colley avait également présenté cette thèse dans son ouvrage de 1992 *Britons. Forging the Nation*, New Haven: Yale University Press, p. 354 : « *There was another, self-referential reason why the British embraced anti-slavery so vigorously from the 1780s onwards. Doing so was a way of reaffirming their unique commitment to liberty at a time when war with America, and unsuccessful war at that, had called it widely into question. [...] after the American war anti-slavery was increasingly seized on a a means to redeem the nation, as a patriotic act.* »
3. Brown, *op. cit.*, pp. 228-258.

4. 1783-1787 Réactivation des réseaux transatlantiques de l'abolition : de l'influence nord-américaine à la différence britannique puis aux divergences nationales

a) « L'internationale quaker » ou l'influence nord-américaine

Nul n'a mieux montré que David Brion Davis, dans *The Problem of Slavery in the Age of Revolution 1770-1823,* comment les Quakers nord-américains ont facilité la mise en œuvre de l'abolitionnisme britannique, dans le cadre plus large d'une « internationale quaker », constituée des réseaux communautaires, spirituels, familiaux et économiques qui liaient entre eux les Quakers d'une rive à l'autre de l'Atlantique. On a vu que John Woolman avait terminé sa vie de témoin quaker antiesclavagiste à York, mais il ne fut pas le seul Nord-Américain à ainsi porter la bonne parole d'Amérique en Europe. Auparavant, son mentor, John Churchman, s'était également rendu en Angleterre avec un jeune Quaker, John Pemberton, appelé ensuite à diriger le *Philadelphia Meeting for Sufferings* et à organiser l'antiesclavagisme en Pennsylvanie. En 1774, un autre Quaker nord-américain, William Dillwyn, élève de Bénezet, fait un voyage en Angleterre, muni de lettres d'introduction pour Sharp et John Wesley qu'inspirent les écrits d'Anthony Bénezet. C'est à cette occasion qu'il fréquente également Joseph Woods, George Harrison, John Lloyd, Thomas Knowles, Samuel Hoare Jr., Joseph Gurney Bevan, et Philip Sansom, qui tous vont participer plus tard au lancement du mouvement abolitionniste en Grande-Bretagne. Dillwyn s'installe en Angleterre définitivement en 1781. En 1783 s'organise à Londres un comité spécial sur la traite au sein du *London Meeting for Sufferings* : d'après Davis, cette initiative répond pour partie aux prières des visiteurs quakers nord-américains, Dillwyn, mais aussi John Pemberton, qui vient également d'arriver. Davis raconte l'anecdote d'une activiste quaker, Rebecca Jones, qui arrive à Londres en 1784, où elle y rencontre six autres ministres nord-américains de la communauté quaker, qui sont presque tous engagés dans la cause antiesclavagiste. Ces Américains installés à Londres canalisent également des fonds de la communauté britannique pour soutenir des projets américains, tels l'École des Noirs (*the Negro School*) de Bénézet[1]. Thomas Clarkson, qui cherche à publier son essai sur la traite (*An Essay on the Slavery and Commerce of the Human Species*), s'oriente vers l'imprimerie du Quaker James Phillips, lui-même membre du comité sur la traite du *London Meeting for Sufferings* : il y rencontre Dillwyn. Mais Bevan est également un ami de Phillips, dont l'imprimerie est située à proximité des banques quakers, comme Lloyd.

1. Davis, *Slavery in the Age of Revolution*, pp. 227-230, 23-236.

b) Au-delà de l'influence : la montée d'une nouvelle génération de Quakers britanniques

David Brion Davis ne suggère cependant pas que l'influence nord-américaine (même celle des co-religionnaires quakers) ait été acceptée facilement et de bonne grâce par les Quakers britanniques. On l'a vu précédemment : ceux-ci sont plus prudents que leurs frères nord-américains, dans la mesure où leur position dans la société britannique est moins assurée (ce sont des *Dissenters*, qui doivent protéger leur position minoritaire dans la Grande-Bretagne anglicane, alors que les Quakers de Pennsylvanie, par exemple, ont longtemps gouverné et dominé cette colonie). Il appartient à Christopher Brown de reprendre cette thèse et de la mener plus loin.

Comme Davis, il note l'imbrication des deux mouvements : en 1761, le *London Yearly Meeting* interdit bien à ses membres de participer à la traite, et confirme ainsi pour la métropole la décision prise en 1758 par les Quakers de Pennsylvanie. Bénezet compte sur les Quakers anglais pour diffuser ses ouvrages, adopter ses idées et les défendre auprès des autorités. Ce que font les Quakers les plus illustres, tel David Barclay qui promeut auprès du *Board of Trade* les pétitions antiesclavagistes des colonies en 1773. Mais Brown, à l'instar de Davis, pense que ce soutien est cosmétique : John Woolman, le visiteur de 1772, embarrasse davantage qu'il ne convainc et ses pamphlets antiesclavagistes sont retirés de l'édition anglaise de ses œuvres publiée à Londres en 1775 ; pendant la guerre d'indépendance américaine, les Quakers britanniques préfèrent militer pour la paix que contre l'esclavage et la traite, et sont alors prêts à intervenir auprès du Parlement et des ministres les plus importants pour défendre cette première cause, mais seulement elle. Ils restent sourds aux appels du *Philadelphia Meeting for Sufferings*, qui les implore, en 1780, 1781 et 1782, d'accorder à la question de l'antiesclavagisme l'attention nécessaire.

L'apport particulier de Brown consiste à expliquer l'enthousiasme abolitionniste des Quakers britanniques après 1783, par la convergence d'une indéniable influence nord-américaine (présence de nombreux ministres de la foi quaker à Londres en 1783, voir plus haut) et de la montée en puissance d'une jeune garde au sein de la communauté quaker anglaise. Les Américains remettent en cause la communauté anglaise, dont la discipline s'est relâchée ; par ailleurs les succès de l'antiesclavagisme en Amérique du Nord prouvent que l'action morale des Quakers peut contribuer efficacement à l'amélioration plus générale d'une société. Depuis 1782, de jeunes hommes (William Birkbeck, Jonathan Hoare, Samuel Hoare Jr.,

Joseph Gurney Bevan, James Phillips en particulier) ont remis en question les dirigeants de la communauté, et pris la direction de celle-ci : ils sont favorables aux idées nouvelles, à la philosophie des droits naturels, et veulent que leur communauté trouve un nouveau souffle spirituel, ancré dans l'action de réforme séculière. Les Américains qui s'expriment lors du *London Yearly Meeting* de juin 1783 en faveur de l'abolition bénéficient donc du soutien d'un groupe qui va s'impliquer rapidement dans la campagne abolitionniste, par l'entremise du sous-comité sur la traite, ou du comité de propagande antiesclavagiste[1]. À l'issue de cette réunion, les Quakers envoient une pétition à la Chambre des Communes, où ils recommandent l'abolition de la traite : sa réception favorable aiguillonne les Quakers qui, trois jours plus tard, créent un comité de 23 membres, le « *Committee on the Slave Trade* ». En juillet, six Quakers entreprennent une campagne de propagande. Alors que le pamphlet de Benjamin Rush n'avait pu trouver d'imprimeur à Londres en 1773 en dépit du soutien de Granville Sharp, l'imprimerie de James Phillips devient la source de toutes les publications antiesclavagistes, nord-américaines ou britanniques, quakers, Évangéliques ou d'inspiration personnelle, comme l'essai de Thomas Clarkson en 1786, on l'a vu. La communauté quaker finance la diffusion gratuite de milliers, puis de dizaines de milliers d'exemplaires de ces textes, qui sont distribués aux personnes de pouvoir et d'influence, et en particulier, celui que rédigent en décembre 1783 au nom de la communauté William Dillwyn et John Lloyd, *The Case of our Fellow-creatures, the Oppressed Africans Respectfully Recommended to the Serious Consideration of the Legislature of Great Britain by the People Called Quakers.* Bien sûr, explique Brown, les Quakers ne réussirent pas à enclencher le débat politique entre 1783 et 1787 : Wilberforce et Clarkson, non-quakers, vont trouver dans cette campagne une motivation sublime qui comble leur désir d'héroïsme. Peut-être les Quakers, trop discrets, n'avaient-ils pas les qualités requises pour mener cette campagne à la victoire finale. Cependant, lorsque se crée en 1787 la *Society for Effecting the Abolition of the Slave Trade*, elle hérite des fonds et des militants de l'association antiesclavagiste quaker[2].

c) Divergences entre les mouvements britannique et américain : le tournant de 1787 aux États-Unis

Une fois la guerre d'Indépendance terminée, les Quakers reprennent dans le mouvement nord-américain la place prioritaire qui était la leur auparavant. Des sociétés antiesclavagistes se créent, où ils jouent un rôle déterminant, comme la *Pennsylvania Society for Promoting the Abolition*

1. Brown, *op. cit.*, pp. 391-419.
2. *Ibid.*, pp. 419-443.

of Slavery, for the Relief of Free Negroes Unlawfully Held in Bondage, and for Improving the Condition of the African Race (1784), ou la *New York Manumission Society* (1785)[1]. Tels leurs co-religionnaires britanniques, qui cherchent à obtenir une action législative, ils tentent d'influencer la convention fédérale de 1787 où se préparent l'avenir de la nation et ses nouvelles institutions. Ils sont confiants : avant de disparaître, cette même année 1787, le Congrès Continental a voté l'Ordonnance du Nord-Ouest. Dans ce texte, une clause déclare l'esclavage interdit dans le Nord-Ouest, immense territoire qui se développe entre l'Ohio, le Mississippi et les Grands Lacs.

Cependant la Constitution américaine de 1787 entérine plusieurs compromis sur l'esclavage : l'abolition définitive de la traite est repoussée de vingt ans ; le nombre d'esclaves d'un État est pris en compte pour l'attribution du nombre de sièges pour chaque État, ce qui renforce le pouvoir des États du sud face à ceux du nord ; les esclaves en fuite qui se cachent au nord doivent être rendus à leurs propriétaires. Certains Quakers visionnaires jugent alors que ce texte fondateur est « *founded on* **Slavery** *and that is on* **Blood**[2] ». Les jeux ne sont pourtant pas faits et nombreux sont ceux qui pensent que l'esclavage est voué à l'extinction. À l'automne 1787, le Quaker Moses Brown réussit à faire voter une loi qui interdit la traite dans le Rhode Island, l'État qui bénéficie le plus de ce commerce[3].

Conclusion

Dès la fin du XVIIe siècle, les Quakers nord-américains prennent l'initiative de divers écrits et actions antiesclavagistes. Dans la deuxième moitié du XVIIIe siècle, cette communauté impulse la dynamique du mouvement antiesclavagiste anglo-américain, et trouve dans le Grand réveil anglo-américain, puis la Révolution américaine — qui s'accompagne d'une guerre où les soldats noirs jouent un rôle non négligeable —, des relais intellectuels et d'opinion qui aboutissent à des décisions d'émancipation d'esclaves, immédiate ou graduelle, à l'échelle des États ou simplement privées, uniques dans le monde occidental. Dès le début de la guerre d'Indépendance, en outre, la traite est également remise en cause par les nouveaux États-Unis. Pourtant en 1787, sans que les uns ou les autres le sachent encore, le témoin de l'initiative antiesclavagiste est passé aux Britanniques. En Grande-Bretagne, une nouvelle génération de Quakers s'empare de l'antiesclavagisme comme d'une cause qui peut régénérer leur communauté, et peut-être toute la société ; ils sont suivis par de fortes personnalités non-quakers, des Évangéliques anglicans, des politiques, et

1. Davis, *Slavery in the Age of the American Revolution*, pp. 216-217.
2. William Rotch à Moses Brown, cité par Davis, *Slavery in the Age of Revolution*, p. 325.
3. Rappleye, *Sons of Providence*, p. 248.

toute une opinion, pour qui cette campagne morale redonne un nouveau sens aux valeurs britanniques. Aux États-Unis, les Quakers et les autres militants antiesclavagistes continuent quelque temps à obtenir des progrès spectaculaires, au niveau des États : en 1804, tous les États du nord et du centre ont passé des lois d'émancipation graduelle, alors que la campagne contre la traite redémarre seulement en Grande-Bretagne. Pourtant le mouvement américain est déjà sur le déclin, et les différentes mesures prises jusque-là pour limiter ou interdire la participation des citoyens américains à la traite atlantique ont eu peu d'effet... Mais ceci est une autre histoire.

Religion and Slavery: a Powerful Weapon for Pro-Slavery and Abolitionist Campaigners

Olivette Otele

In the second half of the 16th century, Queen Elizabeth I tried to answer the demands of dissenting groups regarding religious, political and social affairs by founding a suitable compromise between followers of the Church of England, Catholics, land owners and peers. A series of Acts were passed between 1558 and 1559. Yet these measures were deemed inadequate by religious dissidents who refused to conform to church rituals and who distrusted a clergy they viewed as being corrupt. The group primarily gathered Quakers, Presbyterians, Baptists and Congregationalists. A century later, those who came to be known as the Dissenters enjoyed less political freedom. They had to wait for the Act of Toleration in 1689 to be granted freedom of worship but they were nonetheless barred from holding office. Those who refused to comply were imprisoned. Some of the dissenters were among early colonists of North America and the West Indies. The Glorious Revolution of 1688 marked a turning point in the way religion was considered in the country. The authority of the Anglican Church on political matters was transferred to Parliament. Yet as William Gibson[1] noted, this transfer was accompanied by the idea that the Church should be "a voluntary association". John Locke who embodied that school of thought, promoted what was referred to as a "reasonable model of Christianity".[2] Individuals had the right to refuse religion or simply the authority of the Church of England. The war against Catholic France that came shortly after this intellectual movement had an impact on the new form of religious freedom. The Church of England epitomised unity while Catholicism represented tyranny. The war was exalting protestant fervour. As for dissenters, prevented from working as civil servants, most of them turned to trade and thus strengthened Britain's commercial ties with the rest of Europe and with the Americas. By the 18th century, they were as involved in the transatlantic slave trade as most traders from other religious denominations. Given the notoriety of so lucrative a trade, there seemed to be no reason for the governing bodies and the middle class trading circles for abolishing it. Yet, the revivalist movement that swept across Britain in the 18th century would question the legitimacy of that commerce.

1. William Gibson, *Religion and Society in England & Wales: 1689-1800*, London: Leicester University Press, 1996, p.2.
2. *Ibid.*

The aim of this article is to understand the reasons that led the dissenters, also known as Nonconformists in the 18th century, to fight for the abolition of the transatlantic slave trade. We will articulate our analysis around two points. Firstly we shall explore the early dissenters' place in society, their common beliefs, before studying the birth of the second wave of dissenters known as the Evangelical movement. Secondly, we will chart the most influential groups, inquire into their scope of action such as the abolition of the slave trade, the nature of the links between those groups while analysing the ways in which unexpected events forced those anti-slavery groups to redefine their abolitionist strategies.

"Old Dissent"[1] counted among them, a group called the Congregationalists. They believed that God's churches should be local small churches. These churches should only submit to God and not to any other religious denomination such as the Church of England or even a synod of chosen leaders; for that reason, 16th century Congregationalists referred to themselves as the Independents. Baptism of children was amongst the various rituals they followed. As for the Presbyterians, they were among the most oppressed religious groups in the late 17th century. Persecution did not prevent them from designing a complex church organisation they considered fairer. The aim of the system was to act as a safeguard against the natural tendencies of men to self interest. They formed an organised church government after 1688 with a governing body composed of "elders"[2] overlooking the work of church presbyteries. For instance, below the church presbyteries, there was an assembly of representatives that registered the demands and concerns of ordinary church members. They believed that each person could be saved not because of their deeds but through their faith in Jesus Christ. The Quakers also suffered from persecution. The sect was founded by Leicestershire born George Fox.[3] At a time when a portion of English believers seemed to be disillusioned by church leaders, Fox gathered a few friends to discuss how their religious beliefs could be put to use and impact on people's lives. The group was also referred to as "Friends" or "Friends of the Truth". The Quakers—those who "trembled in the name of God"—moved beyond the scope of religion and became involved in social and political matters in the second half of the 17th century. Opposed to the Calvinist idea of predestination, they strongly adhered to the precept of salvation by faith. According to them, "God's Inner Light" through revelation, was an individual experience. Once the believer had been touched by God's light, he or she was led by the divine

1. As opposed to "New Dissent" such as the Methodists.
2. Presbyterians derive their name from the Greek term 'elder'.
3. George Fox, *The Autobiography of George Fox from his Journal*, London: S. Z. Partridge 1886.

hand. Nevertheless each person had the choice to follow or not that inner light, and that choice was called free will.

By the end of the 17th century, English society was going through changes that put emphasis on moral conduct. Societies for the reformation of manners were created. Dissenters who had been at the forefront of reforms regarding morality were once again persecuted. The Tory government that took the lead in Parliament passed the Occasional Conformity Act in 1711 and the Schism Act in 1714. They were aimed at disqualifying dissenters who had been granted special rights for public office. These acts resulted in the migration of these groups to the colonies. Yet, dissenters had gained ground in the country. As Dr Evans's lists[1] established, dissenters were not small and marginalised groups at the beginning of the 18th century. They accounted for 6 to 7% of the general population in 1715. Dissenters, barred from public office, mainly succeeded in commerce. Commerce was vital for the country at the beginning of the 18th century. The Transatlantic slave trade in particular seemed to hold the promise of a better future for those who had entrepreneurial skills, be they from the upper or the middle-class. Religion did not seem to represent an impediment either to institution-owned plantations such as the one belonging to the Church of England in Barbados by 1710, or to individual trading ventures organised by dissenters. As David Brion Davis contended, "by the early eighteenth century there were Quaker planters in the West Indies and Quaker slave merchants in London, Philadelphia, and Newport".[2] Religion, it was argued saved those poor creatures from their pagan cannibal customs.[3] This argument helped men and women trading in human beings to reconcile mercantilism with Christian ethics. The new century would bring hope and wealth but it would also be marked by new values.

Eighteenth century Britain was characterised by major economic, social, religious, scientific and political changes. On the eve of Europe's industrial revolution, the intellectual and political scenes were dominated by humanist ideas of the Enlightenment and natural rights. In Britain, at least two worlds co-existed: the world of the rich marked by abundance mainly for those who had invested in trade. These people came from the upper class or belonged to the entrepreneurial middle class. The two groups found common interests in money making.

John Wesley is generally considered to be the initiator of the Evangelical movement that changed the way Christianity was perceived in Britain

1. George Fox, *op.cit*, pp.95-97.
2. David Brion Davis, *The Problem of Slavery in the Age of Revolution: 1770-1823*, Ithaca: Cornell University Press, 1975, p.42.
3. Basil Davidson, *The African Slave Trade*, Abingdon: Currey Publishers, 1961.

in the 18th century. Raised as a follower of the Church of England, John Wesley's interest in theology increased upon his arrival at the University of Oxford. He became part of a group of friends devoted to Christianity and to personal discipline. They met to discuss matters relating to the doctrine of salvation by faith. They visited prisons and deprived communities where they spread the gospel. The group was mocked and became known as "the Holy Club", the "Bible Moths" or the "Methodists" in reference to their excessive rigour. On a journey to America, Wesley met a religious group called the Moravians. This encounter would have a lasting impression on young Wesley. Once back in England, he continued to meet the Moravians and in 1738, he experienced conversion. This prompted him to move away from the Anglican Church and soon after, he decided to set up his ministry and he began his Evangelical mission. Wesley extensively toured major cities and the English and Welsh countryside. Wesley and his followers believed that when one experienced revelation, the person was to be born anew in Christ. He or she had experienced a renewal of faith that went beyond the first awakening that took place when he or she first came to Christ. That experience was supposed to take the believer on to a higher level of commitment; that included evangelising those who were still living in darkness. It meant to spread the good news or the gospel of the death and resurrection of Jesus Christ. One could argue that Wesley's emphasis on the doctrine of salvation by faith did not set him apart from previous dissenting movements. Yet, his theological views did touch people's lives because, as Thomas A. Langford puts it, "He consistently turned theological reflection to practical service. Theology, in his understanding, was to be preached, sung, and lived".[1] The constant transfer from inner life to the outer world and vice versa was most salient in his perception of Grace. According to Wesley, "Grace is the source; faith is the condition of salvation".[2] Langford explained:

> Justification by grace through faith was a central motif in John Wesley's thought. He was emphatic: Salvation is the work of God. Salvation is a gracious gift of God and it must not be confused with human achievement, with the exercise of human will, or with the faithful pursuit of a Christian style of life."[3]

One could object that if indeed salvation was the ultimate example of God's grace, what was the value of Christian deeds? After all, if believing in God was enough to benefit from his goodness and grace what was the need for the believer to do good. The answer according to Thomas Langford

1. Thomas A. Langford, *Practical Divinity: Theology in the Wesleyan Tradition*, Volume I, Nashville: Abingdon Press, 1983, p.17.
2. Langford, *op.cit.*, p.23.
3. *Ibid*, p.23.

was to be found precisely in the idea of God's grace. "Redemption is by God through faith. But faith is embodied in love. Regeneration—spiritual rebirth—is given by God, and the resulting new life is expressed in love of God and neighbor."[1] Wesley travelled the country, unrelentingly preaching to a growing number of people. In Bristol for instance, he chose to preach before or after the Anglican Church service time to give a broader audience the opportunity to come and listen to him. When forced out of premises, he followed the path of the Quakers by choosing open-air preaching. Banned several times from preaching in Bristol, Wesley and his followers always managed to find agreement with enthusiastic supporters who would then put pressure on local authorities. Disapproval not only came about open-air preaching but also about people's reactions to Wesley's words. It was not unusual to hear cries, moans and other signs of religious fervour considered by the established church to be indecent. Another attack threatened to split the movement in the years 1738-1740, when Wesley and his friend Whitefield publicly expressed their disagreement over the question of predestination. Wesley believed in unconditional salvation whereas George Whitefield believed that a small group of people were elected by God and because they were especially chosen, "they could not fall from grace".[2] The split over the theological question would last and lead to the creation of two distinct branches of Methodism: Arminian Methodism defended by Wesley and Calvinist Methodism supported by Whitefield. It was in the 1770s that Wesley turned his attention to the question of the slave trade. He had travelled to America and was well aware of the treatment of slaves on plantations, but it was the Somerset Case that prompted him to speak out against that commerce. Unexpected events shaped the involvement of the Evangelical movement in the abolition of the slave trade.

The history of transatlantic slavery is a history of paradoxes. It was shaped by trading interests as well as by violence, subjugation and rebellion. Recent studies have analysed the ways in which slave revolts that started in the 17th century, greatly influenced public opinion over the use of enslaved Africans in the plantation.[3] At home, very specific cases brought the question of abolition in the political arena. Some historians have argued that because most slaves were working in plantations, a vast majority of the British population was unaware of their living conditions and antislavery groups argued that those conditions were far better than

1. *Ibid.*, p.18.
2. Kenneth Morgan, *John Wesley in Bristol*, Bristol: Bristol Branch of the Historical Association, 1990, p.9.
3. Olivette Otele, « Abolition de l'esclavage et émancipation, des périodes d'effervescence propices aux oublis », dans *Histoire de l'esclavage britannique : des origines de la traite transatlantique aux prémisses de la colonisation*, Paris, Michel Houdiard Éditeur, 2008, pp.165-217.

those of poor English communities.[1] Yet, the relatively important number of black people in England could not go unnoticed.[2] In 1765, civil servant Granville Sharp befriended a young black man who after having been beaten by his owner was left as dead. He had recovered barely enough to seek free treatment delivered by Granville's brother, a doctor who provided treatment for the poor in London. It took young Jonathan Strong two years to recover part of his former strength and health. In the meantime, Sharp became very concerned with the treatment of slaves working as servants in London and later on, with plantation slavery. Lisle, Jonathan Strong's former master, found out that the young man had recovered and tried to have him kidnapped and sent back to the harsh field work of the Caribbean Islands. Sharp intervened and took the case to Chief Justice Lord Mansfield. The debate about the abolition of the slave trade became, from that moment on, a legal matter in Britain. Eventually, Mansfield decided that no slave-owner had the right to force a slave to go back to the West Indies. Strong, whose health had remained precarious after Lisle's beating, finally died in 1770. Deeply moved by the debate, John Wesley published a pamphlet entitled, *Thoughts Upon Slavery.*[3] Wesley informed his fellow men and women about the slave trade; the way it started, how it was conducted in Africa and about the horrific treatment of slaves on the plantations. Wesley also contrasted African life of Muslim Negroes with life on the plantations.

> The Mandingos [says Monsieur Brue] are rigid Mahometans, drinking neither wine nor brandy. They are industrious and laborious, keeping their ground well cultivated, and breeding a good stock of cattle. All the Mahometan Negroes constantly go to public prayers thrice a day; there being a Priest in every village, who regularly calls them together; and it is surprising to see the modesty, attention, and reverence which they observe during their worship. [...] Banished from their country, from their friends and relations for ever, from every comfort of life, they are reduced to a state scarce anyway preferable to that of beasts of burden. [...] The time they work in the West Indies, is from day-break to noon, and from two o'clock till dark; during which time, they are attended by overseers, who, if they think them dilatory, or think anything not so well done as it should be, whip them most unmercifully, so that you

1. Brycchan Carey, *British Abolitionism and the Rhetoric of Sensibility, Writing, Sentiment, and Slavery, 1760-1807*, Basingstoke: Palgrave Macmillan, 2005, pp.124-27, for the comparison between the living conditions of slaves and chimney sweepers.
2. From 10,000 to 20,000 black men and women were said to live in Britain, during the period of the British slave trade by Kathy Chater, "Black People in England, 1660-1807" in *The British Slave Trade: Abolition, Parliament and People*, (eds) Farrell, Unwin and Walvin, Edinburgh: Edinburgh University Press, 2007, pp.66-83.
3. John Wesley, *Thoughts upon Slavery*, 1774, http://gbgm-umc.org/umw/wesley/thoughtsuponslavery.stm, July, 2008.

> may see their bodies long after wealed and scarred usually from the shoulders to the waist.[1]

Wesley urged owners to think about saving their soul, for on judgement day, God would remember that they did not extend justice and mercy to enslaved Africans. Wesley did not campaign against slavery the way other antislavery movements did. He used his sermons to raise awareness and to appeal to his fellow Christians regarding the sin they were committing by subjugating other human beings. In a debate marked by what Brycchan Carey called "sentimental diversion", Wesley's *Thoughts Upon Slavery* was "within the tradition of political sermon".[2] In his work on the rhetoric of sensibility and more specifically on a passage of *Thoughts Upon Slavery*[3], Carey contends that:

> [...] inflammatory though it undoubtedly is, it also makes use of many of the conventions of sentimental rhetoric. It constructs a sentimental argument founded in the idea of sympathy, and posits a sentimental hero-here conspicuous by his absence. The implied reader (or listener) of this passage[4] is simultaneously a slave trader and a man of no sensibility. [...] The passage is also marked by its use of sentimental signifiers such as tears, groans, and hearts, by its determination to bring private feelings into public sphere, and by its overheated and excessively woeful tone.[5]

The religious group that was the major driving force against the slave trade and slavery was the Quakers. In the early days of the transatlantic slave trade, enslaving other human beings seemed to contradict the idea of free will defended by the Quakers. In the second half of the 17th century George Fox was warning those who had slaves overseas against the offence of mistreating them. During his visit to Barbados, he encouraged owners to take better care of their slaves. The idea of abolishing that commerce was not part of any religious movement's public discourse until the 18th century. It was a Quaker from Philadelphia, Anthony Benezet who publicly spoke about the evil of the slave trade. Benezet, who had been teaching slave children, dismissed the idea of European intellectual superiority over Africans. His anti-slavery pamphlets reached England at a time when

1. Wesley, *op.cit.*, Chapter II, paragraph 7 and Chapter III, paragraph 7.
2. Brycchan, *op.cit.*, "Feeling Out loud: Sentimental Rhetoric in Parliament, the Pulpit, and the Court of Law" in *British Abolitionism and the Rhetoric of Sensibility: Writing, Sentiment and Slavery, 1760-1807*, Basingstoke: Palgrave Macmillan, 2005, pp.144-185.
3. Wesley, *op.cit.*, Chapter V, paragraph 3.
4. *Ibid.*, "Are you a man? Then you should have an human heart. But have you indeed? What is your heart made of? Is there no such principle as compassion there? Do you never feel another's pain? Have you no sympathy, no sense of human woe, no pity for the miserable? When you saw the flowing eyes, the heaving breasts, or the bleeding sides and tortured limbs of your fellow-creatures, was you a stone, or a brute?"
5. Carey, *op.cit.*, p.151.

slavery-derived wealth was benefiting a good part of British middle class families. Benezet managed to convince Quakers in Philadelphia and Pennsylvania to join the movement for Abolition. Philadelphian Quakers urged their British counterparts to get involved in the movement. The *"Quakers' Yearly Meeting Minutes of 1727"*[1] reveals that some members expressed their opposition to the slave trade but it took British Quakers more than fifty years to form a group that could proudly declare that none of their members owned slaves in the West Indies. Yet, Quakers in the mid 18th century did not seem to have much influence on the political and social spheres. In fact, their influence within the large British Anglican society was limited. They had been involved in trade since the 17th century and had developed commercial ties nationally and internationally. These networks would soon be put to use during the abolition campaign.

The second major event outside the influence of Evangelical revivalist groups that determined the course of the debate about the abolition and therefore had an impact on these movements was the Zong Affair. On September 1781, a slave vessel commanded by Luke Collinwood set sail to West African coasts. As the result of overcrowding, disease and malnutrition, six crew members and sixty enslaved Africans had died by November. Captain Collingwood decided to take drastic measures claiming that for safety and economic reasons, slaves had to be thrown overboard. Indeed, the law stated that owners could only claim insurance if slaves had died of natural death. The natural death clause included disease and suicide but also killing during insurrection. 132 slaves were thus killed but Collingwood died before getting back to Britain. Owners claimed money on the basis that there was not enough water on board so Collingwood had to kill the slaves to preserve crew members. Yet the insurance company refused to pay for the loss because they found out that the ship contained about 420 gallons of water when it set ashore in Jamaica on December 1781. The case was taken to the tribunals in 1783. John Lee, the Court of Admiralty's Solicitor-General who represented the owners, contended that slaves were goods and chattel property and as such their being thrown overboard should not be an issue. What was at stake was the efficiency of Collingwood as commander of the ship and his responsibility regarding the management of food and in that case, water. The case nearly escaped the abolitionists. It was former slave Olaudah Equiano who alerted Granville Sharp about the legal battle that was taking place between insurers and owners. Shocked by the lack of interest Londoners showed and by the fact that the death of those slaves did not lead to any condemnation, Sharp and

1. "*London Yearly Meeting Minutes*", 25th 3 month 1727", Ref. YM/M6/ 457-458 in *Quaker faith and Practice*, London: Library of the Society of Friends.

Equiano highly publicised the story. That gruesome episode would expose even more the realities of the transatlantic slave trade.

In June 1783, the London Society of Friends set up a committee of 23 members.[1] Their aim was to find ways to fight for the abolition of the transatlantic slave trade. The committee was called the Meeting for Sufferings. They drew up a petition signed by 300 Quakers out of the 20,000 Quakers who lived in Britain. They sent the petition to Parliament but no noticeable outcome followed. From this initial group, six members[2] wrote and disseminated anti-slavery pamphlets and drawings. The recipients were well-established merchants and elite school students, all Quakers and non Quakers. Copies of the pamphlets were also distributed to politicians on their way out after parliamentary sessions. Nevertheless, the group was suffering from bad publicity. They were perceived as a sect with extreme views. Their refusal, for instance, to call noble men "my Lord" or to address ordinary men as "Mister" because it reminded them of Master, was often ridiculed.[3] The anti-slavery movement became efficient when London, Manchester, Bristol and other local committees realised that they had to work together. Providence would lead a young scholar called Thomas Clarkson towards the Quakers. As the son of a clergyman who had died in Clarkson's early years, he had followed his father's path towards theology at the University of Cambridge. One of the most prized competitions was the Latin essay competition. The theme that year was slavery. In 1785, Clarkson won the competition, finished his studies and went to London to have his Latin essay, translated into English, published. With the help of a Quaker friend of his family, he was introduced to James Phillips a printer and bookstore owner. Under Phillips's supervision, the manuscript was entitled, *An Essay on the Slavery and Commerce of the Human Species, particularly the African, translated from a Latin dissertation, which was honoured with the First Prize in the University of Cambridge for the year 1785 with additions.* It was published in 1786. In his essay, Clarkson exposed his perception of slaves living in the Caribbean and as Hochschild explained:

> [...] he argued not that color doesn't matter, but rather that Africans might not be permanently black after all. Skin color, he claimed, must be linked to

1. John Barton, William Dillwyn, George Harrison, Samuel Hoare Jr., Joseph Hooper, John Lloyd, Joseph Woods, James Phillips and Richard Phillips.
2. William Dillwyn, George Harrison, Samuel Hoare Jr., Thomas Knowles, John Lloyd and Joseph Woods.
3. Adam Hochschild, *Bury the Chains: the British Struggle to Abolish Slavery*, Basingstoke: Macmillan, 2005, p.107.

climate, for are not children of African slaves in the New World often lighter-skinned than their parents.[1]

A year before his essay was published Clarkson was introduced by his Quaker friends to the work of an Evangelical Anglican minister, James Ramsay, who had spent many years in the Caribbean islands preaching to both the Europeans and often at his own peril, to the slaves. Ramsay's *Essay on the Treatment and Conversion of African Slaves in the British Sugar Colonies* which was published in the summer of 1784, made great impression on Clarkson. Ramsay's accounts of the suffering of slaves posited him as a valuable witness for the abolitionists but more importantly at a time of religious divide, his affiliation to the Anglican Church was greatly appreciated by the Quakers. They came to realise that without the support of prominent Anglican ministers their cause would be marginalised. The Anglican Church was also experiencing a form of Evangelical revival. This revival prompted some of its followers to try and address the question of injustice and poverty. The slave trade was targeted. Early Anglican evangelical movements were not concerned with the slave trade and if they were, it was because they had invested in that commerce. A chapel at Lock Hospital for Penitent Prostitutes was built with money invested in plantations by Reverend Martin Madan. Captain John Newton continued his work in the slave trade even after his conversion. The slave owner the Countess of Huntingdon who had George Whitefield as her chaplain and who promoted the work of three black slaves Ukawsaw Gronniosaw, John Marrant and Phyllis Weatley, joined the Methodist church. Yet, because she did not want to lose her connections with the Anglicans, she created the Countess of Huntingdon's Connexion, a religious denomination. In was in the 1780s that evangelical Anglicans started to question the legitimacy of the slave trade. Circles that had previously been focusing on saving British souls turned their attention to slaves.

The Teston Circle and the Clapham Sect are two examples of Anglican revival groups that campaigned for Abolition. The Teston circle referred to a group of devout Christians who lived in Teston, Kent. Under the patronage of Sir Charles Middleton, James Ramsay had become parson of Teston in 1781. The Teston Circle helped him to publish his essay on slavery in 1784. The group was concerned with the welfare of slaves living in the West Indies. They funded schools for slaves but as Christopher L. Brown contends[2], they were more in favour of improving the living conditions of slaves than considering manumission. Nevertheless, by 1787, they had

1. Hochschild, *op.cit.* p.92.
2. Christopher L. Brown, *Moral Capital: Foundations of British Abolitionism*, Chapel Hill: North Carolina University Press, 2006.

joined the antislavery movement. The "Clapham Sect" was a group that became fully formed as an antislavery club after 1787. The name "Clapham Sect" was coined in 1844. Prior to that date, Clapham members were mostly referred to as the "Saints". Members of the group lived in a small village in Surrey, near London, called Clapham. The village gathered an important number of evangelical Christians involved in trade and in politics. The initiators of the group were Henry Venn, rector of Clapham and John Thornton, a rich merchant. Both men transmitted what they considered to be high moral values to their family and children. Succeeding his father as a leading figure in the group, Henry Thornton and other members took on the ambitious task of reforming British society. They actively worked for prison reform and they became involved in missionary work. Social equality was not their main concern as they believed that a well ordered society was based on class distinctions. They reckoned nonetheless that the duty of those who were well-off was to do philanthropic work. They also supported religious education and funded poet and philanthropist Hannah Moore's schools. It was in 1784 that Hull born MP William Wilberforce joined the Clapham group. The same year he was approached by Reverend Thomas Clarkson. The Committee for Abolition of the African Slave Trade was formed in 1787. It gathered nine Quakers as well as Granville Sharp, William Wilberforce and Thomas Clarkson, three leading names in intellectual, political and evangelical Anglican circles. From that moment on, their battle involved petitioning and lobbying. Despite major set backs due to proslavery campaigners and international events such as the slave uprising of Saint Domingue in 1791 and Napoleon's war against Britain in 1803[1], an act abolishing the slave trade was passed on March 1807.

At the end of the 18th century leading evangelical men and women agreed on the reformation of manners. The motivation to change their world was their commitment to a new religious trend called evangelical Christianity. One can nonetheless wonder whether that kinship in religion when it came to campaigning for abolition, did not have invisible and yet well-defined boundaries. Indeed, Olaudah Equiano who had been involved in the fight against the abolition of the slave trade was not officially part of the Committee for the Abolition of the African Slave Trade in 1787. On several occasions, he provided Sharp with information on runaway slaves who needed help. He informed Sharp about the Zong Affair. As a dedicated Christian, he provided the reader in his autobiography, *The Interesting Narrative of the Life of Olaudah Equiano or Gustavus Vassa, the African*

1. The uprising of 1791 created an unsettling atmosphere in the British West Indies. A war broke out between France and Britain in 1793. It ended in 1802 and Napoleon re-established slavery in the French colonies the same year.

published in 1789, with an insight into his conversion and relationship with Christianity. Whether it was because too visible a black presence would have hindered the work of the Committee by antagonising part of the population or because he was already involved in a committee of twelve leading African men called "Sons of Africa", we can only speculate about his blatant absence in the Committee. This point nevertheless leads us to suggest that Christianity might not have been the unquestionable feature that prompted Evangelical Christians to adopt an antislavery stand; even though they posited themselves as "the true Christians" and hence implying that proslavery campaigners were not "true Christians".

Indeed, most slave traders were devout Christians and their position regarding the use of Africans in plantations varied greatly. Some of them believed that slavery saved Africans from paganism. Others, such as Edward Long, a slaver and judge in Jamaica considered that black slaves were closer to animals in their appearance and their behaviour than they were to Europeans. Some people—such as Lady Nugent, who as the wife of the governor of Jamaica stayed on the island between 1801 et 1807—viewed plantations as a mere economic means much needed by Britain but she had no doubt about the intellectual abilities of black people.[1] For others, slaves had to accept their bondage as slavery was the result of the malediction of Ham.[2] Some of these arguments were also defended by a significant number of antislavery campaigners. In fact the closeness of pro- and anti-slavery campaigners was often based on a racial consensus that stemmed from a particular interpretation of the Bible. What needed to be redefined was the value system attached to evangelical readings of the Bible. Wilberforce's pamphlet contextualises the theological and social issues that sustained the debate as far as evangelical Christians were concerned. In his pamphlet Wilberforce defines what he considers to be true Christianity. He does not seek to convert non-Christians but directly addresses the common pitfalls of "professed Christians".

> The generality of professed Christians among higher classes, either altogether overlook or deny, or at least extenuate the corruption and weakness here in question. They acknowledge indeed that there is, and ever has been in the world, a great portion of vice and wickedness; [...] we must not expect to find them traced in their true origin. [...] The bulk of professed Christians are used to speak of man as of a being, who naturally pure, and inclined to all virtue,

1. Philip Wright, *Lady Nugent's Journal of Her Residence in Jamaica from 1801 to 1805*, Kingston: University of West Indies, 2002.
2. Otele, *op.cit.* p.173.

> is sometimes, almost involuntarily, drawn out of the right or is overpowered by the violence of temptation.[1]

The crucial point Wilberforce was making was that his fellow Christians had become self indulgent and less inclined to take responsibility for their own mistakes. Human beings were inheritably sinful. Contrary to Rousseau's idea, the 'Children of nature' meaning slaves in Wilberforce's context, were even worse.

> They appeared incapable of conjugal affection, or parental fondness, or filial reverence, or social attachments; uniting too with their state of barbarism, many the vices and weaknesses of polished society. [...] But you give up the heathen nations as indefensible, and wish rather to form your estimate of man from a view of countries which have been blessed with the light of revelation. True it is, and with joy let us record the concession, Christianity has set the general tone of morals much higher than ever found in the Pagan World.[2]

The answer according to Wilberforce was to implant Christianity in these Children of nature. Freeing them had to be done gradually as they needed to be prepared for the religious responsibilities that came with freedom. Gradual emancipation would become a bone of contention between abolitionist Elizabeth Heyrick and Wilberforce in the 1820s. Wilberforce's arguments may not have been shared by most evangelical Christians; they were not even shared by one of his closest friends Prime Minister William Pitt who nonetheless brought the topic to Parliament in 1788. It appeared that if indeed the fight for the abolition of the slave trade, and later on for emancipation, was a reaction against an era dominated by personal achievement and by what was seen as decadence, paradoxically, engaging in the campaign seemed to have been eventually guided by individual motives.

We tried to understand the reasons that led the evangelical movement of the 18th century to work for the suppression of the transatlantic slave trade. In order to do so, we had to explore briefly the history, the beliefs and the scope of action of early religious dissenting groups such as the Congregationalists, the Quakers and the Presbyterians. We established that as members of those persecuted groups were prevented from entering civil service, they turned to trade and a part of them left for North America and the West Indies. This analysis then led us to study the most influential evangelical groups such as the Methodists, The Teston Circle and the Clapham Sect. We contended that the motive for their involvement in the social questions of justice and freedom and in particular their questioning

1. William Wilberforce, *A Practical View of Christianity*, (1797), Massachusetts: Hendrickson Publishers, pp.13-14.
2. *Ibid.*, pp.16-17.

of the legitimacy of a trade that thrived on the work of enslaved Africans, came at a time when wealth in 18th century Britain was accompanied by moral decay, self interest and poverty for the labouring class. We also established that despite their commitment, the leading force behind the abolition movement—the Quakers—had to redefine their strategy due to unexpected events such as, for instance, the Zong Affair. They also had to move beyond the boundaries of their group to secure the support of evangelical Anglicans such as Thomas Clarkson and William Wilberforce. They had to use the social codes of a society that saw the rise of a "rhetoric of sensibility".

Works Cited

Brown, Christopher L., *Moral Capital: Foundations of British Abolitionism*, North Carolina University Press, Chapel Hill, 2006.

Carey, Brycchan, *British Abolitionism and the Rhetoric of Sensibility: Writing, Sentiment and Slavery, 1760-1807*, Basingstoke, Palgrave Macmillan, 2005.

Davis, David Brion, *The Problem of Slavery in the Age of Revolution: 1770-1823*, Ithaca: Cornell University Press, 1975.

Farrell, Unwin, Walvin, *The British Slave Trade: Abolition, Parliament and People*, Edinburgh: Edinburgh University Press, 2007.

Gibson, William, *Religion and Society in England & Wales: 1689-1800*, London: Leicester University Press, 1996.

Hochschild, Adam, *Bury the Chains: the British Struggle to Abolish Slavery*, Basingstoke: Macmillan, 2005.

Jennings, Judith, *The Business of Abolishing the British Slave Trade: 1783-1807*, London: Frank Cass Publishers, 1997.

Langford, A., Thomas, *Practical Divinity: Theology in the Wesleyan Tradition*, vol.I, Nashville: Abingdon Press, 1983.

Morgan, Kenneth, *John Wesley in Bristol*, Bristol Branch of the Historical Association, Bristol, 1990.

Otele, Olivette, *Histoire de l'esclavage britannique : des origines de la traite transatlantique aux prémisses de la colonisation*, Paris, Michel Houdiard Éditeur, 2008.

Thomas Clarkson, ambassadeur et promoteur de la première campagne (1787-1807)

Françoise Le Jeune

Lors des commémorations de 2007, les expositions retraçant la première campagne britannique contre la traite négrière ont beaucoup mis en avant le rôle central de deux des membres du comité de Londres, Granville Sharp et William Wilberforce. Granville Sharp dès 1765, avait présenté et défendu la cause des esclaves noirs détenus sur le sol anglais devant les tribunaux[1]. Il était à l'origine du célèbre Somerset Case dont la presse, nationale et provinciale, s'était faite l'écho en s'intéressant pour la première fois à la cause des esclaves[2]. Quant à William Wilberforce, député de York, proche du Premier ministre William Pitt, il avait présenté inlassablement la question de la traite des esclaves devant le Parlement britannique. Entre 1788 et le vote de la loi de 1807 qui mettait fin à la traite, Wilberforce avait défendu annuellement la cause des esclaves achetés par les négriers britanniques et transportés dans des conditions inhumaines vers les colonies britanniques. Son talent d'orateur, sa force de conviction, soulignés par les députés acquis à la cause, firent de lui un acteur essentiel de la cause qu'il défendait.

Ces deux hommes étaient des « *moral entrepreneurs*[3] » sans lesquels la campagne contre la traite négrière n'aurait sans doute pas convaincu les juges, puis les députés. Cependant, on oublie parfois de prendre en compte le travail de Thomas Clarkson. Ce dernier faisait partie du comité de Londres au même titre que Granville et Wilberforce. Il participa activement au travail de propagande auprès des parlementaires et du public en Grande-Bretagne, puis en France, en parcourant le pays et en activant des réseaux de comités contre l'esclavage, mais surtout en apportant des preuves tangibles que le commerce des esclaves était un pêché, un crime, un anathème pour la nation britannique. Dans *The History*

1. James, Walvin, *Black and White, the Negro and English Society, 1555-1945*, London: Allan Lane, Penguin, 1973, p. 119. "*By 1768, Sharp was accepted—by both black and white alike—as the principal white defender of black interests in England.*"
2. Le jugement final de Lord Mansfield établissait que la loi anglaise ne reconnaissait pas à un propriétaire d'esclave en fuite, le droit de le capturer ou de le kidnapper pour qu'il soit vendu. (Seymour, Drescher, *Capitalism and Antislavery: British Mobilization in Comparative Perspective*, London: Basingstoke, Macmillan, 1986, p. 37).
3. Le terme est utilisé par David Brion Davis pour mentionner ces hommes qui se sont emparés du discours idéologique sur l'esclavage pour le transformer en actions ou campagnes en faveur de réformes de la société. David Brion Davis, *The Problem of Slavery in Western Culture*, Ithaca, New York: Cornell University Press, 1966, p. 172.

of the Rise, Progress and Accomplishment of the Abolition of the African Slave Trade by the British Parliament[1], Thomas Clarkson retrace son inlassable activité de promoteur de la cause antiesclavagiste auprès du Parlement, mais aussi son travail d'ambassadeur de cette cause auprès des Français. De son engagement dans le comité de Londres, à partir de 1787 et jusqu'en 1794, année durant laquelle sa santé l'empêcha de prendre la route pour poursuivre sa « mission » (*duty*), comme il décrit sa démarche, Clarkson prend note du développement de la campagne auprès du public rapidement convaincu du bien-fondé de la campagne, le peuple légitime, qu'il oppose à la lenteur de la procédure parlementaire en raison de l'inhumanité de ces représentants du peuple.

C'est donc le rôle de ce troisième « *moral entrepreneur* », celui dont le travail de promotion de la cause abolitionniste à travers le pays fut essentiel, que nous allons examiner ici, à travers sa propre analyse de la dynamique de ce mouvement populaire que fut le soutien du public entre 1787 et 1792, alors que leurs députés restaient sourds à la cause des esclaves noirs.

I. Le débat intellectuel sur la question de la traite et de l'esclavage (1760-1787)

En 1785, lorsque Thomas Clarkson, en dernière année de théologie à Cambridge, remporte le prix de la composition latine, sa connaissance de la question de l'esclavage est fort solide. Pour répondre au sujet proposé par son directeur de faculté, à savoir « *Is it lawful to enslave the unconsenting?* », l'étudiant Clarkson avait consulté tous les traités, textes polémiques et sermons publiés sur le sujet. Ses sources principales étaient Anthony Bénézet, le Quaker américain dont les textes avaient été publiés en Grande-Bretagne par l'entremise du réseau quaker. Il avait lu John Wesley, le méthodiste, et ses *Thoughts Upon Slavery* publié en 1774, les textes de James Ramsay, pasteur anglican évangéliste, ainsi que les pamphlets de Granville Sharp. Il s'était intéressé au discours des Lumières françaises, en particulier aux propos sur l'esclavage dans *L'Esprit des Lois*, dans lequel Montesquieu démontre que l'esclavage s'oppose au droit naturel. Clarkson mentionne avoir lu les Lumières écossaises et particulièrement *Wealth of Nations* d'Adam Smith, paru en 1776. Il explique avoir été « transporté » par ces lectures, ému par la situation ignoble dans laquelle les esclaves étaient vendus, transportés puis traités dans les plantations. Il évoque,

1. Thomas, Clarkson, *The History of the Rise, Progress and Accomplishment of the Abolition of the African Slave Trade by the British Parliament*, (2 vols), London: Longman, Hurst, Rees and Orme, 1808.

dans son *History*, une forme de « révélation » à la lecture de ces textes, qui lui indiquèrent qu'elle était sa nouvelle mission[1].

En d'autres termes, Clarkson s'était familiarisé avec un ensemble de nouvelles idées philosophiques, religieuses et économiques qui circulaient dans les sphères intellectuelles dans cette deuxième partie du XVIIIe siècle[2]. La traite négrière et l'esclavage, son corollaire, étaient devenus intolérables à ces intellectuels ou à ces hommes d'église pour des raisons diverses qui faisaient appel à la « raison » et aux convictions religieuses de chaque individu.

Ainsi, ce ne sont pas des idées nouvelles que Clarkson présentait dans *An Essay on Slavery and Commerce of Human Species, particularly the African, translated from a Latin Dissertation*[3], ou dans les essais qu'il publia au cours des années suivantes[4], mais une synthèse convaincante de toutes les thèses accessibles aux lettrés mais souvent éloignées des préoccupations de la population. La coexistence de discours religieux évangéliques et de discours philosophiques des Lumières dans les textes de Clarkson, des thèses souvent antinomiques en réalité, montre une coïncidence partielle des deux ensembles de discours sur la notion d'humanisme et de loi naturelle.

Dans ce premier essai, Clarkson s'inspire au préalable d'écrits évangéliques sur la bonté (« *benevolence* ») pour expliquer aux Britanniques que la bonté est une valeur morale essentielle et que ce concept a une utilité sociale, particulièrement dans l'abolition du commerce des esclaves. Les Chrétiens doivent y avoir recours pour sauver leurs semblables africains menacés par la violence et le désir du gain des marchands britanniques. La bonté naturelle des Britanniques triomphera naturellement du pêché lorsqu'ils seront sensibilisés à la cruauté de l'esclavage et aux souffrances des individus transportés, puis soudoyés sur les plantations. À l'appui de ses propos, il ajoutera des dessins et des gravures dont nous parlerons plus loin. Par ailleurs, Clarkson croit au progrès moral de la nation britannique, marquée du sceau de la Providence. La nation britannique composée d'une

1. « If the contents of the Essay were true, it was time some person should see these calamities to their end », Clarkson, *History, op. cit.*, vol. 1, ch. 1 p. 28.
2. « The ground was prepared by changes in philosophical and theological ideas », Roger, Anstey, *The Atlantic Slave Trade and British Abolition, 1760-1810*, London: Macmillan, 1975, p. 22.
3. Thomas, Clarkson, *An Essay on the Slavery and Commerce of the Human Species, particularly the African, translated from a Latin Dissertation, which has been honoured with the first prize in the University of Cambridge, for the year 1785*, London: T. Cadell and J. Phillips, 1786.
4. Oldfield note à ce sujet : « *Running to just 16 pages, and small enough at 110 mm x 150 mm, to pass easily from hand to hand, these publications and short pamphlets, were intended to introduce the readers to the subject of the slave-trade* » in J. R., Oldfield, *Popular Politics and British Anti-Slavery, the Mobilization of Public Opinion against the Slave Trade, (1787-1807)*, London: Portland, Frank Cass, 1995, p. 44.

population de croyants et représentée par les membres du Parlement auxquels il s'adressera sans relâche à travers ses pamphlets.

Au discours évangélique, Clarkson mêle le discours des Lumières. Il fait appel à la raison de ses lecteurs en leur proposant des faits et des preuves irréfutables. C'est la démarche qu'il suivra auprès du Parlement lors de ses témoignages devant les députés. Clarkson fait état de la souffrance des esclaves transportés dans des soutes de négriers. Il s'appuie sur des observations produites par James Ramsay et Granville Sharp sur le tonnage des bateaux. Ce sont donc des actions criminelles que le Parlement doit juger pour condamner ceux qui témoignent devant eux que le commerce est légal et qu'ils peuvent posséder des individus et les revendre comme un objet ou un animal dont ils seraient propriétaires.

Puis lorsque l'argument économique est avancé par les marchands et les planteurs qui s'inquiètent d'un empire sans commerce d'esclaves, Clarkson cite Adam Smith pour démontrer à ses lecteurs que le commerce protégé dont se vantent les planteurs est en fait payé en grande partie par les Britanniques eux-mêmes. « *At every point, the mercantile system sacrificed the interest of the consumer of goods, to that of the producer and the merchant. Indeed the home consumers have been burdened with the whole expense of maintaining the empire*[1]. » Le libre-échange avec l'Afrique, avec les colonies françaises et britanniques des Antilles ou les Amériques, rapporterait davantage à la nation et aux consommateurs eux-mêmes que ce commerce de monopole.

Par l'intermédiaire d'un ami quaker, Clarkson l'évangéliste publie sa composition traduite en anglais chez James Phillips, l'imprimeur quaker. Son pamphlet est à l'origine de la création du comité de Londres, en mai 1787, qui prend le nom de *Committee for the Abolition of the Slave Trade*. Autour de Clarkson, le comité compte les neuf Quakers qui étaient les auteurs de la première pétition contre le commerce des esclaves, déposée auprès du Parlement en 1783. Le groupe de Quakers et Clarkson contactèrent le député anglican évangéliste, William Wilberforce car le comité s'était essentiellement regroupé pour distribuer le pamphlet de Clarkson auprès des parlementaires britanniques afin d'intercéder auprès d'eux au nom de la cause abolitionniste. Oldfield explique que : « *The London Committee was conceived as a vehicle 'for procuring such information and Evidence for distributing Clarkson's Essay [on the Inhumanity of the Slave Trade']*[2]. »

1. Extrait de *Wealth of Nations*, cité par l'auteur, Thomas, Clarkson, *An Essay on the Slavery and Commerce of the Human Species, particularly the African, translated from a Latin Dissertation, which has been honoured with the first prize in the University of Cambridge, for the year 1785*, London: T. Cadell and J. Phillips, 1786, p. 7.
2. Oldfield, *op. cit.*, p. 43.

II. Du débat intellectuel à la promotion des idées abolitionnistes auprès du Parlement

Pour mettre en marche une campagne de cette envergure, au départ sur le terrain politique puis auprès du grand public, il fallait utiliser différentes pratiques de « *lobbying* » que les Quakers du comité de Londres avaient déjà pratiquées lors de la pétition de 1783. Clarkson avait aussi de nombreuses idées en la matière. Il s'agissait de faire connaître la cause, celle de l'inhumanité de la traite négrière, par le biais de la publication et de la diffusion de textes et sermons. Parallèlement, il fallait constituer un réseau efficace de comités dans les comtés pour diffuser l'information, proposer des conférences, rallier la population au moment de la signature des pétitions. On pouvait aussi avoir recours à des supports visuels ou des objets ayant trait à la cause abolitionniste, qui pouvaient toucher et émouvoir le grand public, ces classes moyennes et ouvrières qui ne pouvaient s'exprimer directement au Parlement.

Thomas Clarkson s'impliqua dans l'ensemble de ces activités de propagande : à travers la publication de ses essais mettant en avant l'éventail des arguments nécessaires à la compréhension de la traite négrière par le public. Dès 1787, après une longue visite d'observation à Liverpool où il put monter à bord de nombreux bateaux par l'intermédiaire de son ami Middleton[1], il publia *A Summary View of the Slave Trade and the Probable Consequences of Its Abolition*[2]. Dans les conférences qu'il donnait à travers le pays, il eut recours à sa malle (« *African box* ») contenant des objets africains ou des instruments de torture ayant trait à l'esclavage. Mais la démarche de propagande auprès du public était liée à une première étape essentielle, l'introduction d'une motion auprès du Parlement. Pour Clarkson et les quakers, les députés et les Lords devaient être convaincus de l'inhumanité du commerce des esclaves.

Dans un premier temps, le comité de Londres avait pris la décision de concentrer sa campagne sur la traite négrière qui, nécessairement, par ricochet, mettrait rapidement fin à l'esclavage dans les plantations des Antilles, pensaient-ils. Pour éviter l'amalgame entre traite et esclavage dans l'esprit des députés, au sein desquels le lobby des planteurs était toujours puissant en 1787, il s'agissait tout d'abord de convaincre les parlementaires de l'inhumanité de la traite et du fait qu'économiquement la Grande-Bretagne ne bénéficiait aucunement de ce commerce.

1. Charles Middleton, ami du Comité de Londres, ami personnel de Clarkson et grand amiral en charge des ports britanniques auprès de l'Amirauté.
2. Thomas Clarkson, *A Summary View of the Slave Trade*, London: James Phillips, 1787.

Il semblait clair aux abolitionnistes londoniens que le débat devrait d'abord se tenir au Parlement britannique. Wilberforce, soutenu par le Premier ministre lui-même, était persuadé que les preuves apportées par le texte de Clarkson suffirait à convaincre rapidement les députés qu'il fallait mettre un terme à la traite. La distribution du premier texte de Clarkson, *Essay on the Inhumanity of the Slave Trade*, à deux mille exemplaires au départ, visait tous les députés et les Lords, ainsi que quelques personnes influentes en dehors des deux Chambres.

Mais, la motion déposée par Wilberforce en février 1788, qui demandait l'examen de ses propositions pour mettre un terme à la traite lors de la session parlementaire de 1788-89, ne fut acceptée qu'à condition d'un examen préalable du bien-fondé de cette requête par une commission du *Privy Council*. Pour ce faire, le *Privy Council* demandait des preuves, des faits, des témoignages auprès de Wilberforce et auprès de ses opposants, le lobby des marchands et les députés planteurs qui étaient déjà intervenus auprès des deux chambres pour demander une enquête préliminaire pour ralentir le débat.

C'est la nécessité de collecter des preuves et de sélectionner des témoins ayant assisté à l'inhumanité de la traite, ainsi que quelques marins victimes eux-mêmes des mauvais traitements sur les « négriers », qui amena Clarkson sur les routes de Grande-Bretagne pour le comité de Londres. Il est intéressant de prêter attention à cette première visite dans les comtés pour comprendre comment Clarkson collectait des informations et promouvait la cause de l'abolition de la traite auprès de la population.

Le temps était compté car, selon Clarkson, il fallait que le *Privy Council* ait écouté des témoignages des deux parties avant le début de l'année 1789, afin de rédiger un rapport, de l'imprimer et de donner le temps aux Lords et députés de le lire. Le début des débats était prévu pour le mois d'avril 1789 et un vote devait intervenir avant la fin de la session parlementaire, sinon le projet de loi serait abandonné. Par ailleurs, l'examen des témoins fut ralenti par la maladie du roi, qui interrompit la session parlementaire pendant plus de cinq semaines.

Pour collecter un grand nombre d'informations en peu de temps, Clarkson proposa au comité de Londres d'accélérer la création de réseaux de comités afin de leur faire parvenir un tableau comportant une série de questions destinées à interroger des témoins, anciens marins ou boscos à la retraite, anciens chirurgiens sur des négriers, marchands convertis, particulièrement autour de Bristol et de Liverpool[1]. Lui-même équipé de

1. « *My idea was that they should be printed on a small sheet of paper, which should be folded up in seven or eight leaves of the length and breadth of a small almanac, and then be sent to our different*

cette liste de questions prit dans un premier temps la route du sud et des côtes de la Manche, entre le Kent et la Cornouailles :

> *I thought it proper before I took my departure to form a system of questions upon the general subject. These I divided into six tables. The first related to the productions of Africa and the disposition and manners of the natives. The second to the methods of reducing them to slavery. The third to the manner of bringing them to the ships, their value, the medium of exchange and other circumstances. The fourth to their transportation. The fifth to their treatment in the colonies. The sixth to the seamen employed in the trade. These tables contained together 145 questions.*[1]

Lors de ses visites à Poole, Plymouth et Exeter, Clarkson en profite pour créer des réseaux de correspondants autour de comités « *to act in harmony with that of London for the promotion of the cause*[2]. » La plupart des membres fondateurs de ces comités sont quakers et font partie du réseau de diffusion de l'imprimeur Phillips. Ce sont les premiers comités de province après la création de ceux de Bristol et de Manchester, fondés à la suite du comité de Londres. Clarkson continuera à étoffer les réseaux dans les villes moyennes au fur et à mesure de ses déplacements dans les provinces dans les années suivantes. C'est par ces correspondants, acquis à la prose et à la cause de Clarkson, particulièrement après avoir lu son dernier pamphlet, *Essay on the Impolicy of the African Slave Trade*[3], paru la même année, en 1788, que ce dernier reçoit des adresses de témoins à contacter. Persuadé qu'une partie du public apporte déjà son soutien au comité, il pense que les témoins seront facilement convaincus de venir témoigner devant le *Privy Council*.

Loin s'en faut, car parmi les témoins que Clarkson rencontre et qu'il interroge grâce à ses tableaux de questions, nombreux sont ceux qui, bien que convertis à la cause après avoir assisté à des scènes de barbarie sur les bateaux négriers, refusent de témoigner ou de voir leur témoignage consigné par écrit. Clarkson indique : « *After having travelled upward of 1600 miles and having conversed with 47 people, I could only prevail upon 9*[4]. » À la suite de ces neuf témoignages précieusement ramenés à Londres, Clarkson n'obtient finalement qu'une personne qui accepte de témoigner devant les Lords. Selon Clarkson, ces témoins sont choqués par ce qu'ils ont vu, particulièrement les chirurgiens de bord, mais ils craignent pour leur « *patronage* » si leur député venait à apprendre leur implication dans

---

correspondents. These when they had them, might examine persons capable of giving evidence, who might live in their neighbourhoods, and return us their examinations by letter. », Clarkson, *History, op. cit.*, vol.2, p. 9.

1. *Ibid*, p. 9
2. *Ibid*, p. 10.
3. Thomas Clarkson, *Essay on the Impolicy of the Slave Trade*, London: James Phillips, 1788.
4. Clarkson, *History, op. cit.*, vol. 2, ch. 1, p. 11.

la cause abolitionniste, « *they feared to injure their prospects in life* », explique Clarkson.

III. Les auditions devant la Chambre – Clarkson, témoin et avocat

L'oligarchie du Parlement, la non-représentation des classes moyennes, sont des éléments que Clarkson cite comme obstacles à l'avancée de la cause de l'abolition de plus en plus populaire auprès des Britanniques. Il prend pour exemple la première pétition de 1788, envoyée par le comité de Manchester, soutenue par de très nombreuses signatures mais dont l'absence de représentants au Parlement nuit à sa valeur. Pour évoquer le poids de la hiérarchie sociale et des « *rotten boroughs* », il prend aussi le cas d'un médecin de Liverpool dont il avait collecté le témoignage et qu'il retourne voir avant de présenter son nom, en tant que témoin, aux Lords du *Privy Council*. Ce dernier refuse finalement de se présenter au Parlement. Clarkson est agacé par la lâcheté du médecin et par sa bassesse, avant de comprendre que son salaire et le train de vie de sa famille dépendent de ses riches clients, essentiellement des marchands ou d'anciens planteurs :

> *The reader may now conceive the many miserable hours I must have spent, after such visits, in returning home; and how grievously my heart must have been afflicted by these cruel disappointments, but more particularly where they arose from causes inferior to those which have been now mentioned, or from frivolous excuses, or idle and unfounded conjectures, unworthy of beings expected to fill a moral station in life.*
> *Yes, O man! Often in these solitary journeyings have I exclaimed against the baseness of thy nature, when reflecting on the little paltry considerations which have smothered thy benevolence, and hindered thee from succouring an oppressed brother. And yet, on a further view of things, I have reasoned myself into a kinder feeling towards thee.*[1]

La mascarade des entretiens du *Privy Council* semble de plus en plus évidente au comité de Londres. Clarkson est toujours à la recherche de témoins acceptant de se présenter devant les Lords, pour contrecarrer les témoignages fallacieux apportés par l'autre camp. L'un des témoignages — qui sera consigné dans le rapport du *Privy Council* — fait état d'une vie idyllique sur les bateaux négriers où les esclaves auraient tout le confort d'une croisière de passagers de première classe. Pour y répondre, Clarkson ne peut faire état que de questionnaires écrits et de trois témoins qui seront finalement convoqués par les Lords. À ces derniers, il propose en dernier recours de leur présenter son « *African Box* ». Cette malle dotée de plusieurs compartiments contient des objets africains et des

1. *Ibid*, p. 21.

outils utilisés pour soumettre ou torturer des esclaves. Les objets africains ont été collectés auprès des bateaux négriers à Bristol ou Liverpool, où Clarkson se déplace régulièrement pour collecter des informations auprès des marins fraîchement débarqués, de retour d'Afrique et des colonies. Dans sa présentation devant le *Privy Council*, il sélectionne des bois et des produits agricoles pour leur démontrer que l'Afrique n'est pas un pays sans ressource et qu'il est inutile de la piller de ses hommes, alors qu'elle pourrait devenir un partenaire économique important dans une pratique de libre-échange. Il s'agit aussi de leur prouver que l'Afrique n'est pas un continent inférieur à l'Europe, que les Africains pourraient développer leur propre économie si les Blancs les laissaient en paix.

En dernier lieu, Clarkson sélectionne des objets de torture utilisés régulièrement sur les bateaux négriers et mentionnés dans les témoignages écrits des marins interviewés : « *Thumb-screw, speculum oris and chains and shackles of different kinds, collected at Liverpool. To these were added iron neck and collars, and other instruments of punishment and confinement used in the West Indies*[1]. »

Durant la phase de lecture du rapport du *Privy Council* par les députés et les Lords, et en préparation de l'argumentation de Wilberforce dans le débat qui allait suivre au Parlement, Clarkson reprit la plume pour contrer les idées des groupes adverses, les marchands et les planteurs, auprès des députés, mais surtout auprès de la population qu'il fallait continuer à convaincre de la nécessité d'abolir la traite immédiatement. Clarkson était convaincu que les parlementaires, contrairement au peuple, n'étaient pas sensibles à l'argument moral, au discours évangélique ; il fallait donc revenir à un discours constitutionnel ou économique pour leur faire entendre raison :

> *It was soon perceived to be the object of our opponents, to impress upon the public, the preference of regulation to abolition. I attempted therefore to show the fallacy and wickedness of this notion in* An Essay on the Comparative Efficiency of Regulation or Abolition as applied to the Slave Trade.[2]

Fidèle à ses pratiques de diffusion, le comité de Londres fit imprimer le texte rapidement en plusieurs milliers d'exemplaires, envoyés aux membres du réseau et aux parlementaires. Quant au discours de Wilberforce à l'assemblée le 12 mai 1789, il s'appuyait sur l'argumentation de Clarkson et particulièrement sur les propositions listées par ce dernier dans son *Essay on the Impolicy of the Slave Trade*.

1. Clarkson, *History, op. cit.*, vol. 2., p. 13.
2. *Ibid*, ch. 1, p. 79, Thomas, Clarkson, *An Essay on the Comparative Efficiency of Regulation or Abolition, as applied to the Slave Trade. Shewing that the latter only can remove the evils to be found in that commerce*, London: James Phillips, 1789.

Par ailleurs, Clarkson faisant suite à une idée que lui avait soumise son correspondant de Plymouth, fit circuler un plan de coupe d'un bateau négrier, « *which was designed to give the spectator an idea of the sufferings of the Africans in the Middle Passage.* » Clarkson en fait les commentaires, en utilisant des mesures précises pour indiquer l'espace réduit de la soute dans laquelle les esclaves étaient entassés, confinés et enchaînés. Il intègre ce plan en coupe et ses mesures dans son *History* pour rappeler à ses lecteurs que cette preuve visuelle fut un coup de maître pour rallier à la cause le public lors de conférences en province et dans les ports de Bristol et Liverpool :

> *At this point, it seemed to make an instantaneous impression of horror upon all who saw it, and as it was therefore very instrumental in consequence of the wide circulation given of it, it served the cause of the injured Africans.*[1]

Cependant si l'utilisation du plan en coupe d'un négrier fit verser une larme à plus d'un Chrétien que Clarkson rencontra durant ses années de campagne à travers le pays, il ne sembla pas émouvoir les parlementaires britanniques, qui, au contraire, cherchaient à réviser la loi sur le tonnage des bateaux négriers britanniques. Le projet de loi Dolben, du nom du Lord qui l'avait présentée en 1788, indiquait que le « confort » des esclaves sur les bateaux négriers pouvait être amélioré en revoyant le nombre d'esclaves embarqués à la baisse. Cette mesure était un compromis suffisant pour la plupart des parlementaires pour éviter de discuter de l'abolition de la traite. Aussi le plan en coupe du négrier *Brookes* de Liverpool, et les commentaires de Clarkson sur l'exiguïté de la soute dans laquelle étaient entassés les esclaves, permit à certains députés — associés aux marchands —, de souhaiter revoir à la hausse le tonnage (!) d'esclaves embarqués, alors que d'autres constatèrent que le projet de loi Dolben avait même surestimé le nombre d'esclaves pouvant être enfermés dans les soutes[2].

En 1788, comme les années suivantes lorsque Wilberforce présenterait sa motion sur l'abolition du commerce des esclaves devant le Parlement, la cause abolitionniste ne fut pas entendue. Environ un tiers des députés soutenait la cause pour des raisons humanistes, mais le reste de l'assemblée semblait soit peu intéressée par le sujet, soit soutenir les lobbys des marchands et des planteurs. Le comité de Londres subit son premier échec. Dans ce commentaire écrit vingt ans après les faits, Clarkson semble peiné par l'inhumanité de ces députés :

1. Clarkson, *History*, *op. cit.*, vol. 2, p. 80.
2. « *After measuring the Brookes from Liverpool, the House of Commons realized that the Dolben Bill had allowed 150 more slaves on board than could actually have lived there. Before the Bill restrictions, it had carried 609 slaves!* », Clarkson, *History*, *op. cit.*, vol. 2, p. 83.

It would be idle not to confess that circumstances had occurred, which wounded us deeply. Though we had foiled our opponents at their own weapons, and had experienced the uninterrupted good wishes and support of the public, we had the great mortification to see the enthusiasm of members of Parliament beginning to cool; to see a question of humanity and justice (for such it was when it was delivered into their hands) verging towards that of commercial calculations, and finally to see regulation [the Dolben Bill] substituted for abolition.[1]

IV. Clarkson, ambassadeur de la cause abolitionniste en France

Dans son premier grand discours à la Chambre, William Wilberforce avait souhaité que le Parlement britannique soit le premier en Europe à voter l'abolition du commerce des esclaves afin que d'autres empires, la France, l'Espagne, le Portugal, suivent leur exemple vertueux. Pour se justifier face aux critiques des députés qui lui rappelaient qu'arrêter la traite, c'était permettre aux Français de renforcer leur propre commerce en affaiblissant les colonies sucrières britanniques dans les Caraïbes, Wilberforce cita une lettre de Necker dans laquelle ce dernier faisait part de son souhait de mettre fin à la traite négrière dans l'Empire français. Necker, ainsi que Louis XVI, avaient reçu dans un volume magnifiquement relié les deux premiers essais de Clarkson, envoyé par le comité de Londres[2].

Aussi, à la suite du vote négatif des parlementaires britanniques en 1789, Wilberforce suggère à Clarkson de se rendre en France afin de persuader les membres influents de la « Société des Amis des Noirs » de faire voter au plus vite, par l'Assemblée Nationale, l'abolition de la traite dans leur Empire. Clarkson préférait reprendre la route pour collecter de nouveaux témoignages pour convaincre les Parlementaires lors d'une prochaine audition. Wilberforce lui indiqua que le contexte politique français — l'élaboration d'une nouvelle constitution basée sur de nouveaux principes de liberté, d'égalité et de fraternité —, était propice au vote d'une loi sur l'abolition. Une fois les Français convaincus pour des raisons philosophiques de mettre fin à la traite, les parlementaires britanniques ne pourraient qu'accepter de suivre leurs rivaux, sur la même voie, pour des raisons économiques :

Mr Wilberforce was of opinion that as commotions had taken place in France, which then aimed at political reforms, it was possible that the leading persons concerned in them might, if an application was made to them judiciously,

1. *Ibid*, vol. 2, p. 87.
2. La même année d'autres volumes reliés sont envoyés aux cours d'Europe et aux ambassadeurs britanniques. Le comité contacte Benjamin Frossard de Lyon, abolitionniste convaincu, de traduire les essais de Clarkson en français.

be induced to take the slave-trade into their consideration and incorporate it among the abuses to be done away.[1]

À Paris, Clarkson rencontre les membres de la « Société des Amis des Noirs », le duc de la Rochefoucauld, le marquis de La Fayette, le comte de Mirabeau, le marquis de Condorcet, Clavière, Brissot et quelques autres dont il découvrira au bout d'un mois qu'ils étaient des espions à la solde de planteurs et des marchands du Havre. Lors d'une première rencontre, Clarkson convainc les « Amis » de demander une audience le plus rapidement à Necker afin de mettre la question de l'abolition de la traite à l'ordre du jour de l'Assemblée. En contre-partie les Français demandent au comité de Londres une pétition qui serait envoyée à l'Assemblée nationale. Clarkson refuse de s'engager dans cette démarche politique, laissant aux Français le soin de gérer leur propre campagne sans intervention de la part des Britanniques. Une certaine presse à la solde des planteurs français dénonçait sa présence à Paris. Clarkson était déjà traité d'espion et d'agitateur ; il reçut des lettres de menace. Il ne souhaitait pas nourrir une rancœur auprès du gouvernement britannique ou du Parlement en faisant connaître sa présence à Paris.

À Paris, il rencontre des députés créoles venus de St Domingue, qui attendent eux aussi une audience auprès de l'Assemblée pour réclamer l'égalité de leurs droits politiques et un siège de député pour représenter leur île. À plusieurs reprises, Clarkson mentionne le fait qu'ils perdent patience et qu'ils envisagent de prendre les armes à leur retour si la constitution ne leur reconnaît pas une existence légale[2]. Lorsque la révolte de St Domingue éclatera en 1791, Clarkson rappellera aux députés britanniques les réelles circonstances politiques de cette rébellion, là où les MPs ne voyaient que sauvagerie et barbarie du Noir contre le colon blanc. À ce titre, Clarkson se fera traiter de Jacobin par les députés britanniques.

Les Français sont divisés sur le moment le plus opportun pour déposer un projet de loi sur la traite. La Fayette pense qu'il faut attendre que la constitution soit complètement terminée et qu'une nouvelle assemblée soit élue pour proposer une réforme sur le commerce d'esclaves. Seul Mirabeau envisage un dépôt de motion immédiatement. Il donne d'ailleurs son discours à relire à Clarkson, en lui demandant de lui fournir preuves et témoignages nécessaires pour convaincre les députés de la nécessité d'abolir la traite rapidement, avant d'interdire complètement l'esclavage. Clarkson, persuadé par le tribun que ses recherches feront avancer la cause en France, puis en Grande-Bretagne, reprend son travail de collectes de

1. Clarkson, *History, op. cit.*, vol. 2, p. 89.
2. *Ibid*, p. 108.

sources auprès de témoins ayant séjourné dans l'île de Gorée[1]. Il apporte aussi à Mirabeau des informations et des observations recueillies par son propre frère sur les bateaux marchands, en 1788, dans le port du Havre.

Pour poursuivre son travail de promotion de la cause abolitionniste auprès des députés français, normalement plus libéraux que les députés britanniques, Clarkson se fait envoyer un ensemble de documents déjà utilisés auprès des parlementaires de son pays et auprès de la population britannique, pour les toucher et les émouvoir, « *as preparatory to the motion of Mirabeau* ». On y trouve ses essais, des images en couleur de scènes de traite, mais aussi son plan du négrier *Brookes* :

> *A large packet, for which I had sent from England arrived. It consisted of above a thousand plan and section of a slave-ship, with an explanation in French. Also about 500 coloured engravings made from two views taken in Africa [one view representing a mother and child refusing to board a slave-ship]. I had collected by this time one thousand of my Essay on the Impolicy, which had been translated into French language.*[2]

Le résultat est immédiat parmi les membres du clergé : « *this distribution had not been long before I witnessed its effects.* » Clarkson est convoqué par l'Abbé Grégoire et l'archevêque de Chartres, ainsi que par quelques députés, touchés en tant que chrétiens par les arguments de Clarkson. L'archevêque d'Aix lui avoue avoir été converti à la cause abolitionniste dont il avait entendu les arguments auparavant, sans avoir été convaincu. Mais les lobbys des planteurs et marchands se réveillèrent aussi à la suite de cette distribution intempestive de tracts par un espion anglais. La rumeur arrive même au roi, qui demande à lire en français les textes de Clarkson. Pendant ce temps, Clarkson continue de collecter des preuves pour Mirabeau, qui finalement lui fait part de l'impossibilité de trouver des députés favorables à une motion et un débat, au vu de la situation politique de la France en décembre 1789.

Clarkson rentre à Londres, déçu d'avoir perdu son temps auprès des Français alors qu'il aurait pu, explique-t-il, consacrer les six derniers mois à œuvrer pour la cause abolitionniste en Grande-Bretagne. Clarkson en conclut que les parlementaires britanniques, comme les parlementaires français en dépit de leurs discours épris de liberté et d'égalité, sont tout aussi oligarchiques. Les assemblées servent à faire avancer les prérogatives

1. Thomas, Clarkson, *Letters on the Slave-Trade, and the State of the Natives in those Parts of Africa, which are contiguous to Fort St Louis and Goree, etc.*, London: James Phillips, 1791. Série de lettres envoyées à Mirabeau à partir d'informations recueillies auprès de Français ayant séjourné au Sénégal.
2. Clarkson, *History, op. cit.*, vol. 2, p. 109.

des possédants, marchands et planteurs, contre le progrès moral et les intérêts des peuples. Clarkson radicalise son discours.

V. Le discours radical de Clarkson face aux échecs successifs de la loi sur l'abolition de la traite au Parlement

Dans son *History* publiée en 1808, Clarkson fait état de chaque débat à la Chambre des Communes, de chaque argument avancé par les anti-abolitionnistes, citant des noms, des propos, souvent choquants. Clarkson oppose ces débats longs et biaisés à l'infatigable ténacité de Wilberforce face à l'indifférence des députés ou de leur inhumanité. Il y consigne, pour chaque nouvelle motion, son inlassable quête de nouveaux témoins à présenter aux députés. En effet, à chaque présentation d'une motion, presque tous les ans jusqu'en 1807, les députés britanniques exigent d'entendre de nouveaux témoins, de nouvelles preuves. Les audiences sont ouvertes désormais, mais les députés semblent se lasser, même les plus acquis à la cause, par les mêmes histoires racontées chaque année. Pour Clarkson, cependant, chaque nouvelle motion signifie un nouveau voyage à travers le pays, à la recherche de nouveaux témoins.

Mais Clarkson est désormais convaincu que les parlementaires, contrairement au peuple, ne sont pas sensibles à l'argument moral, au discours évangélique. Il indique dans ses mémoires avoir été affecté davantage que ses amis du Comité par le peu de réactions des députés devant les preuves souvent insoutenables qu'il leur avait apportées lors des auditions successives. En collectant ces centaines de témoignages sur les routes et en lisant la dizaine de lettres qu'il recevait quotidiennement rapportant les atrocités du transport des esclaves et de leur enlèvement sur les côtes africaines, envoyées par des marins ou des boscos, Clarkson était le premier exposé à la barbarie humaine. Dans son rapport de 1808, il raconte à ses lecteurs ces nombreuses nuits sans sommeil, hantées par des images d'esclaves torturés, ou ces milliers de kilomètres parcourus à cheval à travers le pays, souvent en vain.

> *It had fallen to my lot, more than to that of any other person, to know these evils, and I seemed almost inconsolable of the postponement of the question. I wondered how members of Parliament, and these Englishmen [merchants and planters] could talk as they did on this subject, how they could bear for a moment to consider their fellow-men as an article of trade.*[1]

Clarkson est convaincu qu'il existe un décalage inadmissible entre le Parlement et le peuple britannique sur le sujet de la traite négrière. À

1. Clarkson, *History, op. cit.*, vol. 2, p. 87. Cette remarque est répétée annuellement à chaque échec de la motion présentée par Wilberforce.

plusieurs reprises, à la suite des échecs successifs de motions, soutenues par des pétitions, Clarkson souligne l'extraordinaire écart entre l'humanité du peuple britannique et l'inhumanité des députés qui à ses yeux deviennent de plus en plus illégitimes comme représentants du peuple : « *It was some consolation to us to know that our cause had not suffered with their constituents,* the people. *These were still warmly with us*[1]. »

On atteint le summum de la division entre le peuple et son Parlement en 1792, lorsque des pétitions arrivent de toutes parts, émanant des comités abolitionnistes qui les font signer par des milliers de Britanniques :

> *In 1791 this prejudice [the prejudice of the MPs against the committee] arrived at its growth… But the nation had never deserted the cause during this whole period. It is much to the honour of the English people, that they should have continued to feel for the existence of an evil which was so far removed from their sight.*[2]

Par ailleurs, le public, et particulièrement les classes moyennes et supérieures, boycottent les produits provenant des Antilles britanniques. Clarkson note qu'il s'agit d'une réaction spontanée à la suite du rejet du projet de loi en 1791. Clarkson décrit cette démarche comme émanant directement et spontanément de comités de province en signe de protestation contre le Parlement et son soutien du lobby marchand : « *But at this moment their feelings [the people's] began to be insupportable. Many of them resolved, as soon as parliament had rejected the bill, to abstain from the use of West Indian produce*[3]. »

Clarkson qui parcourt le pays en 1792, en distribuant son dernier essai, en fait une collection de preuves irréfutables contre l'atrocité du commerce des esclaves, telles qu'elles avaient déjà été présentées au Parlement, rencontre inlassablement des comités qui se mobilisent pour faire signer des pétitions : « *Public meetings took place, and after this petitions were sent to parliament; and these so generally, that there was not a day for three months, Sundays excepted, in which five or six were not resolved upon in some places or other in the kingdom*[4]. » Cette année-là, en dépit de la force de l'argument populaire, du nombre de pétitions qui atteignent un record jamais atteint — « *they breathed the voice of the people* » —, comme l'explique Clarkson, le Parlement rejeta à nouveau la motion de Wilberforce, en proposant à la place d'abolir progressivement le commerce des esclaves pour l'interdire en 1796.

1. *Ibid*, p. 133 (passage mis en valeur dans le texte).
2. *Ibid*, p. 247.
3. *Ibid*, p. 248.
4. Clarkson, *History, op. cit.*, vol. 2, p. 251.

D'après Clarkson, en promettant d'abolir progressivement le commerce des esclaves, les députés cherchaient à amadouer le peuple. C'était une manœuvre politique qui consistait à repousser le débat et à renvoyer cette nouvelle proposition devant les Lords pour gagner du temps, une session parlementaire. La manœuvre réussit puisque les classes moyennes recommencèrent à manger du sucre. En commentant le rejet de la motion en 1792, Clarkson rappelait que la rétribution de Dieu finirait par s'abattre sur ceux qui pêchaient contre l'humanité, et contre le droit naturel du peuple « *in the year 1792, when the national enthusiasm was so great, the good were as distinguishable from the bad, according to their disposition to this great cause, as if the divine Being had marked them… on the day of judgment*[1] ».

Ce n'est qu'en février 1807 que Clarkson semble retrouver foi en son Parlement, un Parlement dont les députés ont été renouvelés en partie puisque que désormais les électeurs de la *upper-class* prenaient en compte les positions de leur député sur le commerce des esclaves. Parallèlement, ces mêmes électeurs commençaient à rejeter les « *nababs* » et les planteurs qui revenaient, enrichis par des pratiques illicites, s'acheter une députation en Grande-Bretagne. En observant la manière dont les députés se comportent au moment du vote final de la loi, Clarkson trouve chez ces nouveaux parlementaires un certain enthousiasme « *which was of moral nature* ». Quant à ceux qui par le passé avaient critiqué et dénigré la cause, Clarkson observe qu'ils s'éloignèrent au moment du vote. Clarkson souligne l'engagement vertueux de ces nouveaux députés au nom des Africains opprimés.

En 1808, lorsque Clarkson conclut son *History*, il revient sur l'expérience nationale que le pays a vécue ces vingt dernières années. Pour l'anglican évangéliste, la longue lutte que viennent de mener les abolitionnistes, parlementaires ou simples individus, a été un test de la Providence envoyé à la nation britannique. Clarkson y voit une forme de rédemption nationale, nécessaire aux Britanniques pour distinguer au sein de leur nation le bien du mal :

> *It [the very agitation of the question] has been useful also in the discrimination of moral character. In private life it has enabled us to distinguish the virtuous from the more vicious part of the community.*[2]

Mais on reconnaît, dans ces remarques finales, un certain discours radical que Clarkson a souvent eu du mal à dissimuler malgré ses emportements contre l'inhumanité des députés. Clarkson souligne ici la nécessité de réformer le Parlement, qui ne représente plus le peuple britannique, et particulièrement les classes moyennes dont l'accès au vote est toujours

1. *Ibid*, p. 413.
2. *Ibid*, p. 412.

limité. Ceux dont les valeurs morales sont justes devraient être représentés par des leaders à leur image, comme cette campagne contre la traite l'a montré à de maintes reprises.

> *It [the debate over the slave-trade] has separated the moral statesman from the wicked politician. It has shown us who, in the legislative and executive offices of our country are fit to save, and who to destroy, a nation.*[1]

Conclusion

En 1808, Clarkson n'envisage pas nécessairement de poursuivre la campagne pour obtenir l'abolition de l'esclavage. Pour lui, il semble essentiel de faire respecter l'application de la loi sur le commerce des esclaves en contrôlant les bateaux en partance des ports britanniques. Il note avec plaisir que la mère-patrie et ses ex-colonies américaines appliquent la même année, en 1808, l'interdiction du commerce des esclaves, faisant triompher ainsi l'esprit anglais de liberté à travers une partie du monde, qu'il décrit comme « *a national virtue.* » C'est ce patriotisme et la nécessité de convaincre les autres empires d'arrêter la traite qui le font reprendre sa démarche d'ambassadeur en direction de l'Europe. Clarkson se rendra à Paris en 1814 en préparation du Congrès de Vienne, le lieu où la question de l'abolition de la traite sera discutée l'année suivante et inscrite dans le texte final.

Étrangement, en conclusion de son *History*, si Clarkson mentionne le fait que les Africains sont désormais libérés de la menace britannique, il ajoute que ce sont les Britanniques qui sont libérés collectivement de la barbarie que la nation nourrissait en son sein : « *We have been freed (alas, if it be not too late!) from a load of guilt, which has long hung like a mill-stone about our necks, ready to sink us to perdition*[2]. » Si la métaphore du « *Ancient Mariner* » se voulait poétique, les termes semblaient mal choisis dans le cadre de la traite négrière. Clarkson suggérait que la campagne abolitionniste avait été menée pour libérer le peuple britannique du poids de la culpabilité engendrée par deux siècles d'esclavage dans l'Empire britannique.

1. Clarkson, *History, op. cit.*, vol. 2, p. 412.
2. *Ibid*, p. 414.

Bibliographie

Thomas, Clarkson, *An Essay on the Slavery and Commerce of the Human Species, particularly the African, translated from a Latin Dissertation, which has been honoured with the first prize in the University of Cambridge, for the year 1785*, London: T. Cadell and J. Phillips, 1786.

—, *A Summary View of the Slave Trade*, London: James Phillips, 1787.

—, *Essay on the Impolicy of the Slave Trade*, London: James Phillips, 1788.

—, *An Essay on the Comparative Efficiency of Regulation or Abolition, as applied to the Slave Trade. Shewing that the latter only can remove the evils to be found in that commerce*, London: James Phillips, 1789.

—, *Letters on the Slave-Trade, and the State of the Natives in those Parts of Africa, which are contiguous to Fort St Louis and Goree, etc.*, London: James Phillips, 1791.

—, *The History of the Rise, Progress and Accomplishment of the Abolition of the African Slave Trade by the British Parliament*, (2 vols), London: Longman, Hurst, Rees and Orme, 1808.

Roger, Anstey, *The Atlantic Slave Trade and British Abolition, 1760-1810*, London: Macmillan, 1975.

David Brion Davis, *The Problem of Slavery in Western Culture*, Ithaca, New York: Cornell University Press, 1966.

Seymour, Drescher, *Capitalism and Antislavery: British Mobilization in Comparative Perspective*, London, Basingstoke: Macmillan, 1986.

J. R., Oldfield, *Popular Politics and British Anti-Slavery, the Mobilization of Public Opinion against the Slave Trade, (1787-1807)*, London: Portland, Frank Cass, 1995.

James, Walvin, *Black and White, the Negro and English Society, 1555-1945*, London: Allan Lane, Penguin, 1973.

Women's Role in the British Anti-Slavery Movement, 1787-1840

Véronique Molinari

"Where they existed, they did everything", George Thompson wrote to Anne Knight about Ladies' anti-slavery societies in 1834. *"They formed the cement of the whole Antislavery building—without their aid we never should have been united."* Thompson's tribute to the work done by women in the campaign for the abolition of slavery is not the only one. George Stephen, writing to Harriet Beecher Stowe in 1854, also acknowledged that anti-slavery meetings had been little attended before it was agreed to admit women and attributed the change *"to the affectionate influence which women rightfully exert in persuading their male relatives to join in matters that interest their best feelings"*. *"Yet"*, he pointed out, *"their admission was long resisted on the ground that their presence lowered the dignity of the subject."*[1]

Women's contribution to the anti-slavery movement certainly deserves some attention, not only because of what it tells us about women's status in the early 19th century, but because of the impact it had on the form and direction of the campaign. Not only did women play a key role in the mobilization of public support that was essential to the fight, they also exerted concerted and effective influence on the anti-slavery crusade and were the ones who, to a large extent, steered the movement from gradualism to immediatism.

The campaign against the slave trade

The campaign against the slave trade that started in the late 1780s was initially a predominantly male movement as both social conventions and their exclusion from the political sphere precluded women from taking an active and formal part. The *Society for the Abolition of the Slave Trade* set up in 1787 by Thomas Clarkson and Granville Sharp was an exclusively male organization and there never was at that time any question that women might be allowed to sign the petitions that were submitted to Parliament—not to mention voting or sitting in one of the two Houses.[2] Women were not totally absent from the fight—poetesses such as Hannah

1. George Stephen, *Antislavery Recollections in A Series of Letters Addressed to Mrs Beecher Stowe*, London: Thomas Hatchard, 1854, Letter xiii, 5th October 1854, p.198.
2. In 1792, Norwich radicals suggested sending a separate women's petition to Parliament but the petition never materialised. A few ladies' names later appeared on some petitions but this participation, when it was discovered, was both unexpected and undesirable.

More, Anna Laetitia Barbauld, Helen Maria Williams, Ann Yearsley and Maria and Harriett Falconar contributed a large amount of poetry between 1788 and 1791[1] and records show that women represented about ten per cent of the financial supporters of the *Society for the Abolition of the Slave Trade*[2]—but their contribution was limited and mostly of an informal kind.

Women's involvement in the campaign began on a larger scale when, following the defeat of a bill presented to the House of Commons by Wilberforce in 1791, the *London Committee for the Abolition of the Slave Trade* decided to change its tactics and appeal directly to the people through public meetings, lectures, petitions and pamphlets. As the government had refused to act, William Fox explained in a popular pamphlet, it was now up to the people to put an end to the slave trade by refusing to purchase and abstaining from the use of West Indian slave-grown sugar.[3] Women's contribution was essential to the new campaign. As a journalist concluded in a report on abstention: *"City meetings might make resolutions upon resolutions in such a business to little purpose indeed, unless we first gain over our wives and daughters"*.[4] As with other reforms that courted women's support, men's appeals for them to become active on behalf of distant slaves were founded on moral arguments and the recognition of woman's moral "influence" in society. Women therefore focused on the evil of consuming slave-grown produce while men concentrated on lobbying Parliament, an approach which, as Midgley points out, *"had the effect of assigning responsibility for slaver to the buyer—commonly female—of slave-grown sugar and cotton in Britain, as much as to the slave holder in the West Indies. In other words, women's approach 'brought home' the issue of slavery, turning it from an issue of colonial and commercial policy into a domestic matter"*.[5] In the following decades, in keeping with propriety and respectability, women were nevertheless meant to operate within a sphere of activity largely separate from the men's.[6]

1. J. R. Oldfield, *Popular Politics and British Anti-Slavery, The Mobilisation of Public Opinion against the Slave Trade 1787-1807*, Manchester: M.U.P., 1995, p.135.
2. Clare Midgley, *Women against Slavery, The British Campaigns 1780-1870*, London: Routledge, 1995, p.17. Midgley also notices that only a quarter of female subscribers appeared to be related to male subscribers, which suggests a decision taken independently of male relatives. These women were mainly of the 'middling sort'—wives and daughters of merchants, professionals, manufacturers and shopkeepers—drawn from Quaker, Unitarian and Evangelical families.
3. William Fox, *An Address to the People of Great Britain on the Utility of Refraining from West Indian Sugar and Rum*, 1791. The pamphlet passed through thirteen editions and 100,000 was distributed within a year.
4. *Chester Chronicle*, 2/12/1791, dans Clare Midgley *op.cit.*, p.37.
5. Clare Midgley, *op.cit.*, p.202
6. At the peak of the abstention campaign (1791-2) an estimated 300,000 people participated in the boycott of slave-grown sugar. Karen I. Halbersleben, *Women's Participation in the British Antislavery movement 1824-1865*, Lewiston: The Edwin Mellen Press, 1993, p.12.

The Campaign against slavery: from gradualism to immediatism

Although the transportation of slaves in British ships as well as their importation to British colonies was finally outlawed in 1807, it soon became obvious that the legislation was not effective and that the institution itself showed no sign of weakening. New organisations were then formed to campaign against slavery, the most important of which was the *Society for the Mitigation and Gradual Abolition of Slavery Throughout the British Dominions*, known as the *Anti-Slavery Society*, founded in 1823. The *Society* sought to improve the lives of the slaves in British colonies and obtain the abolition of slavery through a gradual process, arguing that demanding too much all at once would alienate Parliament. Its members included men such as Thomas Clarkson, Henry Brougham, William Wilberforce and Thomas Fowell Buxton. Throughout this period, the movement remained mostly conservative and Parliament-based, which, once again, precluded the organised contribution of women. When petitions against slavery were resumed, from 1810, women were still rarely allowed the right to sign them.

However, as the 1820s progressed and the failure of the 1807 legislation to hasten emancipation became clear, impatience with the lack of visible accomplishment in Parliament grew. It was at that time, in 1824, that Elizabeth Heyrick, the first woman to appear on the abolitionist scene, published her influential pamphlet, *Immediate not Gradual Emancipation*, which immediately went into three editions in Britain. Opposition to slavery, Heyrick argued, was not only a political issue but a Christian crusade.

> Should the numerous petitions to Parliament be ultimately successful; "she wrote,"—should the prayer for gradual emancipation be granted; still, how vague and indefinite would be the benefit resulting from such success [...] who can calculate the tears and groans, the anguish and despair; —the tortures and outrages which may be added, during the term of that protracted interval, to the enormous mass of injuries already sustained by the victims of West Indian bondage? [...] Why then in the name of humanity, of common sense, and common honesty, do we petition Parliament, year after year, for a gradual abolition of this horrid system [...]? Why petition Parliament at all, to do that for us, which, were they ever so well disposed, we can do more speedily and more effectually ourselves? [...] The very able mover of the question in Parliament last year, proposed that our colonial slavery should be suffered— "to expire of itself, —to die a natural death. —But a natural death, it never will die. —It must be crushed at once, or not at all. While the abolitionists are endeavouring gradually to enfeeble and kill it by inches, it will gradually

> discover the means of reinforcing its strength, and will soon defy all the puny attacks of its assailants.
> Away then with the puerile cant about gradual emancipation. Let the galling ignominious chains of slavery be struck off, at once, from these abused and suffering, these patient, magnanimous creatures.[1]

The tract was a violent attack on gradualism and a passionate plea in favour of the immediate emancipation of the slaves in the British colonies. The British people, not Parliament, were to be the means through which the evil of slavery was to be removed. This position differed radically from the official policy of the *Anti-Slavery Society* that believed in gradual abolition. The leadership of the organisation attempted to suppress information about the existence of this pamphlet and William Wilberforce gave out instructions for leaders of the movement not to speak at women's anti-slavery societies.

Heyrick then organised a sugar boycott in Leicester and with the help of Lucy Townsend, Mary Lloyd, Sarah Wedgwood and Sophia Sturge, helped to form the *Birmingham Ladies Society for the Relief of Negro Slaves*[2] on 8th April, 1825. Many of the founding members came from prominent Quaker families but key positions were taken by evangelical women, such as Lucy Townsend. In many ways, the *Birmingham Ladies' Society* acted as a national rather than a local organisation. Its district treasurers, responsible for collecting funds and arousing local interest, were scattered not only through the Midlands but further afield. In 1826-27, the *Society* handled over £823 (more than half the sum received in subscriptions and donations by the national *Anti-Slavery Society* in 1827) and distributed nearly 35,000 items of propaganda.[3]

Following the lead provided by Heyrick, a new generation of antislavery leaders, men and women, sought to reorganize the antislavery movement for a more direct assault on the institution of slavery. Gradual, intermediate programmes that deferred real emancipation and methods such as petitioning, deemed inefficient, were rejected. The slave trade could not be effectively suppressed until slavery itself was abolished. This shift in strategy from gradualism to immediatism, itself to a large extent initiated by women, is what opened the door of the movement for women's participation in an organised way, first as auxiliaries to men's groups, then as independent associations. Following the *Birmingham Ladies' Society*, other

1. Elizabeth Heyrick, *Immediate, not Gradual Emancipation*, London: Hatchard, 1824, pp.12-19.
2. Later the group changed its name to the *Female Society for Birmingham*.
3. Louis & Rosamund Billington, "'A Burning Zeal for Righteousness': Women in the British Anti-Slavery Movement, 1820-1860", in Jane Rendall (ed.), *Equal or Different, Women's Politics, 1800-1914*, Oxford: Blackwell, 1987, p.86.

independent women's groups were soon created. This included groups in Nottingham (led by Ann Taylor Gilbert), Sheffield (Mary Ann Rawson and Mary Roberts), Leicester (Elizabeth Heyrick and Susanna Watts), Glasgow (Jane Smeal), Norwich (Amelia Alderson Opie and Anna Gurney), London (Mary Anne Schimmelpenninck, Mary Foster), Darlington (Elizabeth Pease), Chelmsford (Anne Knight) and, later, Edinburgh (Eliza Wigham). To Elizabeth Heyrick, the creation of Ladies' Anti-Slavery Associations was essential to the success of the cause and she called other women to join or form such associations:

> Though we have no voice in the senate, no influence in public meetings, though no signatures of ours are attached to anti-slavery petitions to the legislature, yet we have a voice and an influence in a sphere, which, though restricted, is no narrow one. To the hearts and consciences of our own sex, at least, we have unlimited access. By dispelling their ignorance, disseminating among them correct information of the nature and consequences of West Indian slavery, and dissuading them from all participation in its guilt, by a conscientious rejection of its produce, we may withdraw its resources and undermine its foundations [...] Let us emulate the truly Christian zeal of the first institution of Ladies' Anti-Slavery Associations, and strive to our utmost ability to increase their activity and to multiply their number.[1]

Women wishing to act on behalf of the slaves were recommended three kinds of attack: spreading information about the evils of slavery, raising money for the national organisation and promoting the use of free produce. This move towards the creation of women's associations did not go unopposed. Wilberforce, for one, believed that *"for Ladies to meet, to publish, to go from house to house stirring up petitions"* were *"proceedings unsuited to the female character as delineated in Scripture"*[2] and objected to their activities being reported in the *Anti-Slavery Monthly Reporter* (the organ of the *Anti-Slavery Society*). Such positions however became a minority. In the absence of progress in Parliament, extra-parliamentary activities became essential to the campaign and the *Anti-Slavery Society* had no choice but to acknowledge the growing importance of women's contribution. By the early 1830s, there were 73 women's organisations campaigning against slavery. Most of these supported the immediate emancipation of slaves and saw gradualism as dangerous to the cause.

The first anti-slavery society in Britain to call for the immediate emancipation of slaves was a female one: the *Sheffield Female Society,* in 1827. Other women's groups quickly followed and attempted to persuade the leadership of the *Anti-Slavery Society*. The fact that women were excluded

1. Elizabeth Heyrick, *Apology for Ladies' Anti-Slavery Associations*, London: Hatchard, 1828, pp.8-11.
2. Wilberforce, 31 January 1826, in Clare Midgley, *op.cit.*, p.48.

from the committee of the *Anti-Slavery Society* and, unlike delegates from local men's auxiliaries, they could not speak or vote at the *Society*'s annual meetings, made it difficult for them to influence directly the Society to change its gradualist policy. Other methods, however, could be used. Abstention from slave-grown sugar was one of those but not the only one.

Ladies' anti-slavery associations had promoted the slave-grown sugar boycott systematically from 1825. Members of women's anti-slavery societies throughout Britain canvassed door to door, handing out pamphlets arguing that using East Indian sugar was a moral obligation to avoid complicity in the sin of slaveholding. By 1828 the *Anti-Slavery Society*, lamenting the lack of progress achieved by its own approach of petitioning for amelioration and gradual abolition, issued appeals to women which acknowledged that abstention was now one of the main channels left for achieving progress towards emancipation. When, that same year, Heyrick published *Appeal to the Hearts and Consciences of British Women*, 1,500 copies were bought by the *Anti-Slavery Society* for distribution. In it Heyrick explained:

> BY THE SIMPLE SUBSTITUTION OF EAST FOR WEST INDIA SUGAR, THE SLAVE-OWNERS THEMSELVES CONFESS THAT SLAVERY MAY BE ANNIHILATED. To effect its annihilation by this simple means, to whom can we appeal with such propriety as to our enlightened and patriotic country-women? In the domestic department they are the chief controllers; they, for the most part, provide the articles of family consumption; instead of purchasing that luxury, the cultivation of which constitutes at once the chief profits and oppressions of slavery, they can substitute that which is the genuine produce of free labour, and by so doing become a blessing to existing and unborn millions. By the simple substitution of East for West India sugar, they may save their impoverished country the annual tax of THREE MILLIONS now paid in the direct support of slavery; they may save the annual sacrifice of more than two thousand lives of British soldiers in the ignoble enterprise of maintaining a system abhorrent to British Law and British feeling.[1]

Women could also attempt to influence national policy by arousing public opinion thanks to pamphlets, petition drives and canvassing. Literature and lectures depicting the cruelties and physical outrages inflicted on black women and their children and relating attacks on the sanctity of the home, body and family were thought to be particularly effective in appealing to women's maternal feelings and sensitive nature.[2]

1. Elizabeth Heyrick, *Appeal To The Hearts And Consciences Of British Women*, Leicester: A. Cockshaw, 1828, p.6.
2. *"The sensitive nature of woman must dispose her to regard with peculiar hostility an institution which rudely tears asunder all the strongest ties of nature, and subjects the sex to the most degrading and brutal coercion"*. Elizabeth Heyrick, *Apology for Ladies' Anti-Slavery Associations, op.cit.*, p.3.

Finally, women, who, in some areas, such as Manchester, made up over a quarter of all subscribers, could certainly exert financial pressure on the *Anti-Slavery Society* for a change of policy. Thus, when in April 1830 the *Female Society for Birmingham* submitted a resolution to the National Conference of the *Society* calling for the organisation to campaign for an immediate end to slavery in the British colonies, Heyrick, who was treasurer of the organisation, suggested that the society should threaten to withdraw its funding if the organisation did not support this resolution.[1] This was a serious threat as the *Birmingham Society* was one of the largest local society contributors to central funds and was extremely influential over the network of ladies' associations, which had supplied over a fifth of all donations the previous year. As a consequence, the *Anti-Slavery Society*, at its May 1830 conference, agreed to drop the words "mitigation and gradual abolition" from its title. It also agreed to support the *Female Society*'s plan for a new campaign to bring about immediate abolition.

By that time, tensions had started building between abolitionists like Thomas Buxton (who had taken over the role of anti-slavery leader and spokesman in Parliament since Wilberforce's retirement), who favoured the use of parliamentary means to achieve gradual abolition, and the newer generation of abolitionists, such as George Stephen and Joseph Sturge, who looked to more comprehensive means of action for more immediate results. These tensions resulted in an unofficial split within the *Anti-Slavery Society* in 1832. The *Agency Committee*, a subcommittee of the society composed of the more radical abolitionists, chose to forgo parliamentary action to rely on direct appeal to public conscience, emphasizing the moral side of the issue and insisting that immediatism was the only acceptable option. It was the *Agency Committee*, rather than the *Anti-Slavery Society*, that obtained the support of most ladies' societies. The *Birmingham Ladies' Society* thus stopped donating money to the Society and gave it instead to the Committee, soon followed by thirteen other women's groups which, in all, provided nearly a third of the Committee's funds.[2]

The success of the anti-slavery movement through the 1830s rested on a variety of mass agitation techniques such as large public meetings, abstention and petitions and, to achieve this end, abolitionists relied on a

1. *"This Society being anxious not to compromise their own principles, nor to give a sanction to anything which falls short of the standard of Right, will appropriate £50 to the London Gentleman's Anti-Slavery Society when they are willing to give up the word gradual in their title"*, MINUTE book of the Ladies' Society for the Relief of Negro Slaves", 8 April 1830, p.100, in Clare Midgley, *op.cit.*, p.115. As Louis and Rosamund Billington point out, this resolution antedated by six months the speech by the Reverend Andrew Thomson of Edinburgh, attacking slavery as a crime and a sin, which is usually regarded as the beginning of the "immediatist" phase of the campaign against West Indian Slavery.
2. Billington, *op.cit.*, p.90.

network of organisations, paid agents or lecturers and men's and women's local auxiliaries tied to the London parent group. Some of the methods now adopted by the *Agency Committee*—such as hiring paid lecturers to travel part of the country to rouse public opinion—had actually been initiated by ladies' associations a couple of years earlier. Drawing on the methods and organisations they had developed in the previous decade, women's anti-slavery organisations themselves played a major role after 1830 in the work of collecting signatures for petitions asking Parliament for immediate emancipation of slaves. Abolitionism during this period also capitalized on the opportunities created by the imminent reform of Parliament, which extended the franchise to the middle-class nonconformists who comprised its main support. The first reformed Parliament thus received hundreds of petitions from antislavery organisations around the country.[1] The largest of all was presented on the eve of the emancipation debate by the *Ladies' Anti-Slavery Society* under the name "The Ladies of England" and bore 187,000 signatures.[2]

The swing in opinion within the anti-slavery movement in favour of immediatism that started in the early 1830s was therefore to a large extent the result of pressure exerted by ladies' associations on the decision-making hierarchy of the *London Committee*. This conflict between female associations and the male leadership was not the only one. Another one was soon to follow during the campaign of the late 1830s against the apprenticeship system during which some radical women abolitionists opposed more cautious and conservative male members.

The *Abolition of Slavery Act* introduced by the government and voted in July 1833 was a disappointment: though formally abolishing the legal basis of property in people, the Act established a "transition to freedom", a five to seven year apprenticeship interval during which the freed slaves would continue to work for little or no wages on the sugar plantations and £20 million paid to slave owners as direct compensation to cover the loss of "property" (a decision immediately decried as an acceptance of the legality of slave-ownership). Determined not to accept this compromise, antislavery leaders led by Joseph Sturge began a new campaign to inform the British public of the atrocities of the apprenticeship system and formed the *Central Negro Emancipation Committee of the Anti-Slavery Society*. British women, once again, played a major part in this campaign. In 1837, an *English Female Address* was presented to the Queen, containing over 500,000 signatures and the *Darlington Ladies' Society for the Universal Abolition of*

1. Halbersleben, *op.cit.*, p.22.
2. Jack Gratus, *The Great White Lie, Slavery, Emancipation and Changing Racial Attitudes*, London: Hutchinson, 1973, p.229.

Slavery issued an *Address to the Women of Great Britain*, calling them to join or to form anti-slavery societies:

> DEAR SISTERS,
> [...] we plead with you on behalf of 750,000 of your fellow subjects, enduring all the horrors of Slavery, under the delusive name of Apprenticeship; and beseech you by every means you may collectively or individually possess, to come forward in aid of the righteous object, so ardently desired by every friend of justice and humanity,
> THE COMPLETE AND EVERLASTING ANNIHILATION OF THE INIQUITOUS SYSTEM, ON THE FIRST OF AUGUST NEXT. [...]
> Slavery is abolished only in name, whilst its horrors yet exist in unmitigated rigour, and with even increased atrocity [...] Evince your attachment to Anti-Slavery principles and approve yourselves before God and the world, by giving your name and influence to some society established to uphold and diffuse them. If none such exist in your town or neighbourhood, lose no time in urging the formation of one.

Those who had no such possibility were encouraged to "*strive to interest your friends at a distance, stimulate them to send up petitions,* [...] *recommend them to promote the circulation of the valuable periodicals published in elucidation of the subject*" and contribute financially. "*Remember that it is not great or mighty deeds which approve us in the divine sight but the diligence and alacrity with which we employ those means placed in our hands.*"[1]

The apprenticeship system was abolished the following year in the British colonies and, with victory finally achieved; abolitionists focused their attention on worldwide slavery and, in particular, on America, so that a transatlantic Anglo-American anti-slavery alliance developed in the late 1830s-early 1840s. Many women's groups then became auxiliaries of the *British and Foreign Anti-Slavery Society*, which replaced in 1839 the *Anti-Slavery Society*, the *Agency Committee* and the *Central Emancipation Committee*, and an increasing number of British women, like Elizabeth Pease and Anne Knight, became involved in the American women's anti-slavery network. This special link made it inevitable that the split within the American movement that occurred at that time should have repercussions on the British societies.

Conservatives vs. radicals

Tensions between radical abolitionists, centred on William Lloyd Garrison, and moderates, led by New York businessmen Arthur and Lewis Tappan, had been building since the early 1830s. Disagreement concerned

1. Elizabeth Pease and A. D. Miller, *To the Women of Great Britain*, Darlington Ladies' Society for the Universal Abolition of Slavery, Coates and Farmer, Darlington, 1837.

the use of political action to achieve moral reform as well as the expediency of associating the question of women's status to that of slaves.[1] In May 1840, the American conservatives—or "new organisation" group—split away from the more radical "old organisation", loyal to William Lloyd Garrison, to form the *American and Foreign Anti-Slavery Society*. Garrisonians then seized the leadership of the old *American Anti-Slavery Society* and elected women to serve on its governing board.[2] British women abolitionists, as most people, probably remained unaware of these developments until the Garrisonian radicals appointed women to the World's Anti-Slavery Convention held in London in June 1840.[3] It was there that the feuds in the American movement were first revealed to the British abolitionist public, which, so far, had only had occasional hints of dissension. In the following year, every British antislavery society became involved in the controversy and the national movement as a whole split up along lines directly reflecting the fragmentation in America. The London-based *BFASS*, which was reluctant to associate abolition with other radical issues, took a conservative position[4] while in Ireland, the *Hibernian Anti-Slavery Society* sided with the Garrisonians, cutting off official relations with the *BFASS*.

In England a minority of women embraced the position of the American Garrisonians with its emphasis on women's rights. The majority remained conservative and continued to act as auxiliaries to men's groups. In Scotland, however, female societies proved more radical as well as more independent. In Glasgow, the *Ladies' Emancipation Society* remained in the hands of the conservatives (influenced by evangelicals, they argued that seating women at the World's Convention would have been acting in opposition to divine teaching and have obscured women's feminine character[5]) and Garrisonian supporters therefore had to found a new female

1. While Garrisonians began agitating for the recognition of women's equal status within the antislavery movement, the Tappan group thought it tactically unsound to mix abolition with other issues, such as the role/status of women.
2. The *American and Foreign Anti-Slavery Society* only accepted women's membership through auxiliary organizations and denied them the kind of leadership responsibilities that Garrisonian women exercised.
3. Invitations had been issued by the *BFASS* to 35 countries in June 1839 for a World Convention to be held in London the following year to celebrate the end of the apprenticeship system in the British Empire and focus attention on slavery and the slave trade elsewhere. The *Society*, in their initial invitation, had mentioned "delegates" of unspecified sex. In April the Garrisonians informed them that they were appointing a number of women, which was a deliberate challenge to the conventional denial of public platforms to women. The *BAFSS* immediately opposed admission of the American women to the floor of the convention (although they felt obliged to admit them to the proceedings from the gallery of Freemason's Hall, where they were joined by Garrison and other male supporters).
4. Lewis Tappan's conservative group found their main British allies in the national society. Many of the Glasgow, Edinburgh and Dublin abolitionists, however, took the Garrisonian standpoint. See C. Duncan Rice, *op.cit.*
5. Billington, *op.cit.*, p.97.

society: the *Glasgow Female Anti-Slavery Society*. In Edinburgh, although the (male) *Edinburgh Society* remained loyal to the conservative *BFASS*, the *Ladies' Emancipation Society*, headed by Eliza Wigham, broke away and became one of the important British Garrisonian bodies (yet both bodies had identical social and religious backgrounds), spending much time and energy making and collecting goods for the annual Boston Anti-Slavery Bazaar, the sale of which was to raise funds for American antislavery bodies.[1]

Conclusion

Lucretia Mott, one of the Garrisonian women delegates, later confessed in her diary about her experience of the 1840 Anti-Slavery Convention that she was "*much disappointed to find so little independent action on the part of [British] women*" and reported about a social gathering of "Anti-Slavery Ladies": "*we find little confidence in women's action either separately or conjointly with men, except as drudges.*"[2] It is a fact that most British women abolitionists never stopped stressing their avoidance of acting outside their "proper sphere". "*Be not afraid,—we ask you not to do any thing, to unite in any thing unbecoming your sex. The cause concerning which we implore you to take an enlightened and Christian view of your influence and responsibility, is the cause of God and of religion, of justice and humanity*", Elizabeth Pease reassured her readers in her appeal *To the Women of Great Britain.*[3] In that respect, however, the constraints imposed on women by a conventional British society should not be underestimated. The reason why women were allowed to participate in the movement was to a large extent that their contribution was seen as subordinate to that of men, outside the purely political sphere and stemming from motherly concerns, moral feeling and feminine convictions (and therefore not threatening male ascendancy nor "decency"). On the other hand, women's contribution should certainly not be dismissed as merely supportive of men's efforts. Despite their lack of formal and political power at a national level and although restricted by existing social conventions, we have seen that ladies' associations did not hesitate, for more than ten years, to openly criticize the male leadership and exert moral and financial pressure on the national movement, thus influencing the form and direction of campaigns both locally and nationally. Without their contribution, not only would the movement have been less well funded, it

1. Until 1858, when Maria Weston Chapman announced that the Bazaar would in future only accept cash.
2. Lucretia Mott, *Slavery and the 'Woman Question'*, ed. by Frederick B. Tolles, *Journal of the Friends Historical Society*, supplement 23, 1952, p.49.
3. Elizabeth Pease and A. D. Miller, *op.cit.*, p.1.

would also have been less widely supported and shorter-lived. For, while following the abolition of the apprenticeship system, male anti-slavery associations tended to die down,[1] women's societies continued to be active, providing most of the foreign financial aid sent to the American movement until the eve of the American Civil War and completing their transformation from men's auxiliaries to independent organisations. Finally, even though only a minority of British women abolitionists adopted a feminist stance, the anti-slavery campaign can nevertheless be said to have contributed to the emergence of women in public life and, following the 1840 Anti-Slavery Convention, given rise to the movement for women's political equality. Some prominent female campaigners such as Anne Knight and Eliza Wigham, both Quakers and Garrisonians, were thus among the first to campaign for women's suffrage.

Bibliography

Billington L. & R., "'A Burning Zeal for Righteousness': Women in the British Anti-Slavery Movement, 1820-1860", in Jane Rendall (ed.), *Equal or Different, Women's Politics, 1800-1914*, Oxford: Blackwell, 1987.

Gratus J., *The Great White Lie, Slavery, Emancipation and Changing Racial Attitudes*, London: Hutchinson, 1973.

Halbersleben K. I., *Women's Participation in the British Antislavery Movement 1824-1865*, Lewiston: The Edwin Mellen Press, 1993.

Heyrick E., *Apology for Ladies' Anti-Slavery Associations*, London: Hatchard, 1828.

—, *Immediate, not Gradual Emancipation; or, an Inquiry into the Shortest, Safest, and most Effectual Means of Getting Rid of West Indian Slavery*, London: Hatchard, 1824.

Midgley C., *Women against Slavery, The British Campaigns 1780-1870*, London: Routledge, 1995.

Mott L., *Slavery and the 'Woman Question', Lucretia Mott's Diary of Her Visit to Great Britain to Attend the World's Anti-Slavery Convention of 1840*, ed. by Frederick B. Tolles, *Journal of the Friends Historical Society*, supplement 23, 1952.

Oldfield J. R., *Popular Politics and British Anti-Slavery, The Mobilisation of Public Opinion against the Slaver Trade 1787-1807*, Manchester: M.U.P., 1995.

Pease E. & A. D. Miller, *To the Women of Great Britain.* Darlington Ladies' Society for the Universal Abolition of Slavery, Coates and Farmer, Darlington, 1837.

Rice D. C., *The Scots Abolitionists, 1833-1861*, Baton Rouge & London: Louisiana State University Press, 1981.

Stephen G., *Antislavery Recollections, in A Series of Letters Addressed to Mrs Beecher Stowe*, London: Hatchard, 1854, Letter XIII, 5th October 1854.

1. The number of men's societies contributing financially to the *British and Foreign Anti-Slavery Society* thus fell from 20 to 3 between 1844 and 1850 (Midgley, *op.cit.*, 1992, p.125). Methods used by ladies' societies—raising funds, boycotting slave-grown produce—were also certainly more efficient in putting pressure on a foreign country than the parliamentary methods formerly used by men's societies.

Harriet Martineau and the Transantlantic Abolitionist Feminist Nexus

Françoise Orazi

The campaign for the abolition of slavery gave women an opportunity to join in the public sphere and voice their opinions on a political matter, or as many among them would have rather described it, a moral matter with political implications. At the time of course, this was so unusual and controversial that women's active participation in the debate became a debate in the debate as it were, and for many abolitionist militants, the later years of the period under scrutiny went hand and hand with what may be described as a feminist awakening.

Early American feminism provides the most renowned illustration of the connection between abolitionism and "the woman question", as it was called in those days. For instance, Lucretia Mott, the Grimké sisters or Elizabeth Cady-Stanton were all active members of various abolitionist groups. The same kind of connection can be found in British history, though it is less striking and certainly less well-known. However it did play a seminal role in the building and further development of the first organized women's movements historians refer to as first-wave feminism.

The first apparent explanation for the common abolitionist origins of American and British feminism is the predictable cause and effect argument. In a nutshell, women were involved in the abolitionist debates in both countries, there was a reactionary opposition against their involvement on both sides of the Atlantic and, from then on, a number of women were made acutely aware of their status as second-rate citizens, all the more so since their fight was precisely against the subjection of a group of human beings by another group. In a way the struggle against slavery provided women with a mirror image of their own situation in society, whether they were British or American. However, there is also another explanation to be borne in mind when studying this aspect of the debate on the abolition of slavery, namely the extensive contacts between American and British abolitionists, which included numerous and frequent visits and correspondence whether between individuals, abolitionist groups or abolitionist media such as newspapers. Not only did abolitionist women share the same experience of a subjected group struggling to free an enslaved group, they also exchanged views, read the same texts and more broadly, influenced one another. It is therefore not surprising to find that the transatlantic connection was a pillar both of the abolitionist movement and of the beginnings of (organised) feminism.

Within this context Harriet Martineau emerges as a key-protagonist of all three aspects of what may be called the transatlantic abolitionist feminist nexus. She had contributed to the abolitionist literature notably through "Demerara", one of her widely-read *Illustrations of Political Economy* as early as 1832. She then embarked for the United States and spent over a year there, travelling throughout the country both in Southern and Northern States. Her tour of the States turned her into an even stauncher opponent of slavery than she had previously been, and she was to continue to write in support of abolitionism, especially American abolitionism, notably a novel entitled *The Hour and the Man* (1841) and a long article "The Martyr Age of the United States"(1838). She established contacts with several notorious abolitionists and even joined the American debate when she made a public statement against slavery at a Boston Ladies' Anti-Slavery Society meeting.[1] On her return she wrote three books[2] based on her experience, including *Society in America,* which has been likened to Alexis de Tocqueville's *Democracy in America*[3], since both books are a study of American society, based on travels made during the same decade. However it must be noted that Martineau was more interested "in the issue of equality, particularly in matters of race and gender"[4] than Tocqueville seems to have been. Martineau's writings after her visit of the United States, especially those which dealt precisely with this visit, expressed her strong condemnation of slavery, including slavery in the United States, and exposed the contradictions of a political system which claimed to be democratic but nevertheless oppressed the "Negro race" in the most despotic manner. Indeed Martineau's abolitionist conviction was made even stronger both by her encounters with advocates of slavery and with slaves.[5] Conversely her writings also took on a feminist tenor that became stronger as she grew increasingly aware of the unfair treatment of women, notably their exclusion from suffrage, and the need to react like her American abolitionist friends who were showing the way.

1. Harriet Martineau, *Autobiography*, London: Virago, (1877), 1983, p.31. See also *Retrospect of Western Travel*, vol.3 [1838].
2. Harriet Martineau, *Society in America,* London: Saunders and Otley, 1837. Harriet Martineau, *How to Observe Morals and Manners*, London: Charles Knight, 1838. Harriet Martineau, *Retrospect of Western Travel*, London: Saunders and Otley, 1838.
3. This comparison has been made particularly by Susan Hoecker-Drysdale and Robert Nisbet, cf Susan Hoecker-Drysdale (ed.), 'Introduction', *Harriet Martineau: Studies of America, 1837-68*, Bristol: Thoemmes Continuum, 2004, vol.1.
4. *Ibid.*, p.31.
5. Several descriptions of the encounters in question may be found in *Retrospect of Western Travel.*

Thus Martineau may be studied as the thread running through the transatlantic abolitionist feminist nexus, i.e. the theoretical and historical reciprocal influences between abolitionism and feminism, American abolitionists and British abolitionists, American feminists and British feminists.

Martineau's writings on slavery

As said, Martineau's first major contribution to the debate on slavery was *the Illustration of Political Economy* entitled "Demerara".[1] As part of Martineau's series of didactic tales that were meant to explain and vindicate what may be broadly described as an (ideal) British liberal economy, "Demerara" deals with slavery in so far as it attempts to demonstrate its economic absurdity—slavery being taken both as a form of labour and as a form of capital—as Martineau explicitly stated: "[This volume] treats of the respective values of different kinds of labour, and of a particular mode of investing capital".[2]

The original text conveniently contains a summary of the lessons taught by the tale, or rather of the "truths illustrated"[3], according to the author's claim. Rather than follow the original arrangement of these "truths", one may, for the sake of clarity, alternately start with the most obvious and move on to the more complex. Thus the first lesson to be learnt from "Demerara" is that

> Free and slave labour are equally owned by the capitalist. Where the labourer is not held as capital, the capitalist pays for labour only. Where the labourer is held as capital, the capitalist not only pays a much higher price for an equal quantity of labour, but also for waste, negligence, and theft, on the part of the labourer. Capital is thus sunk, which ought to be reproduced.[4]

This is amply illustrated by the text, which insists on the slothfulness of slaves and compares it with the eagerness of paid labourers. For instance, slaves are described as being often late for work. On such an occasion a small conversation occurs between a character (the sister) who has never left Demerara and one who has just returned from England (the brother).

1. The book is named after the part of British Guiana where there was a slave revolt in 1823. Interestingly enough, the death of John Smith, a white missionary who had been imprisoned for having helped to incite the revolt "set off a fury of full emancipationist activity in Britain that lasted until parliament abolished slavery in 1833." Susan Kingsley Kent, *Gender and Power in Britain, 1640-1990*, London: Routledge, 1999, p.206.
2. Harriet Martineau, "Demerara", *Illustrations of Political Economy*, London: Charles Fox, (1832), 1834, vol.2, p.141.
3. *Ibid.*
4. *Ibid.*, p.142.

> "What better can they do in England when people are late at their work? for I suppose people sleep too long there sometimes, as they do here."
> Her brother told her, to her great surprise, that lazy people are punished in England by having their work taken from them; there being plenty of industrious labourers who are glad to get it. She said there was nothing her papa's slaves would like so much as not to have to work; but she had never heard of such a thing being allowed, except on Sundays and holidays.[1]

The second lesson that is meant to be learnt from a study of a slave society also concerns the waste of capital.

> As the supply of slave-labour does not rise and fall with the wants of the capitalist, like that of free labour, he employs his occasional surplus on works which could be better done by brute labour or machinery. By rejecting brute labour, he refuses facilities for convertible husbandry, and for improving the labour of his slaves by giving them animal food. By rejecting machinery, he declines the most direct and complete method of saving labour. Thus, again, capital is sunk which ought to be reproduced.[2]

This argument is derived from the fact that slave-holders must employ their slaves whether they actually need their labour or not, because they must always pay for their maintenance, while an employer may lay off his employees when he does not need them. Therefore slaves are made to do work that could be done by cattle such as cutting grass and bringing it to the cattle rather than simply allowing it to graze. Besides, slaves cannot be employed as skilled workers and it is therefore difficult to introduce machinery. The lack of machinery then means that little profit is made, and that slave-holders cannot afford to feed and dress their slaves properly, so that the slaves suffer from hunger and from the cold and are thus less able to work. All in all, slave-holding implies constant and high expenses, which means that the slave-holder requires a very regular income, thus making it impossible for him to turn some of his land to pasture, let alone to fallow. This, in turn, leads to soil exhaustion, which completes Martineau's demonstration: no sustainable economy can rely on slavery.

The argument then moves on to denounce the consequences of slavery not only on the economy of the colonies specialised in the production of sugar, but on the whole British economic system.

> In order to make up for this loss of capital to slave owners, bounties and prohibitions are granted in their behalf by government; the waste committed by certain capitalists abroad, being thus paid for out of the earnings of those at home.[3]

1. *Ibid.* p.11.
2. *Ibid.* p.142.
3. *Ibid.* p.143.

Because it is unprofitable, an economy based on slavery must be indirectly subsidised, which of course is incompatible with the precepts of liberal economy supported by the author.

> A free trade in sugar would banish slavery altogether, since competition must induce an economy of labour and capital; *i.e.*, a substitution of free for slave labour.[1]

Martineau's typical 19th century liberal faith in free trade leads her to point to the government's responsibility in upholding slavery, as she describes the "legislature" as its true accomplice.

> Let us see, then, what is the responsibility of the legislature in this matter. The slave system inflicts an incalculable amount of human suffering, for the sake of making a wholesale waste of labour and capital. Since the slave system is only supported by legislative protection, the legislature is responsible for the misery caused by direct infliction, and for the injury indirectly occasioned by the waste of labour and capital.[2]

Although "Demerara" primarily focuses on an almost materialistic approach of slavery, it also includes more abstract thoughts such as a reflection on the origins of property, which contains Lockean undertones.

> Property is held by conventional, not natural right. As the agreement to hold man in property never took place between the parties concerned, *i. e.*, is not conventional, Man has no right to hold Man in property. Law, *i. e.*, the sanctioned agreement of the parties concerned, secures property. Where the parties are not agreed, therefore, law does not secure property.[3]

Once more, Martineau's point is that slavery is irreconcilable with a liberal organisation of society, whether economically or politically. In fact the author claims that the necessary paradox of a "free" Government—i.e. one based on law—is that it oppresses slaves even more than a "despotic magistracy".[4]

> In the days of Augustus, one Vidius Pollio, in the presence of the emperor, ordered one of his slaves, who had committed some slight fault; to be cut in pieces and be thrown into his fish-pond to feed the fishes. The emperor thereupon commanded him to emancipate, immediately, not only that slave, but all the others that belonged to him.
>
> In these days, no potentate can thus dispose of the property of a Briton; and it is well. But it is clearly just that while the Briton abjures despotic rule, he should hold none under him in such subjection as to need the interference of despotic vengeance for the redress of their wrongs.[5]

1. *Ibid.*
2. *Ibid.*
3. *Ibid.* p.141.
4. *Ibid.* p.57.
5. *Ibid.*

Finally "Demerara" also indirectly evokes the moral issues of the debate on slavery namely the question of the slaves' humanity, when discussing the poor output of their labour.

> Human labour is more valuable than brute labour, only because actuated by reason; for human strength is inferior to brute strength. The origin of labour, human and brute, is the Will. The Reason of slaves is not subjected to exercise nor their will to more than a few weak motives. The labour of slaves is therefore less valuable than that of brutes, inasmuch as their strength is inferior; and less valuable than that of free labourers, inasmuch as their Reason and Will are feeble and alienated.[1]

Indeed slaves being human beings their reason dictates them to act in their interest, which is necessarily at odds with their owner's interest. Depending on the extent to which their character has been spoiled by slavery, they will either be idle, since they cannot benefit from their work, or wish for their freedom and see their owners as their oppressors.

> But slaves differ from cattle, on the one hand, in yielding (from internal opposition) a less return for their maintenance; and from free labourers, on the other, in not being acted upon by the inducements which stimulate production as an effort of mind as well as body. In all three cases the labour is purchased. In free labourers and cattle, all the faculties work together, and to advantage; in the slave they are opposed: and therefore he is, as far as the amount of labour is concerned, the least valuable of the three.[2]

Out of all of Martineau's writings on slavery "Demerara" is certainly the text that is the closest to an actual abolitionist pamphlet, and contains a systematic and fully developed analysis of the wrongs of slavery. According to Susan Belasco[3], *The Hour and the Man*[4] differs from it in so far that after having observed slavery in the United States, Martineau came "to view slavery as more than an impediment to the greatest economic happiness of the greatest number"[5] and focused on "its cost to human dignity and ability".[6] Its full title, *The Hour and the Man. An Historical Romance*, indicates the author's claim to historical accuracy as the background of her narrative. In the appendix she clarifies the historicity of the characters and plot and states that most characters are based on true people. Therefore her depiction of Toussaint Louverture as a wise, well-read, loyal and just man, who first opposed the Haiti rebellion and only joined it when he heard of

1. *Ibid.* pp.141-142.
2. *Ibid.* p.71.
3. Susan Belasco, "Harriet Martineau's Black Hero and the American Antislavery Movement", *Nineteenth Century Literature*, vol.55, n°2 (Sep., 2000), pp.175-194.
4. Harriet Martineau, *The Hour and the Man. (An Historical Romance)*, London, 1841.
5. Susan Belasco, "Harriet Martineau's Black Hero and the American Antislavery Movement", p.172.
6. *Ibid.* p.172.

the decree of the French Convention by which the slaves of the colony of Saint Domingue were made full fellow-citizens, is all the more potent as it meant to be derived from the few historical sources that were available to her and not merely from her imagination. Obviously this attempt to re-establish Toussaint Louverture as a hero rather than as a cold-blooded murderer remains in itself a militant abolitionist act.

One possible explanation for the difference between the two books is, of course, that the first one was written during the debate on slavery, while the second one was published in its aftermath, at least within the British context. It is indeed evident that since her return from the United States Martineau's writings on slavery also aimed at her American readership as she sought to support American abolitionism. This concern was also clearly at the origins of "The Martyr Age of the United States"[1], which can be read as an appeal to British abolitionists to turn their attention to the difficulties experienced by American abolitionists and lend them their support. By shedding light on the American situation it seems Martineau was trying to remind her fellow citizens that the fight against slavery was not over—it had just been won in Britain.

Writing about slavery as a woman

The fact remains that, at first sight, "Demerara" may appear rather detached from the slaves' ordeal, as if the main reason for rejecting slavery was that it did not make any economic sense rather than because it caused intolerable suffering to human beings. This would, however, be a rather superficial analysis of Martineau's work. First because the condition of the slaves constitutes the background of the tale which includes some rather moving subplots such as the story of little Hester, a twelve-year-old orphan, but mostly, because one should examine the situation of its author when she wrote "Demerara". At the time, it was thought that intellectual neutrality was both possible and a pre-requisite to any analysis of society. Therefore, like Alfred, her mouthpiece in the tale, Martineau chose a neutral and seemingly objective approach.

> "True enough," thought Alfred, who, earnestly as he had endeavoured to keep his mind free from prejudice respecting the institution of slavery, yet entertained a deep dislike of the system.[2]

An unemotional, materialistic treatment of slavery was more likely to convince readers of the need for its abolition. Moreover, writing as a

1. Harriet Martineau, *The Martyr Age of The United States*, Boston, Weeks, Jordan & Co, 1839. First published in the *Westminster Review*, December 1838, printed as a book in 1839.
2. Harriet Martineau, "Demerara", p.7.

woman, Martineau ran the risk precisely of being accused of a sentimental approach, which would have brought discredit to her work. There is no doubt that Martineau was aware of this risk throughout her whole career since she often resorted to an alias—"Disciplus"—when writing articles for newspapers. In her preface to "Demerara" she tackled this very issue as if she was trying to justify her literary choices.

> If I had believed, as many do, that strong feeling impairs the soundness of reasoning, I should assuredly have avoided the subject of the following tale, since Slavery is a topic which cannot be approached without emotion. But, convinced as I am, on the contrary, that the reason and the sensibilities are made for co-operation, and perceiving, as I do, that the most stirring eloquence issues from the calmest logic, I have not hesitated to bring calculations and reasonings to bear on a subject which awakens the drowsiest, and fires the coldest.[1]

There are, to my knowledge, no indications that Martineau was ever publicly condemned, or disapproved of, for her views on slavery in Britain. Even the very fact that she was a woman who wrote about a subject that did not belong to the sphere women were assigned to, did not lead to particular criticism. In fact she may have been less derided for her writings on slavery than for her historical studies, or her studies of political economy. This can either be explained by the fact that abolitionism was seen as stemming from compassion for fellow human beings, which was usually considered a typical female feeling (though, as just said, her writings could hardly be deemed feminine in this respect) or because Martineau was indeed not at her best when dealing with more general and abstract theories, at least according to her detractors.

Bearing in mind that, in the 1830s, abolitionism was more widely accepted in Britain than in the US, it is not surprising that Martineau was able to express her abolitionist views far more freely than her American counterparts or than she herself had been in the United States. During her visit there she experienced "the system of terrorism"[2] which prevailed at the time and made it very difficult for abolitionist militants, especially women, to express themselves. Of this she gave a full account in *Retrospect of Western Travel*[3], but *Society in America*, her political or even (pre)sociological account of the American society, was also strongly influenced by this experience. From then on it seems that her writings echoed both her lifelong awareness of the horrors of slavery as well as a somewhat new, or

1. *Ibid.* pp.VI-VII.
2. Harriet Martineau, *Retrospect of Western Travel*, London: Saunders and Otley, 1838, vol.3, p.148.
3. *Ibid.* pp.148-165.

at least more explicit, awareness of the similarities between the status of women and that of slaves.

Comparison between slavery and the condition of women

The part of *Society in America* entitled "Political Non-Existence of Women" cannot be discussed at length here, but it should be mentioned that Martineau denounced the condition of women immediately after the part entitled "citizenship of people of colour", in the chapter "Morals of Politics", which appears to be an inquiry into the extent to which human equality, the founding principle of the United States, was enforced. This led Martineau to wonder

> One of the fundamental principles announced in the Declaration of Independence is that governments derive their just power from the consent of the governed. How can the political condition of women be reconciled with this?[1]

Looking for a historical explanation to Women's exclusion from politics, Martineau quotes Jefferson,

> Were our State a pure democracy, in which all the inhabitants should meet together to transact all their business, there would yet be excluded from their deliberations,
> "1. infants, until arrived at age of discretion;
> "2. Women, who, to prevent depravation of morals, and ambiguity of issue, could not mix promiscuously in the public meetings of men;
> "3. Slaves, from whom the unfortunate state of things with us takes away the right of will and of property."[2]

and adds

> If the slave disqualification, here assigned, were shifted up under the head of Women, their case would be nearer the truth than as it now stands. Women's lack of will and of property, is more like the true cause of her exclusion from the representation than that which is exactly set down against her.[3]

The rhetorical strategy which is apparent in Martineau's comparing of the disqualification of slaves with that of women, consists in implicitly appealing to abolitionists to see the parallel between the subjection of women and the enslavement of "Negroes" and from that draw the right conclusions.

This kind of comparison between the condition of women and of slaves was a potent feminist argument. John Stuart Mill's *Subjection of Women*

1. Harriet Martineau, *Society in America*, Unders and Otley: New York, 1837, p.148.
2. *Ibid.* p.149.
3. *Ibid.* p.150.

often resorts to it, while the full title of Thompson and Wheeler's feminist pamphlet *Appeal of One-half the Human Race, Women, Against the Pretensions of the Other Half, Men, to Retain Them in Political, and Thence in Civil and Domestic Slavery* is an earlier example. All these works denounced both the injustice of women's social status and the hypocrisy of those who sought to justify it by claiming that women approved of their condition.

> It is pleaded that half of the human race does acquiesce in the decision of the other half, as to their rights and duties. And some instances, not only of submission, but of acquiescence, there are. Forty years ago, the women of New Jersey went to the poll, and voted, at state elections. The general term, "inhabitants" stood unqualified;—as it will again, when the true democratic principle comes to be fully understood. A motion was made to correct the inadvertence; and it was done, as a matter of course; without any appeal, as far as I could learn, from the persons about to be injured. Such acquiescence proves nothing but the degradation of the injured party. It inspires the same emotions of pity as the supplication of the freed slave who kneels to his master to restore him to slavery, that he may have his animal wants supplied without being troubled with human rights and duties. Acquiescence like this is an argument which cuts the wrong way for those who use it.[1]

The comparison was not limited to the exclusion of slaves and women from political representation. All the above quoted authors mentioned the correspondence between the bond connecting master and slave and the bond that linked a husband and a wife, though Martineau, as well as other commentators, conceded that in most cases wives were better off than slaves.

> The Indian squaw carries the household burdens, trudging in the dust, while her husband on horseback paces before her, unencumbered but by his own gay trappings. [...] From a condition of slavery like this, women are found rising to the highest condition in which they are at present seen, in France, England, and the United States,--where they are less than half-educated, precluded from earning a subsistence, except in a very few ill-paid employments, and prohibited from giving or withholding their assent to laws which they are yet bound by penalties to obey.[2]

Feminist leaning of writings on Slavery

Interestingly enough, Martineau had focused her attention on marriage and slavery before her trip to the United States but at the time her goal seemed simply to show how the condition of slavery is really incompatible

1. *Ibid.* pp.152-153.
2. Harriet Martineau, *How to Observe Morals and Manners* London: Charles Knight, 1838, p.174, my underlining.

with marriage. In this extract from "Demerara", a slave named Willy tells his father why he does not wish to get married:

> Because a black man must be first a slave and then a man. A white woman has nobody to rule her but her husband, and nobody can hurt her without his leave: but a slave's wife must obey her master before her husband; and he cannot save her from being flogged.[1]

This particular extract reveals an implicit and underlying feminist theme. Indeed a progressive reader was sure to see the irony of the master-slave relationship becoming a hindrance to marriage because its very nature competed with the husband-wife bond.

Thus in Martineau's work, the condition of women is often brought up when the wrongs of slavery are being discussed. In *The Hour and the Man,* Martineau's hero is a paternal figure, constantly surrounded by family and friends—which serves Martineau's intention to make him a born benevolent leader. Many of the secondary characters are women and Toussaint discusses politics and morals with them as much as he does with male characters. From the point of view of feminism, the most interesting character is certainly a very beautiful young black woman named Thérèse whom Toussaint rescues from the rebellion at the end of the second chapter. She is the slave of a Monsieur Papalier and the reader soon understands that she is also his mistress. When she first appears in the book she is terrified and submissive. She carries an infant who is murdered later because his crying puts the escape of a refugee group at stake. The ensuing dialogue between Papalier and Thérèse reveals Papalier's typical slaveholder selfishness and utter lack of morals.

> "My child!" said Thérèse, fearfully. "Give me my child!" She looked about, and saw that no one seemed to have the infant.
> "I will not let it cry," she said. "Give me back my child!"
> "What is it?" asked Papalier, coming beside her horse. She told her grief, as she prepared to spring down.
> "No, keep your seat! Don't get down," said he, in a tone she dared not disobey. "I will inquire for the child."
> He went away, and returned — without it. "This is a sad thing," said he, leading her horse forward with the rest. "No one knows anything about the poor thing. Why did you let it go?"
> "Have you asked them all? Who snatched it from me? Oh, ask who took it! Let me look for it. I will — I will—"
> "It is too late now. We cannot stop or turn back. These sad accidents will happen at such times."
> "Leave me behind — oh, leave me in the wood! I can follow when I have found it. Leave me behind!"

1. Harriet Martineau, "Demerara", p.61.

> "I cannot spare you, my dear. I should never see you again; and I cannot spare you. It is sad enough to have lost the child."
> "It was your child," said she, pleadingly.
> "And you are mine too, my dear. I cannot spare you both."[1]

Papalier embodies the anti-Toussaint, the barbarous white man as opposed to the enlightened black man, in contradiction of traditional racist notions. Papalier's characterization is done through his detestable relationship to Thérèse, while Toussaint was never affected by the moral degeneracy associated with slavery: he is married and faithful. When Thérèse becomes free, she rebels against her master, refuses to leave the island with him, marries Toussaint's second in command and is redeemed. Thus, for Thérèse, liberation amounts to being freed as a slave and as a woman.

> And I was sinful; but no one told me so. I was ignorant, and weak, and a slave. Now I am a woman and a wife. No more whites, no more sin, no more misery![2]

Like "Demerara" and *The Hour and the Man*, "The Martyr Age of the United States" is a text that bears no apparent connection to the woman question. When Martineau wrote her extended article on the American antislavery movement, her intention was to inform British readers of the great difficulties encountered by abolitionists in America and of their heroic struggle.

> [...] it may be remarked that it is a totally different thing to be an abolitionist on a soil actually trodden by slaves, and in a far-off country, where opinion is already on the side of emancipation, or ready to be converted; where only a fraction of society, instead of the whole, has to be convicted of guilt; and where no interests are put in jeopardy but pecuniary ones, and those limited and remote. Great honour is due to the first movers in the anti-slavery cause in every land: but those of European countries may take rank with the philanthropists of America who may espouse the cause of the aborigines.[3]

Since a large section of the text is dedicated to the Massachusetts Female Anti-Slavery Society, it is also a chronicle of its members' struggle for the recognition of the entitlement of women to intervene in political matters. Thus, Martineau authored a text that includes some passionate feminist statements such as the following.

> If we are not enough grieved at the existence of slavery to ask that it may be abolished in the ten miles square over which Congress possess exclusive jurisdiction, we may rest assured that we are slave-holders in heart, and indeed

1. Harriet Martineau, *The Hour and the Man*, p.40.
2. *Ibid.* p.91.
3. Harriet Martineau, *The Martyr Age of The United States*, pp.3-4.

> under the endurance of the penalty which selfishness inflicts, the slow but certain death of the soul. We sometimes, but not often, hear it said ' It is such an odd, unladylike thing to do!' We concede that the human soul, in the full exercise of its most god-like power of self-denial and exertion for the good of others, is, emphatically, a very unladylike thing. We have never heard this objection but from that sort of woman who is dead while she lives, or to be pitied as the victim of domestic tyranny. The woman who makes it is generally one who has struggled from childhood up to womanhood through a process of spiritual suffocation. Her infancy was passed in serving as a convenience for the display of elegant baby-linen. Her youth, in training for a more public display of braiding the hair, and wearing of gold, and putting on of apparel [...].[1]

However she was not speaking in her own name but merely quoting the words of another, i.e. her life-long friend and appointed biographer Maria Weston Chapman. Once more, Martineau is found to express feminist opinions while claiming that she is merely acting as a neutral reporter of facts, and in the context of abolitionism. "The Martyr Age" was rather influential among abolitionists. It was reprinted by abolitionist societies both in Britain and in the United States. Such a text undoubtedly contributed to the diffusion of feminism as well as abolitionism. But it served another, more practical purpose: by drawing attention to the plight of American abolitionists, especially the women, it could reasonably be hoped that the sympathetic readers would be willing to make a donation to abolitionist societies. Indeed, according to Claire Midgley[2], "financial support was particularly valued by American campaigners, who directed their financial appeal largely towards women".[3] Collectors were sent to Britain and Ireland under the aegis of Maria Weston Chapman to help fund abolitionist papers such as the *Anti-Slavery Standard* or the *Liberty Bell*. Martineau herself contributed both money and articles.[4] All this intellectual and fieldwork contributed to creating a network of women's abolitionist movements that relied on female and transatlantic solidarity. This was even more evident in the later years of the abolitionist campaigns, when male participation was declining while women were increasingly involved (1838 marked the beginning of the political marginalisation of anti-slavery). It can therefore be said that much as abolitionism helped the promotion of

1. *Ibid.*, p.29, here Martineau quoted from Maria Weston Chapman's Boston Female Anti-Slavery Society reports, *Right and Wrong in Boston*.
2. Clare Midgley, *Women against Slavery (The British Campaigns, 1780-1870)*, London: Routledge, 1992.
3. *Ibid.*, pp.125-126.
4. Midgley mentions that Elizabeth Barrett-Browning contributed "two powerful anti-slavery poems" to the *Liberty Bell*. *Ibid.* p.126.

feminist ideas, so female solidarity, or 'sisterhood' as Midgley puts it, was the background that enabled abolitionism to thrive.

In 1840, feminist notions were to be shifted to the foreground of abolitionism. Indeed, several American organizations appointed women as delegates to the first World Anti-Slavery Convention in London. Alongside with Lucretia Mott, Maria Weston Chapman, and Lydia Maria Child, Harriet Martineau was also nominated—as a member of the Massachusetts Anti-Slavery Society—but was unable to go because she was severely ill. All women were denied admission which led to a dispute between those who supported the women's right to attend and those who regarded it as improper. The first day (out of ten) was entirely spent on this debate. It was resolved that women would observe the proceedings from the visitors' gallery. This created a shockwave whose effects are hard to measure exactly but were definitely far-reaching. Anne Knight started her campaign advocating equal rights for women in the wake of the convention. According to Margaret McFadden, Marion Kirkland Reid[1] "attributed her own heightened consciousness about the woman question to the furore aroused by the attempt of American women delegates to be credentialed at the conference."[2] Furthermore, as Elisabeth Cady-Stanton famously recalled, the American female delegates "resolved to hold a convention as soon as we returned home, and form a society to advocate the rights of women."[3] Thus the last year of the debate on slavery was marked by the beginning of organised feminism.

Bibliography

Martineau, Harriet, *Autobiography*, London: Virago, (1877), 1983.

—, "Demerara", *Illustrations of Political Economy,* vol.2 [1832].

—, *How to Observe Morals and Manners* London: Charles Knight, 1838.

—, *Retrospect of Western Travel*, London: Saunders and Otley, 1838. Martineau, Harriet, *Society in America*, London: Saunders and Otley, 1837.

—, *The Hour and the Man. (An Historical Romance)*, London: 1841.

—, *The Martyr Age of The United States*, Boston: Weeks, Jordan & Co, 1839.

Belasco, Susan, "Harriet Martineau's Black Hero and the American Antislavery Movement", *Nineteenth Century Literature*, Vol.55, n°2 (Sep., 2000), pp.175-194.

Midgley, Clare, *Women against Slavery (The British Campaigns, 1780-1870)*, London: Routledge, 1992.

1. Author of *A Plea for Women.*
2. Mc Fadden, Margaret, H. *Golden Cables of Sympathy (the Transatlantic Sources of nineteenth-century Feminism)*, University Press of Kentucky, 1999, p.110.
3. *Ibid*. This resolution led to 1848 first Women's Rights Convention at Seneca Falls.

The Irish Involvement in the Abolition of Slavery (1787-1840)

Joyce Fereres

> Gentlemen, God knows I speak for the saddest people the sun sees: but may my right hand forget its cunning, and my tongue cleave to the roof of my mouth, if to save Ireland, even Ireland, I forget the negro one single hour!
>
> Daniel O'Connell

In 1787, the Society for the Abolition of the Slave Trade was formed in Great Britain and intervened in a period when fierce and obstinate battles for the emancipation of the Catholics were exploding on Irish soil. These struggles had a thunderous resonance which started fading before the mid-19th century as soon as the Abolition Act was given Royal Assent in 1833 and the status of peonage that followed was put to an end in 1838.

As any other people who had been enslaved or involved in slavery and who sought change, the Irish raised their voice, joining the debaters on the abolition of slavery in Great Britain. Irish people may be seen on two opposite sides: slaves and slave traders. Even though it may appear strange that some Irish people may have been against abolition, because of their suffering from Norman times onwards, one has to bear in mind that, in those days, some of the slave traders were themselves Irish.

In this study the location and condition of the Irish slaves and the sudden rise of Irish slave traders will first be briefly reviewed, as well as the Protestant ascendancy of the English. Secondly, the crusade to abolish chattel slavery in the British Empire and in the United States will be presented with the rise of two antithetical movements which, during many decades of debate on the abolition of slavery, asserted their affiliation to the following groups: the Abolitionists on the one hand and the pro-slavery movement on the other hand. In Ireland, the people expressed their objection to slavery with the help of a very charismatic figure, Daniel O'Connell, who appeared to be their mouthpiece and parliamentary spokesman for the movement at the British Parliament. Their actions and their various ways of conveying their points to the largest public, in order to support their views and interests, had crossed oceans and built bridges between Ireland, Britain and what is now the United States, before circling the globe. Last, the evolution of the debating process prior to the initiating of the Abolition of Slavery Act and its official implementation will be observed along with the consequences in these countries and around the world.

I. Irish slaves and Irish slave traders

Understanding the position of the Irish on the question of slavery requires remembering the collective heritage of the Irish both as a nation and as a group who suffered enslavement. The historical experience of slavery of the Irish cannot be separated from the English history, since the colonisation of Ireland by the English military power.

1) White slaves

The origin of the word *slave* refers to the Eastern European Slavs who were taken into captivity to serve masters, in the Middle East and Western Europe, from the 10th to the 16th century. In Western Europe, the white slave trade actually preceded the sale of black captives, which only began in the 15th century with the rise of European empires and their colonies. This was a continuation of the previous form of slavery in ancient Greece and in the Roman Empire, where slavery was defined in terms of social class rather than race. It was only in the centuries before its outright abolition that slavery became a predominantly racial institution.[1]

By the 1790s there were as many as 480,000 slaves at work in Britain's Caribbean colonies. The black race was not the only race in the last 400 years that was subjected to forced labour by many European powers, notably the British, the French, as well as within the American republic. In fact, the race held in slavery the longest was white to start with, namely the Alba, the Scots and the Picts. Hundreds of thousands of Scots were sold into slavery during the time of Colonial America but their early ancestors were enslaved as early as the first century BC.[2] There was also a less commonly known face of slavery, that of the Irish slaves, which occurred as a consequence of colonisation.

Slavery was instituted as early as 1627 in the British West Indies. In the 1640s, according to Thomas Burton's diary, the British government understood that white slave labour was beneficial to the colonial plantations.[3] A debate in the English Parliament focused on the selling of British whites into slavery in the New World. Hundreds of people from the British

1. Lance Selfa, "Slavery and the Origins of Racism", in *International Socialist Review*, Issue 26, November-December 2002. And in Encyclopaedia Britannica, volume 27, pp.294-301.
2. William D. Phillips, *Slavery from Roman Times to the Early Transatlantic Trade*, Manchester: Manchester University Press, 1985, p.18.
3. Thomas Burton, of Brampton Hall, Westmorland, was MP for Westmorland from 1656 to 1659. His diary is a key record of proceedings in the Parliaments of 1656-59. It was edited and published in four volumes in 1828 by J.T. Rutt. See volume 4, pp.253-274.

Isles were captured and crammed into ships and transported to Virginia, Boston, New York, England's colonies of St. Christopher, Barbados, Nevis, Montserrat, Antigua, and Jamaica in the first half of the 17th century. This brought the English new commercial opportunities.

According to the enactment of 1652, beggars and vagrants were also to be captured and shipped to foreign countries or plantations.[1] The conditions of the white slaves were the same as or even worse than those of the black slaves.

2) Irish Slaves

As Sean O'Callaghan expressed in his work, the Irish were persecuted and enslaved during the era of British Imperialism. Furthermore, the English policy in Ireland was punitive and often resulted in the confiscation of land occupied by Gaelic clans and Hiberno-Norman dynasties. England had been involved in a form of domestic colonisation in Ireland. Plantations in 16th and 17th century Ireland were established throughout the country. Although the native Irish landowning class was subordinated in this period and replaced with a Protestant landowning class, the vast majority of the settlers were Scottish who brought Presbyterianism with them. This new Protestant denomination was different from both Roman Catholicism and from the Church of England. They also brought new farming methods and a Puritan style, and these changes led to the creation of the British Protestant ruling class known as the Protestant ascendancy. It was a way of securing the authority of Crown government in Ireland during the 17th century even though there were several rebellions against the Irish and the Anglo-Irish aristocracy.

The reign of Oliver Cromwell after the English Civil War was the starting point of a period of oppression and suffering of the subject Irish population. Religion was at the centre of Cromwell's early life and he shared the religious beliefs of the Puritans. Their common goal was to *purify* the nation and particularly the Church of England and the national political power of Roman Catholic influence. From that time, Cromwell's political ambitions and religious opinions were closely related. The last form of enforced thrall turned into a form of punishment against the Catholics. The latter, and to some extent Presbyterians, were discriminated against under the Penal Laws. The dominance of the ruling class in Irish life persisted until the late 18th century. In several places across Ireland a desperate people rose up, sacrificing their lives to free their nation from bondage. They transmitted the light of Irish freedom, kept carefully burning, to the next generations.

1. According to the Egerton manuscript which can be found in the British Museum.

During the period 1652 to 1659, about 50,000 people, including children, of Irish origin were, against their will, shipped to British imperial colonies in Barbados, England's most popular colony, and to Virginia in permanent exile to serve as slave labour in the plantations.[1] In Barbados, they were joined by another kind of new slaves who were originally prisoners of war, political dissenters from England, Wales, and Scotland.

Irish natives shared a common fate with their African counterparts on the island of Barbados. Those who were *barbadosed*[2] were sold as slaves or indentured servants to British planters. The number of barbadosed Irish is not known but is estimated, widely, from 12,000 to 40,000. Later on while the African trade was flourishing, the Irish population was decreasing during the course of time as a result of being worked to death, as well as racial intermixing with black slaves. The latter aspect was seen by the plantation masters as "a free, unlimited breeding stock of future slaves".[3] Irish slaves were regarded as property to be bought, sold and mistreated.[4] The humiliating conditions of Irish captives on slave markets reached a state of ignominy. Potential buyers undertook the process of cattle-like physical inspections to value the qualities of the slaves.[5] They were also branded with their owner's initials by way of red-hot iron. Irish slaves played an important part as instigators and leaders of various slave revolts. Both groups survived in harsh conditions; the colony subsisted in the turmoil in spite of raids carried out by French and Spanish pirates, and a tropical weather with constant winds that caused storm damage to the crops. These conditions hastened African and Irish slave revolts and they joined together to rise up against English settlers. In 1655, a seditious outburst resulted in the burning of sugar fields on the island. The aim of sparking a general rebellion was not achieved because militia were deployed in time and prevailed. As a grim warning and a peremptory deterrence, they burnt the mutineers alive and hung their heads on pikes which were displayed throughout the public square.[6] By 1786 the dwindling minority of white slaves still remained significant and were known on the island as the *Red Legs*.[7] They were the survivors of their enchained Celtic forebears and bore the testimony to their tragic legacy. The enslavement of Africans in

1. Sean O'Callaghan, *To Hell or Barbados: The Ethnic Cleansing of Ireland*, Dingle, Ireland: Brandon, 2001, p.9.
2. To be *barbadosed* meant to be deported to the West Indies to a life of slavery.
3. Sean O'Callaghan, *op.cit.*, p.168.
4. *Ibid.*, p.111.
5. *Ibid.*, p.113.
6. *Ibid.*, pp.123-125.
7. Originally, they were known as the *rednecks*, derived from the sun-burnt skin experienced by early white slaves in the Caribbean climate.

Barbados continued until 1834 when slaves were emancipated, and then apprenticed for a period of four years.

A similar harrowing process of Irish slave labour migration appeared in the plantations of Jamaica under Cromwell's reign and earlier under the reign of James I.[1] In 1620, forced white slave labour migration to the colony of Virginia had begun. Other Irish slaves were also to be found further back in 1612 on the Amazon in South America. This was the unmentioned dimension of the Irish in white slavery.

The report on the Irish experience of slavery cannot, though, be limited to the picture of Irish slaves. As was often the case in the process of history, subjugated people associated their liberation with the empowerment that allowed them to do to others what they had suffered themselves. Irish slave traders had found an escape to subjugation and a rise in the economic scale and in society. These Irish slave traders are important to our study because they established the base for the pressure groups who fought for the continuation of slavery. A close study of the historical circumstances that favoured their rise allows one to better grasp the conditions of their trade.

3) The Irish slave traders

Many Irish people fled their own country to escape poverty and sailed across the Irish Sea to the shores of England. A vast number of them arrived in Liverpool in a state of grinding poverty and despite their physical weakness they found work in loading and unloading the largest ships in the world. From about 1750 the merchants of Liverpool made huge profits from the slave trade.

Liverpool's population grew rapidly, and by the early 18th century it had reached some 5,000 inhabitants. By 1750, it continued to increase due to the great influx of immigrants, and by 1801 it had reached 77,000. Many of the newcomers were Irish and Welsh, and in the course of time, a few Irish merchants and captains appear to have been engaged in the slave trade. Interestingly, the letter books and ships' logs with surnames of ships' captains from the ports of Bristol and Liverpool are testament to the involvement of captains with surnames of Irish descent.[2]

For example, the name of David Tuohy[3] may be mentioned as he was an Irish Catholic emigrant, and resident of Liverpool. He was someone who benefited from the traffic in human beings as did the Irish-Frenchman and

1. Sean O'Callaghan, *op.cit.*, pp.140-141.
2. Nini Rodgers, *Ireland, Slavery and anti-Slavery*, London: Palgrave Macmillan, 2007, p.98.
3. *Ibid.*, p.99.

armateur, Antoine Walsh[1] (1703-63) whose glaring slave-trading activities afforded him great wealth in St. Malo and Nantes. Liverpool had close ties with Ireland, given Ireland's geographic location, its domination by Britain, and the fact that in the 18th century slavery made up one-third of Europe's and half of Britain's trade. Between the 15th and 19th centuries, European powers transported 11,000,000 enslaved Africans to the Americas. These huge maritime and commercial ventures, the largest in history, demanded a great investment in order to provide Gargantuan profits.

In the new country, the Irish immigrants found a very different form of social hierarchy, one that was based on the colour of a person's skin, which was entirely different from what they had suffered before. The new Irish immigrants had the possibility of integrating into an initially hostile population only by proving that they could be more brutal in their oppression of African Americans than the natives. The Irish, colonised at home, were colonisers abroad.[2] Curiously, Irish connections of African slave trade had not been recorded in Irish History. It had probably been forgotten because it "was regarded as shameful or because the collection of relevant material on Irish involvement with black slavery has been widely dispersed or ill-recorded."[3]

However, the importance of the Irish in global developments surrounding the slave trade cannot be denied. Black slavery made the fortune of some Irish abroad as they participated in the slave trade and in the establishment of slave plantations in the Caribbean.

The economic impact of sugar in the rise of the Catholic middle class played a pivotal role, as well as the importance of supplying the slave trade in the West Indies to the development of Cork in the 18th century.[4] One of Cork's wealthiest merchants in London was Richard Hare. Others like the Roche[5] and the Creagh families[6] from Limerick held slaves in Barbados. Their involvement extended from Nantes to Africa, the Leewards, Rhode Island and South Carolina. The founding president of the Belfast Chamber of Commerce, Waddell Cunningham, amassed a fortune from slavery. In 1754 he became the major shipowner in New York. The Latouche family[7] owned plantations in Jamaica while the Brownes of Westport, with seats in the British Parliament, became "Ireland's premier slave-holding family."[8]

1. *Ibid.*, p.111.
2. *Ibid.*, pp.95 *seq.*
3. *Ibid.*.
4. *Ibid.*
5. *Ibid.*, p.111.
6. *Ibid.*, p.113.
7. *Ibid.*, p.164.
8. *Ibid.*

It came as no surprise that on two occasions, one in Cork (1762) and one in Dublin (1768), slaves had been advertised in Irish newspapers.

Throughout the Irish diaspora two opposite attitudes matter: an Irish affinity with oppressed peoples, and activities of numerous individuals who profited from the slave trade. Although Irishmen of all backgrounds had a connection with slavery, very little of the slave trade profits actually ended up in Ireland.

The economic rise of a Catholic middle class benefiting from slavery had a political and social consequence: it led this newly-born bourgeoisie to look for political representation and social recognition. Paradoxically, the representation of Catholics required their Emancipation, which, in turn, opened the way for the emancipation of slaves in general.

II. Towards abolition

The process of the abolition of slavery started as a religious idea, and was promoted by a Protestant group, the Quakers. The economic and political evolution of the Catholics led the Catholic leader, Daniel O'Connell, to endorse this fight and to give it a political dimension.

1) Catholic emancipation: Daniel O'Connell, the Liberator

O'Connell was fully committed to religious tolerance and freedom. He became involved with the United Irishmen, a group that had been inspired by the French Revolution. He opposed the insurrection of 1798, arguing that the people of Ireland were not ready for immediate freedom. Instead he advocated using the machinery of Parliament to obtain political and religious equality. Ten years later, he became a successful and well-known barrister in Ireland. By 1815, he was acknowledged as the leader of the Catholic Emancipation movement. In 1823, O'Connell formed the Catholic Association with Richard Lalor Sheil and Thomas Wyse. By 1826 the Association had begun supporting candidates in parliamentary elections and O'Connell was elected as MP for County Clare in 1828.

Radical MPs, notably Sir Francis Burdett and Joseph Hume, were in favour of the end of anti-Catholic legislation and urged Parliament to change the law. Even Tories, in particular Sir Robert Peel and the Duke of Wellington, who had been against it in the past, had respect for the political and social upheaval at home. They urged their Conservative colleagues to adopt new reforms before a civil war broke out. The Catholic Emancipation Act was only passed with the support of the Whigs. In two years' time, in 1829, the British Parliament passed the Roman Catholic Relief Act, granting

Catholic emancipation. This spectacular victory meant a step forward to freedom for Irish people.

Daniel O'Connell played a significant part in Ireland's destiny. For years, he had been working relentlessly to change laws and obtain reforms for the Irish people's betterment. He had spent his life challenging the British government, had been running from meeting to meeting and making a great number of speeches in defence of tolerance and freedom. He was indeed Ireland's liberator and, to some extent the liberator of other people who were enchained. The Catholic emancipation and the abolition of slavery were closely linked. A great number of Irish people had been enslaved and sent to the Colonies simply because they were Catholics. In obtaining their full emancipation in 1829, O'Connell freed his people at home and abroad. Thus, the emancipation had a direct impact on the conditions of the Irish Catholic slaves in the British colonies. Moreover, the Emancipation Act was the first step towards the abolition of slavery that was decreed in 1833 and freed all white slaves as well as black slaves. In this perspective O'Connell's speech reveals that he was conscious of the fact that his fight for the freedom of the Irish Catholics was also a fight for the freedom of all slaves.

> Gentlemen, God knows I speak for the saddest people the sun sees: but may my right hand forget its cunning, and my tongue cleave to the roof of my mouth, if to save Ireland, even Ireland, I forget the negro one single hour![1]

As a matter of fact the Emancipation Act of 1829 led consequently to a more general reflection on the status of slaves, concretely realised by the Abolition Act of 1838. His winning of Catholic emancipation and his way of moderating and holding his people led him, in 1840, to reach with them the threshold of a new era.

As said before, focusing on the anti-slavery movement among the Irish would be one-sided, since economic interests had led some Irish to fight for the continuation of slavery.

2) The pro-slavery movement: interests and arguments

The emergence of the slavery and anti-slavery movements is closely linked to the rising and falling fortunes due to the production of sugar in the Colonies and the transatlantic slave trade. In the 17th and 18th centuries, the vast profits had given Britain enormous resources that benefited its economy. By that time, merchants and planters grew wealthier and acquired a powerful political power. They developed lobbies and monopolies which

1. Daniel O'Connell, speech of 1830 cited in Noel Ignatiev, *How the Irish Became White,* New York: Routledge, 1995, p.7.

endowed them with a great influence on the English state's economy. Financial institutions such as banks were founded and fully participated in the growth of the mercantile sectors of the British Empire. Conflicts of financial interests between the colonies and Britain arose after the tariffs and other trade restrictions imposed by the English state. They opened the way to criticism and attacks at the end of the 18th century. Public opinion was awakened by the constant questioning of the different churches about the morality of the slave trade and the ownership of other human beings. The Quakers headed the list of the churches that campaigned against the overproduction of sugar and the illegitimacy of the slave trade. Propaganda against sugar buying spread throughout Great Britain. Then significant decline in the sugar industries of the Colonies slowed down the slave trade. The new economic vulnerability of the two major commercial exchanges favoured the anti-slavery movement. The economic profits brought to all mayors of Liverpool and MPs who were involved in the lucrative slave trade and to the Church of England that also had plantations began to be seriously threatened. Consequently, they did little to question the ethics of the ownership of slaves.

The pro-slavery arguments evolved when the anti-slavery movement began to challenge slavery's moral legitimacy. Justifications for slavery arose in the late 18th century and Parliamentary debates facing the threat of the masses' uprisings reinforced their position on slavery, asserting that slavery had a positive influence upon society[1] and the alternatives of abolition were inconceivable. Pro-slavery supporters argued that Britain would suffer great economic distress if it were to withdraw from the slave trade. The end of slavery would have a bad effect on ordinary working people in Britain. They further asserted that British withdrawal would not result in a reduction of the trade.

The arguments of the pro-slavery movement was that people should think first about Britain's prosperity at home and not be concerned that it may depend on the ill treatment and enslavement of others in the Caribbean. The people who supported slavery made their own propaganda and challenged the abolitionists. The latter therefore had to convince people that ending slavery was the right thing to do.

The organisation of the abolitionist movement grew on the basis of these social and political circumstances. Significantly, its success was due to the original views and methods of a man who had forward-looking views

1. John Cary, *A Discourse on Trade and Others Relative to It*, London: Routledge Thoemmes Press, 1992, p.8.

both about non-violent political fights and about the emancipation of his own people.

3) The Abolitionist movement (1783-1788): struggle and organisation

The slave trade system provoked little protest until the 18th century. The Quakers and other evangelical religious groups such as the Methodists and the Presbyterians in Britain and in the United States had been the precursors. They criticised and condemned the violation of man. Subsequently, moral disapproval of slavery was widespread in Colonial countries. A multitude of societies against slavery flourished everywhere in Britain, Ireland and America. This movement was originally founded for the ending of the transatlantic slave trade but developed into a larger vision of mankind and turned to a fight for absolute abolition of slavery.

The Quakers were originally called the "Friends of Truth" and later became "The Society of Friends". The origins of their testimony against slavery and slave trade can be traced back to an Englishman, George Fox from Fenny Drayton, Leicestershire, who had been inspired to the point of preaching a gospel of brotherly love. During the reign of Charles II, followers of Fox refused to attend Anglican services or to pay tithes. A great number of them were arrested and imprisoned in England. Some were transported as slaves while others were killed at their meetings. By 1660 the number of the Societies of Friends grew to 20,000. They sent missionaries to Ireland, Scotland, Wales and the American Colonies, but their regard for all human beings to be treated equally before God and their disregard for peoples' ranks and titles meant persecution throughout the 17th century. In the 18th century, they became involved in politics and social reform. From the 1750s, Colonial American Quakers called on British Quakers to take action against slavery. They were the first group to denounce slavery. In 1783, the Quakers presented a new petition against slavery, more substantial than the first one in 1727, to Parliament and played a prominent role in the Anti-Slavery Society. By the early 19th century, there were about 25,000 Quakers in Britain.

They wrote and distributed anti-slavery literature and lobbied Parliament. They pursued lobbying activities for abolition in Britain. By 1785 the Anti-Slavery Movement drew the attention of Anglicans Thomas Clarkson and Granville Sharp, and the Evangelical William Wilberforce. They became interested in the cause and in 1787 the Society for the Abolition of the Slave Trade was formed with nine Quakers out of the twelve members involved and with Wilberforce as its Parliamentary spokesman who since 1791 had regularly introduced a motion in favour of abolition. Like the Quakers, they collected all kinds of evidence, travelled, raised money, lobbied and took the necessary task of spreading anti-slavery literature to arouse public opinion against the slave trade. Among anti-slavery societies which were flourishing all over the country and overseas, another pioneering anti-slavery group appeared in Birmingham in 1824, the Female Society for the Relief of British Negro Slaves. Women also played an important role in the anti-slavery movement. The British Parliament passed the Abolition of the Slave Trade Act in 1807. It made slave trade in the British colonies as well as the transportation of slaves on British ships illegal. Quakers were involved in the formation of the Anti-Slavery Society in 1832 and the BFASS, the British and Foreign Anti-Slavery Society in 1839. The latter lasted during the whole period and still exists today as the Anti-Slavery International.

The stage was set for the political struggle. The battle could start.

III. The Irish voice in the fight for the Abolition of Slavery

As Noel Ignatiev wrote, "Ireland had an old anti-slavery tradition, going back to the Council of Armagh in 1177, which had prohibited Irish trade of English slaves. It was a common boast that in seven centuries no slave had set foot on Irish soil."[1] By 1788, the Dublin Chamber of Commerce proudly observed with great satisfaction that "the traffic in human species does not appear to have ever been carried on from their kingdom."[2]

Anti-slavery international meetings took place in Ireland, England and the United States and in 1841, sixty thousand Irish issued an Address to their compatriots in America calling upon them to join with the abolitionists in the struggle against slavery. At the top of the list of signatories was the name of Daniel O'Connell, well known throughout Ireland as "the Liberator".[3] O'Connell had founded the Catholic Association which was the first mass political party in History. According to Ignatiev, he was "acknowledged as the first modern agitator in developing the methods of grass roots organising and the mass meeting". At a time when Catholics were prohibited from holding public office, he had led the campaign for Catholic emancipation.[4]

O'Connell had been elected by poor rural voters to the House of Commons and also held the honorific post of Lord Mayor of Dublin. He then led a new campaign against the Act of Union of 1800 and to restore an Irish parliament under the Crown. Most of his speeches were published

1. Noel Ignatiev, *How the Irish Became White*, p.7.
2. Nini Rodgers, *op.cit.*, p.159.
3. Noel Ignatiev, *op.cit.*, p.9.
4. *Ibid.*, p.6.

in newspapers and particularly in the Catholic and Irish press. He was the most popular figure in Ireland and among Irish throughout the world.[1] He first entered Parliament in 1830. A year before, he denounced slavery and American hypocrisy. His attacks were particularly scathing and made the Americans resentful of him. After one of his fiery anti-slavery speeches in London, he received a letter in 1838 from a group of prominent Irish living in Philadelphia.[2] They were the first to express their concern about slavery but attempted to define the resentment of the Americans for the immigrant group to which they belonged and confessed their painful feeling of insecurity. That same year another group, the American Anti-Slavery Society, thanked him for his support even though his declarations were severe. O'Connell was warmly encouraged to go further in his denunciations for the slaves' sake. With James Haughton, a Dublin grain merchant and Unitarian, he founded the Hibernian Anti-Slavery Society. Like O'Connell, he was a supporter of the repeal of the Act of Union of 1800. He retained some links with the United States by being the regular correspondent of the North American Anti-Slavery Journal, William Lloyd Garrison's *Liberator.*[3] Garrison was in some ways the American equivalent of O'Connell. He and other members of the Society, notably the black abolitionist Frederick Douglass, met their Irish counterparts when touring the Esmerald Isle. It was established practice that black American abolitionists crossed the ocean to visit the European coasts.

One cannot deal with these historical events without analysing their literary counterpart, since literature has always played the role of a mirror of politics in Ireland. A few names may be mentioned even if space does not allow for the development of the contribution of Irish writers to the anti-slavery attitudes, notably Mary Leadbeater and Mary Birkett. Poet Hugh Mulligan, author of *Poems Chiefly on Slavery and Oppression* (1788), was an Irish emigrant and was acknowledged as an influential personality in the anti-slavery movement. Other novelists known for comparing poor Irish people with West Indian slaves comprise Maria Edgeworth.[4] The links between Catholic and slave emancipation, including the similar Irish slave relationship, were quite obvious.

O'Connell had many causes for which to struggle. The three main issues started with the Catholic emancipation, followed by the repeal of the Union Act of 1800 and the abolition of slavery. The three issues were all grounded on freedom, each connected to the other. By emancipating the

1. *Ibid.*, p.7.
2. Philadelphia was the Quakers' fief.
3. Noel Ignatiev, *op.cit.*, p.9.
4. Nini Rodgers, *op.cit.*, pp.230 *seq.*

Irish Catholics the British Government knew that there was no alternative. Ireland was in an era of demands, and it was time for the society to change and it was slowly, progressively changing. Oppression was heavy and voices claiming their immediate freedom were rising so loudly that it took them five years to see the actual abolition of slavery. Even though the abolition was revealed gradually in the course of time it took some seven years to almost disappear in Great Britain and the Colonies. Gradual abolition happened to be necessary for various reasons, mainly economic and social. Time was required to prepare British society for the effects of the end of slavery on the one hand and freed slaves to integrate into a new way of life and learn the ways of a free society on the other hand.

Conclusion

Suffering and social injustice could only elicit wrath or revolt towards a government policy in spite of economic interests at stake. Irish Catholics were among the first victims of slavery, in particular white slavery. The echo of their suffering and their death resounded strongly and was finally heard by those who always proclaimed that the human being, his ideas and his faith are more important than material and economic interests. The role of the Irish people in the abolition of slavery changed the fate of both their people and all the others who fell under the yoke of slavery. The first step to freedom and to the end of slavery for Irish people was to obtain their religious emancipation. They were unable to influence the British Parliament concerning the abolition of slavery as they were discriminated against by what was left of the Penal Laws. The Catholic Relief Act in 1793 enabled Catholics to obtain more rights but not to have a full equal standing. Actually, by the 1820s they had the right to vote in elections, but were not allowed to sit in Parliament. Thus their power was limited. The Irish people knew that the political battle they were pursuing would lead them to emancipation. They found in O'Connell their liberator, the man who knew how to use his political abilities to open the path to freedom in obtaining Catholic emancipation. The involvement of Irish people in the debate for the abolition of slavery was significant not only on the political scene, but also on the literary, religious, social and international sides. The involvement of the Irish people in their desire for emancipation was impressive and their fight relentless. They stood up to the struggle they delivered against their oppressors. The Irish people, small in number but large in bravery, courage and will, knew and still know how to keep alive the light of what they have always been characterised by: *the fighting spirit*.

Bibliography

Akenson D., *If the Irish Ran the World. Monserrat 1630-1730.* Montreal: The McGill-Queens University Press, 1997.

Cary John, *A Discourse on Trade and Other Matters Relative to it,* London: Routledge-Thoemmes Press, 1992.

Ignatiev Noel, *How the Irish Became White,* New York: Routledge, 1995.

MacIntyre Angus, D., *The Liberator, Daniel O'Connor and the Irish Party, 1830-1847,* London: Hamish Hamilton, 1965.

McCafferty K., *Testimony of an Irish Slave Girl,* New York: Viking Press, 2002.

Moody T.W., Vaughan W.E, ed., *A New History of Ireland,* IV, *Eighteenth-Century Ireland, 1691-1800,* Oxford: Clarendon Press, 1998.

O'Callaghan S., *To Hell or Barbados: The Ethnic Cleansing of Ireland,* Dingle, Ireland: Brandon Books, 2001.

Rawley James, *London, Metropolis of the Slave Trade,* Columbia, Miss.: University of Missouri Press, 2003.

—, *The Transatlantic Slave Trade,* New York, London: W.W. Norton; Toronto: G.J. McLeod, 1981.

Rodgers Nini, *Ireland, Slavery and Anti-slavery,* London: Palgrave Macmillan, 2007.

Scully Denys, "Statement of the Penal Laws which Aggrieved the Catholics of Ireland", in Nicholas Lee (ed.), *The Catholic Question in Ireland, 1762-1829,* Bristol: Thoemmes Press, 2000.

"... The state of slavery is not recognised by the laws of this Kingdom, and is inconsistent with the principles thereof"[1]

The Scots and the Problem of Slavery

William Findlay

"... for, as long as but a hundred of us remain alive, never will we on any conditions be brought under English rule. It is in truth not for glory, nor riches, nor honours that we are fighting, but for freedom—for that alone, which no honest man gives up but with life itself". As this extract from the *Declaration of Arbroath* of 1320 proudly proclaims, Scottish national identity was intimately linked to the notion of "freedom" from its origins and over the following centuries this credo gradually became enshrined in the national consciousness. Yet, as Rosa Luxembourg once astutely remarked, a people that haughtily proclaims its freedom can easily be lulled into a false sense of superiority and not realise that all they really possess is that right alone, when the substance of the claim has long since disappeared. So it is reassuring to discover that in the case of the struggle against slavery, Scotland did more than merely proclaim its hostility and that the nation's passion for freedom, in the words of one expert, forged a "history of which the Scots can be rightly proud".[2]

The question of slavery first became a national issue in Scotland through a series of high-profile court cases, which, from the mid-18th century, challenged the legal status of slavery in the country by placing it in a "national" context and linking it to the religious settlement of 1707. The first of these concerned James Montgomery the slave of Robert Sheddan, a merchant from Morrishill in Ayrshire, who, on 21 April 1756, escaped from his captivity while being transported to Virginia in order to be "sold on". Although Montgomery was quickly recaptured in Edinburgh, he challenged the legality of his condition at the Court of Session on the grounds that having been baptised in Scotland his new status should be recognised as incompatible with that of a slave.[3] Despite the fact that

1. Judgement handed down by John Swinton, Sheriff Depute of Perth, in *Knight V Wedderburn*, on 20th May 1774, Court of Session records, National Archives of Scotland (CS235/K/2/2).
2. Cf. Neal ASCHERSON, *Stone Voices: The Search for Scotland*. London: Granta Books, 2002, p.VIII. Also *Forward* by Dr. Desmond M. Tutu to Ian Whyte's, *Scotland and the Abolition of Black Slavery, 1756-1838*. Edinburgh: Edinburgh University Press, 2006.
3. Montgomery had been instructed in Christianity and baptised by the Rev. John Witherspoon, who later became president of Princeton University and a signatory to the American Declaration of Independence. The baptism had been strongly opposed by his master and

Montgomery died before his case could come to trial, the legal precedent had been established which opened the way for other cases. In 1769 a second case was brought before the Court of Session in Edinburgh when Dr. David Dalrymple of Methil in Fife accused his servant, Black Tom, of "pious fraud", by using the pretext of baptism to claim his freedom.[1] Once again, therefore, the legal challenge centred on the transforming and liberating power of religion, for as the accused set out in his statement,

> I am now by the Christian Religion Liberate and set at freedom from my old yoke bondage and slavery and by the Laws of this Christian land there is no Slavery nor vestige of Slavery allowed...[2]

But the case had wider implications since it involved a determined and concerted effort to challenge the very legality of slavery in Scotland by what Dr. Dalrymple called "secessionist militants". Unfortunately, here again, the legal challenge came to nothing as Dr. Dalrymple died before the trial could take place, thus making Spens a free man by default. Yet the courts were to have their say when in 1774 Joseph Knight contested his status as a slave of John Wedderburn of Ballendean (Perthshire) on the grounds that "the act of landing in Scotland freed him from perpetual servitude, as slavery was not recognised in Scotland".[3] Although the Justices of the Peace Court in Perth rejected his claim, Knight appealed to John Swinton, Sheriff of Perth, who found for him declaring that:

> the state of slavery is not recognised by the laws of this kingdom, and is inconsistent with the principles thereof: That the regulations in Jamaica, concerning slaves, do not extend to this kingdom; and repelled the defender's claim to a perpetual service.

Amid rising public interest the case then went to the Court of Session, Scotland's supreme civil court, where Wedderburn argued that the states of slavery and perpetual servitude were different and that in Scots law, Knight, even though he was not recognised as a slave, was still bound to provide perpetual service in the same manner as an indentured servant or an apprenticed artisan. However, in a landmark ruling, the judges rejected Wedderburn's appeal without qualification and found that:

seems to have been done publicly in the church but also discretely since it was not officially recorded at the time. Curiously, on 19th April 1756, the day before Montgomery was due to be taken back to Virginia, he was given a "certificate" by Witherspoon which appears to be an invitation to Christians to assist in his freedom. Cf. I. Whyte, *op.cit.*, p.21.

1. "Black Tom" had been baptised and given the name David Spens (after the minister of the Church) on 1st September 1769.
2. The court records of the Dalrymple vs Spens and Henderson case are to be found in the National Archives of Scotland, CS236/D/4/3 box 104 and CS236/S/3/13.
3. The court records can be consulted in the National Archives of Scotland under reference CS235/K/2/2.

> … the dominion assumed over this Negro, under the law of Jamaica, being unjust, could not be supported in this country to any extent: That, therefore, the defender had no right to the Negro's service for any space of time, nor to send him out of the country against his consent: That the Negro was likewise protected under the act 1701, c.6. from being sent out of the country against his consent.

On an individual level Knight had thus won the right to leave his domestic service as he so wished but more importantly the Court of Session effectively declared that the state of slavery was not recognised under Scots law and that runaway slaves (or "perpetual servants") had the right to the full protection of the courts.[1] Thus, six years after the English courts had provided slaves with the same legal right to protection as other members of society[2], the Scottish legal system had effectively outlawed slavery in that country by giving the question "its first *general determination* in the supreme Civil Court of Scotland".[3]

That Scottish law should have taken such a bold step at this time has intrigued historians and merits detailed examination. The domestic importance of slavery in the country was, after all, relatively marginal both in sociological and economic terms[4]: Scotland having been excluded by the Navigation Acts of 1660 from the slave trade until the Act of Union in 1707.[5] Yet, as has been noted, behind and feeding the legal debate over slavery, were extremely powerful social and religious forces which believed that

1. The Court of Session's decision was reached by a majority of eight to four.
2. On June 22, 1772, Lord Mansfield, gave an important ruling in the case of James Somerset a slave who had been recaptured after resisting his master's attempt to send him back to Jamaica for resale. Mansfield determined that a master cannot by force carry his *slave* out of England and that his status as a servant must be determined under English law alone and that whatever any use of force against that person in England must be permissible under English law. His judgment was deliberately silent regarding the legal status of slaves in England. Mansfield was raised to the peerage in 1756 and became 1st Earl of Mansfield in 1776 but was, in fact, born and educated in Scotland. His historic judgement is perhaps all the more remarkable since his own sister was the owner of at least one black "servant". Cf. George Van Cleve, "Somerset's Case and Its Antecedents in Imperial Perspective". *Law and History Review*, vol.24, n°3, Fall 2006, pp.601-645.
3. The *Caledonian Mercury* of 17th January 1778.
4. If, as has been suggested, there were between 3,000 and 15,000 black people in Britain by the 1780s and perhaps half of them lived in London, the numbers in Scotland were extremely small, perhaps as few as 70 or 80 at any one time. "Slave markets" had been in existence in Glasgow as in various other towns in Britain, though they seem to have been comparatively small (only eight recorded slave sales are known for Scotland) and the length of time for which they existed during the seventeenth and eighteenth centuries is uncertain. Cf. Folarin O. Shyllon, "The Black Presence and Experience in Britain: An Analytical Overview", in J. S. Gundara and I. Duffield (eds), *Essays on the History of Blacks in Britain*, Aldershot: Avebury, 1992, p.203; Norma Myers, *Reconstructing the Black Past: Blacks in Britain, 1780–1830*, London: Frank Cass, 1996, pp.20 and 35.
5. Certain colonial goods particularly needed in England, known as "enumerated goods", including sugar, cotton, ginger, indigo, dyewoods and tobacco, could only be marketed in Britain.

the sanction of religion and morality were subsumed within the common law of the land. In the three cases brought before the Scottish courts the issue took on a particular intensity as it carried echoes of the nation's own historic struggle against oppression, and, consequently, this theme began to resonate inside the wider social debate of the time. As a result, the question of slavery took on a new significance for the Scots, which was far greater than might be assumed from the sociological reality of the country at this time. It became, it has been suggested, a question heavy with symbolic meanings, which connected it to a whole series of questions which the rapidly changing social and intellectual context of the period forced to the surface.[1]

Slavery, for instance, raised serious and sensitive questions for the Church of Scotland as it did for other churches. On purely religious grounds, the state of slavery was denounced as an aberration, an obscenity, a flagrant example of the corruption of modern society, for it compromised the slave's ability to save his immortal soul.[2] At the heart of this corruption was the "guilty *phantasy*", as one of the leading figures of the anti-slavery movement put it, that "man can hold property in man".[3] It was seen as a direct challenge to the Christian notion of free agency, the Master "presuming to replace God in the eyes of the slave". Such "illegitimate authority" which obstructed the slave's quest for salvation, had therefore not only to be denounced but also actively combated by all Christians.

How exactly this could and should be done was less obvious to the church at this time and the arguments and counter-arguments were often caught up in the particular nature of the religious settlement in Scotland. The Church of Scotland, in its official capacity as one of the great institutions of the realm, opted for a cautious approach. Despite having taken a stance against slavery, in general terms, in the mid 1850s, it was not until the abolitionist movement had got underway that the General Assembly of the Church of Scotland finally accepted a debate on the question in 1788. Even at this point, and despite almost overwhelming condemnation of slavery and the slave trade, however, it stopped short of petitioning Parliament on the question, an approach it deemed below its dignity, and

1. Cf. David Brion Davis, *The Problem of Slavery in Western Culture*, Ithaca: Cornell University Press, 1967, and *The Problem of Slavery in the Age of Revolution, 1770-1823*, Ithaca, Cornell University Press, 1975, pp.249-254 and passim. And C. Duncan Rice, "Controversies over Slavery in Eighteenth and Nineteenth-Century Scotland" in Lewis Perry and Michael Fellman (eds), *Antislavery Reconsidered. New Perspectives on the Abolitionists*, Baton Rouge and London: Louisiana State University Press, 1979, p.26.
2. Jean L. Watson, *The Life of Andrew Thomson D. D.*, Edinburgh, 1882, p.111ff.
3. Speech made by Lord Chancellor Brougham on 13th July, 1830.

instead included its protest in the *Annual Address to the Throne.*[1] Protocol however was not the only consideration behind this institutional reluctance, especially in the later stages of the campaign. Inside the Kirk there was also a growing disquiet at the role of secular patronage and how it was "interfering" with the proper running of the House of God. As an institution it chose therefore to tread a fine line on the question of freedom from slavery so as not to become entangled in the debate as to whether it had become "enslaved, and bondaged" itself.[2]

But if the Church of Scotland as a national institution was slow to become involved in the practicalities of the question, on the local level the engagement of its clergy and church members was quite different. Before the first case had been brought before the courts, sermons were already being given from pulpits throughout the country, denouncing the evils of slavery and exulting the transforming power of Christianity.[3] The ceremonial surrounding baptism, in particular, played a significant role in the Scottish context and one which distinguished it from its southern neighbour, for it was a public act involving a profession of faith before a congregation. For many Scots it was, quite simply, equivalent to a rite of passage into the local community where basic assumptions about the sacredness of individual freedom were taken for granted.[4] Furthermore, the notion of "rebirth in Christ" and the sense of Christian brotherhood which it conferred, implied a moral obligation to help the less fortunate in their struggle through life. The extent to which this obligation was taken seriously can be judged from the fact that in the three test cases, as in other similar situations, local church leaders were remarkable in the extent and the variety of the support provided, covering all aspects of this "liberation", from sheltering the runaways, to organising their legal cases and guiding them through the courts.[5] In several cases the actions of individual ministers verged on illegality in their zeal for their

1. It also did this again in 1791 and more forcefully in 1792. But this practice ceased due to the growing feeling that it had no right to "meddle in politics" and should confine its activities to the kingdom "not of this world". Iain Whyte, *Scotland and the Abolition of Black Slavery, 1756-1838*. Edinburgh: Edinburgh University Press, 2006, pp.188 and 204.
2. This unease over the "rights of property holding" and how they impacted on the governance of the Church threatened the very essence of the Presbyterianism settlement in Scotland by blurring the fine line between the jurisdiction of the civil and spiritual authorities. It ultimately resulted in the *Disruption* in 1843 when the Church of Scotland divided into two warring factions.
3. I. Whyte, *op.cit.*, p.28ff.
4. *Ibidem*, p.35.
5. It has been calculated that between 1719 and 1776, there were 36 reported cases of runaway slaves in Scotland, although there are no figures concerning the capture rates. Cf. *Scotland and the Slave Trade. 2007 Bicentenary*. One Scotland: Scottish Executive Electronic Publication, 2007, p.20.

self-appointed mission, prompting a general reluctance among many slave owners to consent to the baptism of slaves and a feeling that the Church was indulging in the "spread of fancies of freedom" among them.[1] Parish congregations and those of surrounding areas were also active in this campaign most visibly in the collection of funds in preparation for legal action and here again the impression is that a discrete network of militancy might well have existed over wide areas of Scotland.[2]

From the latter part of the century and especially after the setting up of the *Society for the Abolition of the Slave Trade* in London in 1787, the nature of Church protest began to change from formal denunciation and essentially reactive involvement to a more proactive and aggressive stance. On 27th February 1788 the Church of Scotland's Presbytery of Edinburgh, under the impulsion of the Rev. Robert Walker of Canongate[3], determined to petition Parliament for the abolition of the African slave trade. This new and more direct approach, calling on the House of Commons to end the trade, quickly caught on and over the following years was emulated by numerous other groups, secular as well as religious.[4] As a result, of the 101 petitions addressed to the House of Commons on the slave trade in 1788, 16 came from Scotland and the majority of these from church bodies. In 1792, the second year of petitioning, the numbers had risen considerably so that 185 of the 519 petitions came from Scotland, thus representing over 35% of the British total. Again church leaders were directly involved in an estimated 50% of these petitions. Petitioning only resurfaced in the post war period and inside a social context which had dramatically changed but even during this phase of the struggle the contribution made by the Kirk remained a major factor in the dynamics of the movement and its uncompromising stance. In this respect it stood in stark contrast to the attitude of the Church of England.[5]

1. NAS CS 235/K/2/2 p.16, 23-24.
2. At the start of the Spens case, for instance, collections were raised in the surrounding churches to meet the legal costs. In the Montgomery case the certificate delivered by his local church on the eve of his escape reads more like a coded message calling on Christian help than a mere attestation of baptism. In several other cases Church intervention would appear to have been on behalf of slaves from outside the parish of origin.
3. Walker became one of Scotland's best known clergymen after being immortalised on canvas as the *Skating Minister on Duddingston Loch* (a painting by Sir Henry Raeburn).
4. Many of these petitions came from areas where the reality of slavery must have been purely notional. General James Grant of Ballindalloch, Banff (Governor of East Florida) in a letter to Lord Cornwallis, dated 22nd April 1792 complained that "Petitions have been pouring in from every part of the Island, and a great number indeed from Scotland, some of them from the Highland Parishes where the Fools who sign the petitions at the Black Smith's shop, which is the Country Coffee House, never saw the Face of a Black…". Charles Cornwallis: Papers, PRO 30/11/270, fo. 95.
5. These contrasting attitudes of the two national churches were visible from the start of the campaigns. In 1788 some 92 ministers of the national churches of England and Scotland

Religious considerations were however not the only arguments behind the anti-slavery movement in Scotland for they were often reinforced by other secular arguments and underpinned by the pivotal role which education played in society.[1] For all the subtle differences in analysis and interpretation which had arisen from the Scottish Enlightenment, a feeling had gradually spread throughout the country that slavery was simply wrong on both moral and economic grounds. Morally it was believed to negate individual freedom of action which was seen as a necessary counterweight to the needs of society as a whole, while for the advocates of the new science of economics it was quite simply unprofitable and ultimately self-destroying.[2] The power of these ideas, especially as they attached themselves to the spreading belief that a no-nonsense "Common Sense" approach to life's problems was the only correct one, seems to have filtered through all levels of Scottish society via an intricate network of universities and grammar schools, an extensive network of clubs, popular literature[3] and the press itself.[4] Gradually a framework of meaning, inside which individual and collective involvement in the struggle against slavery

sponsored between 14 and 22% of abolitionist petitions. But only 9% of the English petitions came from Church of England sources. Among the petitions co-sponsored by civic and religious leaders the Scottish figure was considerably in excess of 50%. In 1831 the Church in Scotland provided 5% of all Scottish petitions while the Church of England contributed just half of that in England. Cf. I. Whyte, *op.cit.*, p.101 and S. Drescher, "Two Variants of Anti-Slavery: Religious Organisation and Social Mobilisation in Britain and France, 1780-1870" in Christine Bolt and Seymour Drescher (eds), *Anti-Slavery, Religion and Reform: Essays in Memory of Roger Anstey*, Folkestone: Dawson publishers, 1980, p.47.

1. The Protestant Reformation in Scotland had, by necessity, placed an immense burden on education. By 1750, according to the standards of the time, there was an estimated 75% level of literacy in the country and the impact of the "written word" on the ordinary people has often been remarked upon. The young Robert Burns, for instance, despite his humble origins had by the age of sixteen read such diverse authors as Shakespeare, Alexander Pope, Locke and the French Enlightenment philosophers. By 1790 Edinburgh boasted 16 publishing houses.
2. Adam Smith, *An Inquiry into the Nature and Causes of the Wealth of Nations,* London, 1776, p.289.
3. Attacks on slavery also found literary expression in Scotland where a recent survey found a significant number of eighteenth-century Scottish poets who touched on the theme of slavery. Cf. James G. Basker (ed), *Amazing Grace: An Anthology of Poems about Slavery, 1600-1810*, New Haven: Yale University Press, 2002, p.XLIV ff.
4. Several Scottish newspapers were particularly supportive of the cause and opened their columns to the protesters. The *Caledonian Mercury*, in particular, was often outspoken in its denunciation of slavery. The *Edinburgh Review*, started in 1802, also became a champion of the cause by elevating the argument above individual cases to a global analysis. The review relentlessly denounced the anomaly of slavery as contrary to the very logic of social and economic organisation which lay at the core of modern civilisation. In article after article it was argued that since the principles of social and economic organisation were immutable and universal, slavery as a glaring deviation from these principles, jeopardised humanity's progress by its very existence. It might also be noted that the *Anti-Slavery Reporter* was founded in 1825 by Zachary Macaulay who was also Scottish and who devoted most of his life to the anti-slavery movement from London.

made sense, began to take shape and staked a claim to the national sense of duty.

It is this sense of duty which helps explain why, in the three key court cases on the question, popular support for the victims of slavery was so spontaneous and forthcoming and took such a variety of forms despite the obvious dangers involved. Individuals volunteered their services spontaneously as in the Spens case when the slave's counsel and agent acted on his behalf without fee and two journalists, Walter Ferguson and William Chalmers, undertook to find the bail of £30; as did others, including Samuel Johnson, in the Knight case. As already noted, John Henderson an ordinary farmer who went to considerable risks to himself and his livelihood in helping David Spens and other unsung heroes, formed part of the more discrete networks which were set up elsewhere in Scotland to help these unfortunate victims in their quest for freedom.[1] It was, no doubt, the strength and depth of this shared sense of commitment which prompted Henderson to warn that if Spens were returned to slavery, "the whole country would be inflamed", in a groundswell of revulsion against "the horrible traffik in humans". Individual initiatives came from other parts of the community as well, noticeably from Scotland's academics who played a key role in the protest movement against the slave trade in the 1780s and 1790s. James Beattie, for instance, Professor of Moral Philosophy and Logic at the University of Aberdeen, drafted one of the first petitions to Parliament on the trade in 1788 and persuaded Aberdeen City Council to do likewise in 1792 while other similar initiatives produced petitions from the University of Glasgow and a whole variety of Town Councils throughout Scotland.

It was however the gradual recognition of the immensity of the task and the wealth, power and influence of the "slave lobby", particularly in the West of Scotland, which encouraged collective rather than individual actions. Organised sections of the working class, such as the local salters and miners of Ayrshire contributed to Spens' costs during his four years' legal battle and took a prominent part in the public protest meetings organised throughout the country. In the context of the period when the labour movement was in its infancy and workers themselves had few positive rights of their own, this struggle held particular poignancy and relevance.[2] When petitioning of Parliament started in 1788, many

1. Iain Whyte refers, for instance, to several instances in Glasgow and Paisley, where ordinary people and local communities actively intervened to help slaves gain their freedom Cf. I. Whyte, *op.cit.*, pp.16 and 36.
2. Cf. Alan B. Campbell, *The Lanarkshire Miners: A Social History of Their Trade Unions, 1775-1974*, Edinburgh: J. Donald, 1979, pp.9-15.

organisations such as the weavers of Paisley, one of the most impoverished sections of the local working class, threw themselves into the fight with great dynamism and an uncompromising denunciation of the slave trade, organising public meetings with the support of church ministers and local magistrates. Similar initiatives were also taken by a variety of guilds such as the Brewers of Paisley, the Journeymen Shoemakers and the Candlemakers of Edinburgh and the incorporated trades of Perth. This last group took upon itself to petition Parliament in 1792 when the town itself declined to do so. Perhaps more surprisingly even the Edinburgh Chamber of Commerce felt compelled to petition the House of Commons in 1792, a petition which focused deliberately on disproving the claim that the slave trade was commercially valuable, but ending with the words:

> that even if this was not the case the feelings of your petitioners as men would overbear their opinion as merchants would lead them to sacrifice somewhat of the convenience and profit of commerce to the rights and principles of humanity.[1]

Again, after the ending of the Napoleonic war, this activity continued although at a more cautious pace. Civic groups who had never sent petitions to Parliament before made their opposition to the trade known in the press. More and more these came from small towns and villages particularly in the north east of the country. These Scottish petitions concentrated their denunciations of a trade which was contrary to the principles of justice, humanity, good policy and religion, denouncing in detail the horrors of slavery and contrasting these with the Scottish traditions of common humanity, justice, civilisation, liberty, and concluding with their absolute belief in the inevitability of divine retribution for these sins. Many also took great care to counter the economic arguments justifying the slave trade and the "patriotic" belief that it was a necessary evil for the nation's maritime survival. In one telling argument, exposing the greed of the traders, it was suggested:

> If profit and advantage abstract from justice, is a good reason for continuing the slave trade, the pirate and the highwayman may urge the same plea for continuing their equally honest, humane and honourable employment.[2]

As in England, the urgency of bringing together all of these forces was seen as vital for the success of the cause. In 1788, the year following the setting up of the *Society for the Abolition of the Slave Trade* in London, an Edinburgh branch was founded under the chairmanship of Lord Gardenstone. By 1792 Scotland boasted five such societies in the main

1. I. Whyte, *op.cit.*, p.70.
2. *Ibidem*, pp.91-99 for details.

urban and industrial centres of Aberdeen, Perth, Glasgow, Paisley and Edinburgh. Although no minute books have survived, indications are that these groups were particularly dynamic in raising awareness of the question and focusing public pressure on petitioning Parliament. The Edinburgh committee, for instance, regularly published tracts and factual articles in the press and took up the challenge of sending a copy of the *Abstract of Evidence* to every parish in Scotland. It was also responsible for co-ordinating the city's massive petition of March 1792 which contained almost eleven thousand signatures, a total exceeded only by London and Manchester in that year. The Glasgow Committee, under the chairmanship of David Dale, father-in-law of Robert Owen, seems to have concentrated its activities on its propaganda efforts and financially supporting other Scottish initiatives. No doubt the ground work done by these groups constituted the bedrock on which, after the ending of the war with France, other societies dedicated to the abolition of slavery itself sprung up. The Glasgow Anti-Slavery Society was founded by one of the city's tea merchants and well-known Quaker, William Smeal in 1822. The following year an Edinburgh group was also set up which quickly rose to become the strongest in Scotland. It was followed by others elsewhere in Scotland such as Aberdeen in 1825 and, by the end of the decade, the setting up of Ladies' Sections. As in the previous phase of action, they concentrated their activities on written propaganda and generating and co-ordinating support for the cause through public meetings and debates. The Glasgow association achieved the remarkable feat of successfully piloting a city petition in 1826, which assembled 39,000 signatures representing nearly a quarter of the population of the city at this time.[1]

Scotland's contribution to the anti-slavery movement was, of course, not confined to the boundaries of the country. Individual Scots were also prominent activists in other parts of the United Kingdom as well. This was the case, for example, in Manchester where the Scottish contribution to the movement was particularly identifiable.[2] But above all it was in London that the leading Scottish figures were concentrated and where their contribution was the most significant because of their firsthand knowledge of the West Indian slave trade. Among these were William Dickson, originally of Moffat, who had served as Secretary to the Governor of Barbados and Doctor James Ramsay, native of Fraserburgh, whose experiences, when published, are said to have exposed the full horrors of slavery to the British

1. *The Glasgow Courier*, 22nd April 1826.
2. Cf. David Turley, "British Anti-Slavery Reassessed", in Arthur Burns and Joanna. Innes (eds), *Rethinking the Age of Reform*, Cambridge: Cambridge University Press, 2003, pp.188-189.

public.[1] Others brought their commitment to the service in different ways. James Stephen, Wilberforce's brother-in-law, Henry Lord Brougham[2] and Sir Charles Middleton MP all contributed their expertise in the legal and political fields in the fight against slavery. Brougham and above all Zachary Macaulay were also particularly active in the propaganda struggle and the fight for the "hearts and minds". Macaulay especially became one of the pillars of the movement because of his almost obsessive veneration for detailed factual evidence which became one of the hallmarks of the *Anti-Slavery Reporter* founded by him in 1823 and which became the official organ of the "London Society for the Mitigation and Gradual Abolition of Slavery throughout the British Dominions".[3] As Iain Whyte, in his remarkable study of the Scottish anti-slavery movement, underlines, all of these men were the product of a distinctive culture where theology and egalitarianism, the notion of progress and of a common humanity were paramount and reasoned argument sacred. All had "northern iron" in their make-up and a propensity for the rigours of the intellectual struggle they were involved in.

By any measure the Scottish response to the problem of slavery and the struggle for its abolition was, as Desmond Tutu suggests, a remarkable one. But, like Dr. Jekyll and Mr Hyde, Scotland was also involved in the "dark trade in slavery"[4] and was a society which had been very heavily committed to the slave trade. Several Scottish towns and industries owed their prosperity directly to the slave trade after 1707 such as Leith, Greenock, Montrose and, of course, Glasgow. Glasgow is undoubtedly the most glaring example of this, for its transformation from "quaint fishing village" to "second city of the Empire" was initially triggered by the city's connection with the tobacco and sugar trades. By the latter part of the eighteenth century, tobacco made up over one third of Scotland's imports and over half its exports. The direct and indirect profits of the slave trade spread wealth also to other parts of Scotland, from Ayrshire in the south to Aberdeenshire in the north.[5] Even after the collapse of the tobacco trade in 1775, Glasgow's slave connection continued through the trade in cotton and the links with the West Indies. The role of the Scots in the slave colonies was likewise particularly significant for, according to one study, they held

1. Dickson also undertook a tour of Scotland in 1792 which was extremely successful in raising awareness of the problem at that time.
2. Lord Brougham founded the influential *Edinburgh Review* in 1823 and later became Lord Chancellor.
3. Circulation rose to around 20,000.
4. *The Glasgow Herald. Weekend Review*. 18th October 2003, p.13.
5. Alexander Allerdyce of Aberdeen was reputed to have transported more African slaves to Jamaica than the entire population of Aberdeen at the time. Richard Oswald from Caithness amassed his fortune from slave trading in Sierra Leone.

a disproportionate proportion of the posts of clerks, factors, bookkeepers and managers on which the slave system depended. In 1812, Samuel Taylor Coleridge noted with some contempt that,

> ... of the overseers of the Slave-plantations in the West-Indies three out of four are Scotsmen, and the fourth is generally observed to have very suspicious cheekbones: and on the American Continent the... Whippers-in or Neger-Bishops, are either Scotchmen, or (monstro monstrosius!) the Americanized Descendants of Scotchmen.[1]

What has been termed "Caledonian Antizyzygy" seems to have been visible in the attitudes of many Scots who clearly forged an invisible barrier between intellectual theory and practical action. Scotland's national poet Robert Burns, for instance, was only prevented working as a "bookkeeper" on an estate in Jamaica by the sudden success of his poems, although among his radical writings we find *The Slave's Lament* written in 1792 and *A man's a man for a' that* in 1795. David Hume, Scotland's great Enlightenment philosopher, likewise could denounce the barbarity of slavery yet "concede" the "innate inferiority of black people".[2] Even in the 1840s, when slavery itself had been abolished and damned by all Scottish Christians as an abomination, the breakaway Free Church felt no unease at compensating for its loss of stipends and church buildings by accepting money from evangelical groups in the American South![3]

Slavery has indeed been, as one commentator suggested, "all things to all men" and in Scotland's case, its complexity and its interaction with the nation's soul-searching at this time of great upheaval is particularly disconcerting. Generalisations about the problem of slavery and the Scots seem therefore to have a tendency to be self-contradicting and are, ultimately, unhelpful apart from one, which does appear to be irrefutable, that "... Scotland's involvement in the rise of black slavery, in its maintenance, and in its ultimate overthrow, was out of all proportion to her size".[4]

1. Kathleen Coburn (ed), *The Notebooks of Samuel Taylor Coleridge, 1772-1834*, vol.III, London: Routlege and Kegan Paul, 1973, entry 1434.
2. David Hume, *Essays Moral, Political and Literary*, vol.II, London, 1754, pp.244-252.
3. A deputation of Free Church ministers on a fund raising tour of the southern United States, accepted a sum of about £3000 from the American Presbyterian Church which was one of the most popular congregations in the slave states and primarily raised by American slave owners. Cf. Nikki Brown, "'Send back the money!' Frederick Douglass's Anti-Slavery Speeches in Scotland and the Emergence of African American Internationalism". Scotland's Transatlantic Relations Project Archive, www.star.ac.uk, April 2004, pp.5-10.
4. C. D. Rice, *op.cit.*, p.24.

Notes sur les auteurs

Laurent Curelly est maître de conférences à l'université de Haute Alsace-Mulhouse. Il est l'auteur de plusieurs articles portant sur la littérature et la civilisation anglaises du XVIIe siècle. Il s'intéresse plus particulièrement à l'histoire de l'Interrègne (1649-1660), et notamment à la politique étrangère de l'Angleterre à cette époque. Il est membre du jury de l'Agrégation interne d'anglais depuis 2006.

Joyce Fereres a été qualifiée pour les fonctions de maître de conférences en 2007. Elle est docteur en Littérature anglaise (XXe siècle). Professeur certifiée, chargée d'enseignement à l'université de Paris XI-Orsay, elle est l'auteur de plusieurs articles, portant notamment sur le thème de l'identité dans *Brothers* de Bernice Rubens et sur la communauté irlandaise de Liverpool dans le roman d'Elaine Feinstein, *The Survivors*.

William Findlay est professeur de civilisation britannique à l'université François-Rabelais de Tours. Il est spécialiste du mouvement ouvrier français et britannique aux XIXe et XXe siècles. Il travaille actuellement sur les divisions religieuses et sociales en Écosse au XIXe siècle et la question de l'identité nationale.

Françoise Le Jeune est professeur à l'université de Nantes. Spécialiste de l'Empire britannique, elle travaille sur les rapports politiques et culturels entre la Grande-Bretagne et ses colonies américaines et canadiennes (1763-1867). Ses travaux récents portent sur les colonies canadiennes et leur représentation dans la Grande-Bretagne victorienne, à travers presse, récits de voyage et rapports parlementaires.

Éric Molina est docteur en Études anglophones de l'université Michel de Montaigne-Bordeaux III, où il a soutenu sa thèse en 2006. Il a été qualifié en 2007 pour les fonctions de maître de conférences. Il enseigne actuellement à la Martinique, où il vit depuis 1992. Il a publié en 2006 *Le Discours antiabolitionniste anglais au siècle des Lumières* chez C'ditions, Fort-de-France, et va publier fin 2008, chez le même éditeur, *Les Théories raciales pré-darwiniennes et le postulat de l'infériorité des Noirs*.

Véronique Molinari est maître de conférences à l'université Stendhal-Grenoble III et l'auteur d'une thèse sur les conséquences du droit de vote des femmes dans l'entre-deux-guerres en Angleterre, publiée en 2001 aux Presses universitaires du Septentrion. Elle a publié de nombreux articles sur la participation des femmes en politique et sur le mouvement féministe britannique ainsi que deux ouvrages : *Le Vote des femmes et la Première Guerre mondiale en Angleterre*, L'Harmattan, 1996, et, avec Catherine-Émilie Corvisy, *Les Femmes dans l'Angleterre victorienne et édouardienne : entre sphère privée et sphère publique*, L'Harmattan, 2008.

Françoise Orazi est maître de conférences à la faculté des Langues de l'université Lumière Lyon 2. Après une thèse sur Leonard Hobhouse elle a continué ses recherches sur le libéralisme, en particulier sur la fin du XIXe et le début du XXe siècle, s'intéressant notamment aux déclinaisons du libéralisme et à ses liens avec le conservatisme, l'impérialisme et le féminisme.

Olivette Otele est maître de conférences à l'université Paris XIII ; elle est l'auteure de *Histoire de l'esclavage britannique : des origines de la traite transatlantique aux prémisses de la colonisation*, Paris, Michel Houdiard Éditeur, 2008. Elle a également écrit l'article « Bristol, Slavery and the Politics of Representation: The Transatlantic Slave Trade Gallery in the Bristol Museum » dans l'ouvrage *Memory / Politics, Cultural Studies*, qu'elle a dirigé avec G. Jordan et C. Weedon, Londres, Routledge, 2009.

Michel Prum est professeur à l'université Diderot Paris 7. Il a fondé en 1998 le Groupe de Recherche sur l'Eugénisme et le Racisme (GRER), qui publie chaque année un ouvrage consacré à l'aire anglophone dans la collection « Racisme et eugénisme », qu'il dirige chez l'Harmattan. Il a co-dirigé en 2007 *Racial, Ethnic and Homophobic Violence* chez Routledge. Il coordonne avec Patrick Tort la traduction des œuvres complètes de Charles Darwin (chez Syllepse puis Slatkine). Il a également co-traduit *La Richesse des nations* d'Adam Smith (Economica).

Marie-Jeanne Rossignol est professeur de civilisation américaine à l'université Paris-Diderot. Elle a publié en 1994 *Le Ferment nationaliste : aux origines de la politique extérieure des États-Unis 1789-1812*, Paris, Belin, 1994, et co-dirigé *L'Amérique : des colonies aux républiques*, avec Lucia Bergamasco, Paris, université Paris-Diderot, 2003. Elle prépare en ce moment un livre sur le premier mouvement antiesclavagiste aux États-Unis.

Achevé d'imprimer sur les presses de l'Imprimerie BARNÉOUD
B.P. 44 - 53960 BONCHAMP-LÈS-LAVAL
Dépôt légal : septembre 2008 - N° d'imprimeur : 808060
Imprimé en France